# Modernism: Evolution of an Idea

NEW MODERNISMS SERIES

Bloomsbury's New Modernisms series introduces, explores, and extends the major topics and debates at the forefront of contemporary modernist studies.

Surveying new engagements with such topics as race, sexuality, technology, and material culture and supported with authoritative further reading guides to the key works in contemporary scholarship, these books are essential guides for serious students and scholars of modernism.

Other titles published in the series:

*Modernism in a Global Context*, Peter Kalliney

*Modernism's Print Cultures*, Faye Hammill and Mark Hussey

*Modernism, Science, and Technology*, Mark S. Morrisson

*Modernism, War, and Violence*, Marina MacKay

# Modernism: Evolution of an Idea

*Sean Latham and Gayle Rogers*

Bloomsbury Academic
An imprint of Bloomsbury Publishing Plc

B L O O M S B U R Y
LONDON • NEW DELHI • NEW YORK • SYDNEY

**Bloomsbury Academic**
An imprint of Bloomsbury Publishing Plc

| 50 Bedford Square | 1385 Broadway |
| London | New York |
| WC1B 3DP | NY 10018 |
| UK | USA |

**www.bloomsbury.com**

**BLOOMSBURY and the Diana logo are trademarks of
Bloomsbury Publishing Plc**

First published 2015

**British Library Cataloguing-in-Publication Data**
A catalogue record for this book is available from the British Library.

ISBN: HB: 978-1-4725-3124-7
PB: 978-1-4725-2377-8
ePDF: 978-1-4725-2532-1
ePub: 978-1-4725-2915-2

**Library of Congress Cataloging-in-Publication Data**
A catalog record for this book is available from the Library of Congress.

Series: New Modernisms

Typeset by Deanta Global Publishing Services, Chennai, India
Printed and bound in India

# CONTENTS

# ACKNOWLEDGMENTS

We would like to thank David Avital, Mark Richardson, and the Bloomsbury team for their immense support in bringing this book to life. We are grateful for support from the Richard D. and Mary Jane Edwards Endowed Publication Fund from the Dietrich School of Art and Sciences at the University of Pittsburgh. This book evolved from many discussions with colleagues and from astute readings by Jonathan Arac, Greg Barnhisel, Peter Kalliney, Celia Marshik, Ryan McGinnis, Adam McKible, Guy Ortolano, Stephen Ross, Daniel Worden, and Autumn Womack. We dedicate this book to our students, whose energy, questions, and ideas have shaped it.

Every effort has been made to locate the copyright holder for the advertisement for the Edison-Dick mimeograph (p. 31).

Alfred Barr, "The Development of Modern Art" (p. 54) used with permission of the Museum of Modern Art.

We thank Indiana University Press and Bonnie Kime Scott for permission to reproduce "The Tangled Mesh of Modernists" (p. 117).

# Introduction:
# Is There a There There?

*What is modernism?* This question has now beset, driven, and often befuddled generations of students and scholars alike. It is not, however, the question this book will answer. That's because there is no such thing as modernism—no singular definition capable of bringing order to the diverse multitude of creators, manifestos, practices, and politics that have been variously constellated around this enigmatic term. As we'll see, even for the experimental authors most often associated with it, modernism was a mobile, expansive, and ultimately unsettled concept. In 1922, Ezra Pound wrote that T. S. Eliot's *The Waste Land* (1922) "is I think the justification of the 'movement', of our modern experiment, since 1900" (*Selected Letters* 180). He praised Eliot for having "modernized himself *on his own*" and sent his own poems to Alice Corbin Henderson to publish in the magazine *Poetry* (1912–) with the note, "I give you your chance to be modern" (24, 40; italics in the original). In the 1930s, Pound still believed that he and Eliot had founded a "movement," but that it remained one "to which no name has ever been given" ("Harold Monro" 590). At the same time, competing claims for the name, origins, and nature of this "movement" or period were proposed, from Gertrude Stein's assertion that she "started the whole thing" by writing *The Making of Americans* (1925) to Virginia Woolf's famous declaration that "on or about December 1910 human character changed" (qtd. in Benstock 18; "Mr. Bennett" 320). No one definition or contention, however, has answered the question.

So make no mistake, the word "modernism" is a problem. Its strange temporality is disconnected from political history (unlike the crisply defined Victorian era) and even from the Western calendar itself, leaving it unmoored from something as vague as twentieth-century studies. Instead, "modernism" insists on a kind of ahistorical, even paradoxical presentism, an art for a boundless now. It became a pervasive term even though many of the figures we now consider foundational didn't think of themselves explicitly as modernists, and even though generations of critics have been dissatisfied with it. Graham Hough believed "Imagism" was the more accurate term for the literary revolution that began around 1910, while Hugh Kenner fashioned a "Pound Era"; others conceived of "Post-Impressionism," "Symbolism," or "Futurism" (see Hough; Kenner; Fry). Furthermore, several Marxist critics have seen "modernism" as anything from a wholly empty category to a dangerous, even nefarious concept (see Anderson; Eagleton; Adorno, *Aesthetic Theory*). Sensing the weird shiftiness of "modernism," Frank Kermode distinguished the pre–Second World War "palæo-modernism" from "neo-modernism," a second phase that arose later, now often called "postmodernism" (*Continuities*). Putting his finger on the problem in a series of lectures in 1987, he observed the strange way the term "modernism" itself, despite its energetic novelty, actually announces a worrisome, even threatening end to aesthetic history: "The reasons we give for choosing periods and authors always change, along with changed valuations. Sixty years ago the propaganda for current changes and preferences was so successful that we now identify that period as Modern (later, Modernist) which of course all periods once were, though none can be henceforth" (*History* 125).

In just the last few decades, furthermore, the once dominant emphasis on modernism as a purely aesthetic concept has been transformed by attempts to understand its imbrication in the social, material, and economic structures of a globally conceived modernity. Thus, scholars might locate the origins of modernism in any number of world-historical events and circumstances, from the women's suffrage movement to the Berlin Conference (1884–85). The result is that "modernism" has become an ingrained yet somehow weightless concept. Lawrence Rainey notes with some amusement that defining modernism and locating its origins has been "something of an academic obsession" particular to scholars of literature, and that, by contrast, this endeavor has not been as pronounced as in other fields ("Introduction" xx). Art historians, he observes, are generally satisfied to point to Édouard Manet's *Le Déjeuner sur l'herbe* or *Olympia* (both 1863), or perhaps to Pablo Picasso's *Les Demoiselles d'Avignon* (1907); music scholars look to the premiere of Igor Stravinsky's *Le Sacre du printemps* (1913);

architectural historians often cite the work of Le Corbusier or Frank Lloyd Wright. By contrast, Susan Stanford Friedman has provocatively argued that modernism across the arts *must* be linked to modernity, and thus might extend across historical periods and geographical boundaries to encompass any cultural response to "accelerated societal change brought about by a combination of new technologies, knowledge revolutions, state formations, and expanding intercultural contacts [that] contribute to radical questions and dismantling of traditional ontologies, epistemologies, and institutional structures" ("Definitional" 507). Seen from this vantage, modernism can include the literature of 1920s Paris, the ceramics of Tang Dynasty, China, and the music of contemporary Afghanistan. The problem, of course, is that in coming to mean so very much, "modernism" also comes to mean so very little.

Thus do scholars, readers, and students alike find themselves increasingly disoriented by the polymorphous term "modernism." Our concern here is not the validity of any individual claim or definition; instead, we will explore the shifting history of the idea and its consequences for how we have tried to understand the arts and cultures of the twentieth and twenty-first centuries. We will examine, that is, the stakes and implications of assertions that modernism began with Charles Baudelaire's *Les fleurs du mal* (1857), that Immanuel Kant was the first modernist, or that an alternative but interlaced tradition began in Booker T. Washington's Atlanta Compromise speech in 1895. There are other books that have traced the background of the modernist spirit or the array of creative texts in which various critics have found something called "modernism." This book is different; our focus is the *formulation* and *reception* of modernism—the ways in which its intellectual and cultural histories have been made. Ours is a work of historiography in the field of modernist studies, which has seen anything but a straightforward trajectory or continuous teleology in its development from a descriptive adjective in aesthetic discussions to a contested concept in discussions of contemporary art and the institutions that shape its meaning, circulation, and reception. So be warned: we offer not a way out of the many problems posed by the term "modernism," but, instead, a way into a daunting yet still pressing set of questions concerning how we have argued about the concept for over a century.

When Gertrude Stein returned from Paris to her childhood home in Oakland, California, she wittily remarked, "There is no there there" (289). As we'll see, the same is true of "modernism." As Kermode realized, the word itself insists on a radical yet paradoxically continuous break with the past—an attempt to locate the artist within a liberated and liberating present somehow freed from the constraints of history. Pound insisted that artists must "Make it new"—a move that evokes rupture and escape as well as marketing and effervescence. The Futurist avant-garde movement embraced this idea, with its manifestos pronouncing a love for explosions, war, and violence, all in an attempt to break definitively with a past that became less a resource for classical order than a fusty burden on the creative mind. By the same token, large-scale movements around the turn of the twentieth century were called the New Woman, the New Negro, the New Imperialism, and, several years later, the New Criticism. To break with the past, however, is also to embrace it as essential to one's own creative project, if only as a negative image of the thing against which the artist must struggle. As this book traces the history of modernism, therefore, it will examine not only the theorists and practitioners themselves, but also their own complicated positions within the institutions, histories, and systems that at once enable and constrain their work.

The itineraries we trace will be various, overlapping, and, at times, contradictory, carrying us through a broad range of critical, intellectual, and aesthetic traditions. This is a short volume, however, so we offer a concise overview and make no attempt to be encyclopedic or comprehensive. The figures we treat made their modernisms through revealing inclusions and exclusions, and we have had to do the same; yet we have aimed to account for, rather than replicate, the patterns of the past. Certain sections of our book will focus more heavily on Anglo-American academic scholarship, not out of bias, but out of historical necessity, so we can trace succinctly the rise and dominance of that branch of work—especially since the midcentury. This will also help explain why "modernism" remains such an "obsession" in English, but barely signifies, for instance, in Francophone discussions of the avant-garde, Symbolism, or literary experimentation in general. Indeed, there is a certain irony in the fact that the English language was belated in accepting the claims to newness carried both by the term and by the aesthetics of "modernism": Manet had been dead for almost thirty years, for instance, when Roger Fry organized the Post-Impressionist show of 1910 in London. This is even reflected in the names of the professional organizations that have developed to study the period. The Modernist Studies Association (MSA) was founded primarily by scholars in the United States, Canada, and England, and its business is conducted entirely in English. Its counterpart on the European continent, however, is called the European Network for Avant-Garde and Modernist Studies and conducts its business in English, French, and German. This complicated alignment with language and the boundaries it creates means that literary theory and criticism will play a central role in our story. But we will focus also on a diversity of disciplines and interests, from cinema and queer studies to book history, celebrity studies, mass media, philosophy, and translation—following the tendrils of the new networks that now carry the field beyond its bastions in individual disciplines. While these fields, their research, and their insights will factor into our account, other books forthcoming in this series will give greater depth to the writers, critics, and cultural figures which, for reasons of space, we are only able to treat partially.

The conversations, debates, and critical revisions of "modernism" did not take place in a single arena; the terms changed as the players shifted positions; the conversations were sometimes parallel, sometimes orthogonal, sometimes deeply intertwined, and sometimes sharply divergent. Modernism will at times appear to cohere as a single, unified concept in this book; but at other times it will emerge as a kind of strange attractor around which different creators, events, objects, and media can be gathered and dispersed. A similar tension between unity and fragmentation was, in fact, essential to the work of many artists and writers who were first labeled "modernist." In "Tradition and the Individual Talent" (1919), Eliot imagined there might indeed be a single thing called the literary tradition, though it stood ineffably beyond the comprehension of any one poet or critic. Reflecting his own bias, he called it the "mind of Europe" and suggested that it contained a "simultaneous order" to which any writer or thinker must fit himself or herself and then channel poetically (38, 39). In a roughly contemporaneous essay, he argued again for the importance of this single, unifying sense of order, finding in the Homeric allusions of James Joyce's *Ulysses* (1922) a means of "giving a shape and a significance to the immense panorama of futility and anarchy which is contemporary history" (*"Ulysses"* 177). To paraphrase Stein, Eliot looked at the aesthetic world and found a "there there": a common history that ordered art while simultaneously helping to cleave authentic accomplishment from mere pretense, genuine art from mass fiction, poetic beauty from sentimental dross, what some critics grew to call "modernism" from the vast expanse of twentieth-century culture.

This tension between tradition and the apparent chaos of "contemporary history" structures much of our thinking about art and literature in the twentieth century. Eliot's reading of *Ulysses*, after all, is wrong in many ways but certainly right in identifying the struggle evident throughout the book's bulk between the apparent chaos of everyday life and the idea that there might be some way of organizing it into something deeper and more cohesive. Stephen Dedalus, himself a kind of figure for Joyce, thus walks along a garbage-strewn beach and looks to make the corpse of a dog, a buried bottle, and even a handbag carried by some women into complex symbols that open onto the deeper truths of the universe. "Signatures of all things I am here to read," he thinks, seeing in that handbag, for example, "a misbirth with a trailing navelcord," a "strandentwining cable of all flesh" that links him to the moment of creation itself (31, 32). Walking on that same beach later in the book, Leopold Bloom doesn't see sacred symbols, but only sand and water before which "all fades" (312). In these echoing scenes resides the very tension over "modernism" itself—an apparent contest between the order that Dedalus so desperately desires and the flotsam of the everyday that washes endlessly in and out at Bloom's feet. Even Eliot, in *The Waste Land*, found it difficult to affirm a belief in the order and tradition he desired. Thus, after assembling the poem's often brilliant lattice of classical and Christian allusions, he concludes with a speaker who confesses that these are merely the idiosyncratic "fragments I have shored against my ruins" (50). Far from discovering the "mind of Europe," the poem, which concludes by pointing to the East (*"Shantih shantih shantih"*), is finally rent by the contradiction between eternal order and everyday chaos it sought to contain.

In their own ways, Eliot and Joyce's Stephen Dedalus looked to the past for some sensible tradition or storehouse of symbols, hoping to find a "strandentwining cable" that might indeed forge a link to the present in a mystical chain of being. For Pound, however, the past was just as fragmented as the present and it was up to the poet or the critic to *impose* form on it. Writing about his own attempt to forge a new order, he used the following metaphor in a 1913 article for the journal *The New Age* (1907–22):

> If you pour a heap of iron filings on to a glass plate they form a heap; no amount of care and thought would make you able to arrange them bit by bit in a beautiful manner. Clap a strong enough magnet to the underside of the plate and at once the filings leap into order. They form a rose pattern on the lines of the electric force; move the magnet and they move in unison. ("Through Alien Eyes" 252)

Creation here becomes the constitution rather than the discovery of form and involves pulling together otherwise seemingly chaotic fragments into an organized pattern, then encouraging others to see it. In a later essay on "Vorticism" (1915), Pound uses this same metaphor, this time insisting that "the design in the magnetised iron filings expresses a confluence of energy" (277). Unlike Eliot, whose fragments have been arranged "bit by bit," Pound evokes the powerful forces of the imagination to make and unmake the past into patterns useful in the present.

As a term and a concept, modernism has wavered for over a century between these two different ways of understanding culture, tradition, and the everyday. For some critics—especially those who first helped formulate the idea—it constitutes a "strandentwining cable" that weaves together a distinct group of writers and artists around shared aesthetic practices. That cable, however, becomes not just a lifeline but also a boundary and a barrier—a way of separating modernism from something else. Over the decades that we will survey in this book, that boundary was drawn in different ways and used to exclude a vast amount of writing and cultural production from different people, different places, and different times. Certain works seem to run steadily through its core, like Joyce's *Ulysses*, Eliot's *The Waste Land*, and Picasso's *Guernica*. Others, like Woolf's *Mrs. Dalloway*, D. H. Lawrence's *Women in Love*, or Jean Toomer's *Cane*, are woven in by some critics or excluded by others. This mode of critical thinking helped galvanize the idea of "modernism" as a substantive concept and thus created a canon of works, but it has often been criticized for its sometimes overt (and sometimes more subtle) twists that exclude women, as well as nonwhite, queer, and postcolonial creators—or include them for strictly formal and not identitarian reasons. As we'll see, this cable runs almost exclusively through Europe and pieces of the Americas, though other critics later graft new strands onto it in an attempt to widen its diversity without compromising its cohesion. Even as its constituent strands change, however, the critical sense remains that only a handful of works are genuinely modernist and that they are bound to one another through a shared set of aesthetic practices.

This cable, however, is more than just an abstract idea, since the mode of thinking upon which it depends had very real historical and institutional effects. It determined what works would be made accessible to students and teachers and thus how modernism itself would be embedded within the larger arc of cultural history and tradition. In doing so, however, it steadfastly ignored, neglected, or excluded the enormous diversity of twentieth-century art and literature. To take one example: in the late nineteenth century, a revolution in media culture began with a fall in printing costs, a rise in literacy, the creation of an international copyright system, and the invention of new printing and distribution technologies. The result was a massive explosion in print culture that then fed into the Edisonian era of the early twentieth century, which saw the birth of new media like film and phonography, followed later by radio and television. Seen from this vantage, the "new media" of our own day are actually only the most recent in a series of media revolutions that have now spanned 150 years, in the process creating a vast yet fractious collection of works too large and too diverse to ever be organized into a single tradition. Modernism's cable, therefore, provides a way of cutting through this extensive archive to select a set of essential works, which are themselves edited, anthologized, taught, and debated as the fine distillates of aesthetic culture. Like Eliot's fragments, they are both boundary and bulwark—a way of "giving shape and significance" to a media-saturated world. As such, they endow "modernism" with sense, history, and purpose—a purpose, as we'll see, that often aligned with the consolidation of national literary, linguistic, and aesthetic traditions alongside a growing fascination in universities and beyond with the art, literature, and culture of the present day. As its tendentious name implies, "modernism" sought not only to segregate some aesthetic objects from the rest of mass culture, but also to invest those objects with a special expressive power—one derived from their deep engagement with *now*—even while all of these objects were connected, as the art critic Clement Greenberg put it, by an "umbilical cord of gold" ("Avant-garde" 1:11).

This understanding of modernism produces a certain map of the modern, its contours running along lines that converge in great cities like Paris, New York, London, and Berlin and even in specific neighborhoods like the Rive Gauche, Greenwich Village, Bloomsbury, and Harlem. In other cases, it attempts to bind together often quite disparate groups of people, such as the Men of 1914 (Joyce, Eliot, Pound, and Wyndham Lewis), the members of Gertrude Stein's coterie (Ernest Hemingway, F. Scott Fitzgerald, and Picasso), the Harlem Renaissance (Langston Hughes, Claude McKay, Zora Neale Hurston, Alice Dunbar Nelson, and W. E. B. Du Bois), and the Bloomsbury Group (Woolf, E. M. Forster, Lytton Strachey, and J. M. Keynes). Other threads emerge as well and are sometimes grafted onto the central cable, like the one running from the Irish Revival through Dublin's Easter Rebellion in 1916—a circuit so powerfully charged that W. B. Yeats wondered late in his life, "Did that play of mine send out/Certain men the English shot?" (345) Sometimes the attempt to preserve a single cable of tradition ends up binding creators and critics together through competition rather than collaboration, producing tensions that eventually undermine the very idea of modernism as a coherent, synthetic term. Indeed, in the early twentieth century, artists themselves sought to weave their own cables in order to cement their place in a larger tradition. Here we can trace competing cables that run from Symbolism to Fauvism to Futurism to Vorticism to Cubism to Surrealism, to the all-encompassing modernism itself (and through it to postmodernism and now to the new modernism). As these brand names suggest, writers and artists were themselves well aware of their institutional futures, and in the pages of magazines, chapbooks, and broadsides, they often competed openly to consolidate a tradition, a movement, and a school—to wrap themselves in the cables that they thought might lend their work permanence. It has now passed to anthologists, critics, teachers, and writers of introductions like ourselves to trace modernism's tangle—to look at how the cable of tradition sometimes knotted, looped, or even snapped as different writers tried to bring some Eliotic sense of coherence to the archive.

The problem with treating modernism as a cable, however, is that it inevitably excludes so much of the boundless cultural production of the twentieth century. In the introduction to their influential anthology *Modernism: A Guide to European Literature, 1890-1930* (1974), Malcolm Bradbury and James McFarlane proclaimed confidently that "Modernism, while not our total style, becomes the movement which has expressed our modern consciousness. . . . It may not be the only stream, but it is in the *main* stream" (28; italics in the original). Few would express such confidence today; rather, it might be possible to see the history of modernism as a history of exclusions such as these and their interactions—hidden or in plain sight—with all that they attempted to occlude. As Pound's image of the iron filings suggests, culture does not necessarily fall along clear boundaries, but can instead be pulled into mutating, contingent patterns. If Eliot's tradition is about subtraction and stasis, Pound's magnetic patterns function by addition, movement, and even disaggregation. New iron filings—in the form of new artists, new works, and new media—are constantly being cast onto the critic's glass plate. Indeed, the more recent history of modernism is characterized precisely by such additions and reorientations. Feminist critics in the 1960s and 1970s helped excavate the work of writers like Hurston, Jean Rhys, H. D., and Mina Loy; here, what might have seemed at first like the addition of new threads to the cable of a still coherent modernism eventually helped fray, and even unwind, it. This was followed by a range of critical and archival interventions that added an ever-growing collection of cultural filings that included works by black poets, subaltern artists, and those who wrote or worked beyond, in only tangential relation to, or even with contempt for, Eliot's "European mind." To this was added work, first in film and then in the other new media of the twentieth century, including photography, sound, and the uncountable number of magazines that carried print and visual culture around the globe. The pile of filings grew also to include texts in new genres and subgenres such as science fiction, film noir, the musical cabaret, the pantomime, and advertising. Our own digital technologies are now making more and more of the twentieth century's archive readily available, piling the glass plate Pound imagined with so many filings that it becomes impossible to see the clear lines of transmission so essential to Eliotic tradition. (A Google search for the term "modernism," for example, returns millions of results, led by a Wikipedia entry that has been edited over 3,000 times.) Seen this way, the term "modernism" becomes not a cable, but a magnet—a critical force field that can be used to pull all of this material into different, often competing or contradictory, shapes detached from a strong sense of "tradition" or affiliation. This archival turn means that modernism gives way to modernisms, to a plural, even pragmatic array of patterns and shapes produced as different critical magnets are dragged through the heaped filings of the twentieth century.

So is modernism a single tradition or a fluid pattern—or something in between, like a shifting tradition of antitraditionalism or self-proclaimed novelty? Rather than answering that, this book explores the tension inherent within the ever-changing idea of modernism in order to trace the life of a polymorphous term. But where to begin, and how to form our own boundaries? We start with the incredibly sharp rise in the use of the word "modernism" and its kin (modern, *modernisme*, *modernismo*, *Modernismus*) in the late nineteenth century. At this time, as we have already seen, writers, artists, and thinkers around the world believed that *something* was happening, that the established conventions of realism, representation, and poetic form seemed to be failing in the face of new experiences, new audiences, and new things. In the arts, for instance, Impressionism opened up a whole range of experiments with form and color that moved away from material reality and toward the expression of some inner truth or vision. Just as color and canvas began to displace the object of representation in painting, so too in literature, traditional poetry and prose began to give way to a series of increasingly radical experiments that would lead to the complete abandonment of meter and rhyme in verse, and to the almost entirely unpunctuated stream of consciousness in the novel. Nor was it just a question of inventing new forms, since the very objects of representation themselves began to change. Picasso painted boxers and prostitutes; Samuel Beckett tried to construct a play in which nothing happens; Stein lyrically described the queer, erotic nature of household objects; William Faulkner tried to imagine the life of a mentally ill man in a family torn by the racism endemic to the American South; Dziga Vertov made a film in which the cities of Odessa, Kharkiv, and Kiev are the main (indeed nearly the only) characters; Rhys wrote brutally honest stories about life on the fringes of bohemian Paris; Joyce and D. H. Lawrence both tested the very bounds of what might constitute art, writing so frankly about sexuality that their books were banned.

These aesthetic revolutions, furthermore, took place within and alongside a series of equally radical technological, social, and political changes—events that had not always registered in the work of critics who first conceived and consolidated the idea of modernism. Women took to the streets to demand and eventually win the right to vote and to take up more visible positions in the public sphere. A small Irish revolt in Easter week of 1916 gave new force to a growing wave of anticolonial struggles that helped to bring European imperialism to an end and to completely remake the global map. Media, communication, and even military technologies—the machine gun, the aerial bomb, and the concentration camp—created new kinds of experience and indeed new landscapes that seemed beyond human comprehension. Nor were these new spaces confined to the devastated fields of Flanders, the ovens of Dachau, or the pulverized cities of Berlin, Guernica, and Hiroshima. Steel and concrete enabled the construction of massive skyscrapers, thus facilitating the growing concentration of national populations in teeming metropolises: new spaces there were lit day and night with the artificial glow of electrical bulbs and traversed by oil-fueled automobiles. The city itself became synonymous with the modern, its dense population, cacophonous voices, and soaring towers so overwhelming that the sociologist Georg Simmel believed it would overwhelm the human mind and the philosopher Georges Sorel feared that individuals would collapse into the violence of mass identity.

Amid such tumult, new kinds of laws arose to regulate the flow of cultures, peoples, and ideas. The sailor-turned-writer Joseph Conrad imagined an "earth girt about with cables" across which information moved in new and unexpected ways (67). Thus a writer or dissident in Buenos Aires, Delhi, Des Moines, or Sydney could connect with someone in London, Paris, or New York, and often did so through the pages of magazines, newspapers, and books. At the end of the nineteenth century, new technologies and new routes of trade made publishing inexpensive and led to a flowering of both local and international print cultures. Thus could Joyce, an obscure Irish writer living in Trieste, become famous in the United States when his *Ulysses* appeared in a New York–based magazine called the *Little Review* (1914–29) after it had been read and forwarded to editors by Pound, himself an American who served as the journal's European Editor from his bases in London and Paris. This unprecedented flow of information fed new political movements, fueled revolutions, built national communities, and opened new spaces between and beyond political borders. Governments passed obscenity, copyright, and libel laws in attempts to regulate this information, even as they also began to declare some of it an "official secret" and turned other parts of it into a tool of statecraft and warfare as propaganda. It wasn't just information that flowed across borders, but also people, and thus laws governing refugees, emigrants, and citizenship also came into being, often alongside the harrowing violence of racist and nativist movements ranging from the American South to the ghettos of Eastern Europe.

All of these changes—aesthetic, technological, political, and legal—form part of what came to be understood as and named a modern body of experiences. Increasingly, "modernism" now refers broadly to the widely distributed networks of writers, artists, and institutions that sought to cast these events into a characteristic form. For our part, we will remain agnostic about the term "modernism" and we will not seek to provide or privilege a single definition of the term. Instead, we will offer a history of the way it has been used, of its power and its incoherence, both of which have traveled globally in ways that a term like "Naturalism" did not. In doing so, we will move between Eliot's "tradition," Pound's "iron filings," and newly visible, often transdisciplinary networks that now seek to connect disparate works, writers, artists, and spaces into a "new" modernism. Chapter 1, "The Emergence of 'Modernism,'" traces the earliest travels of the word "modernism" and its cognates. We follow their diverse, seemingly incommensurable courses as they cohered slowly around a growing sense of cultural, political, and aesthetic crisis exemplified by the papal encyclical against "modernism" in 1907. We then home in on the successful purposing of "modernism" as an expressly aesthetic term at a moment when "modernism" was also becoming a powerful brand in commercial culture before examining the way it became associated with a particular lineage of difficult works. Here we treat modernism primarily as a cable—part of a self-conscious attempt to assemble a tradition that connected a handful of works like Joyce's *Ulysses* and Eliot's *The Waste Land*. This chapter thus includes a brief survey of the critical histories that caused these works to become so tightly bound up as exemplars of modern experience and expression.

Chapter 2, "Cables," then explores the ways in which modernism became (and for many remains) a proxy for aesthetic difficulty, a subtle but profound shift in the concept that allowed it to assemble a canon of works by writers and artists who had varied relationships to the concept's initial formation. This focus on complexity and on the idea that art should be experimental in its aims and resistant to traditional or popular codes of taste was codified by a number of otherwise disparate thinkers. Marxist, New Critical, formalist, and psychoanalytic critics all offered different (though sometimes overlapping) ways of interpreting works that typically privileged form over content. These critical practices themselves coincided with the increasing professionalization of literary criticism within the university; the difficult works and the difficult theories needed to interpret them reinforced the idea that art was formally complex and had to be taught by experts. As difficulty became synonymous with modernism, it also allowed a new field of study to expand considerably the kinds of texts that the term could now encompass.

The evolving definition of modernism, of course, did not take place in isolation, but was instead part of a larger series of debates among critics, historians, scholars, and teachers about the very nature of aesthetic form, narrative content, and linguistic traditions. In this context, the close connection between modernism and difficulty made it appear increasingly isolated, elitist, and apolitical. Even for Marxist critics like Theodor Adorno and Fredric Jameson, who argued that the movement's aesthetics had a political core, the emphasis ultimately fell on "negative dialectics" or a textual unconscious that might register politics but could not intervene in the public sphere (see Adorno, *Negative*; Jameson, *Political*). Chapter 3, "Iron Filings," examines alternative attempts to move modernism away from the relative autonomy of aesthetic difficulty and toward a broader engagement with political and social issues that inhere within an increasingly global modernity. In place of the single cable of difficulty, an array of alternative critical magnets arose, each pulling a particular array of cultural filings into new shapes. Thus do feminist, ethnic, media, and political modernisms begin to cohere within or alongside a growing interest in works that are not evidently experimental, resistant, or difficult. This new pluralism opened up wide new swaths of twentieth-century culture for critical analysis and in the process began to challenge the assumption that modernism itself might be confined to a single place (the West) or a single time (roughly 1890–1940). Amid this enormous expansion, however, modernism becomes less a single tradition or a byword for difficulty than a prismatic way of describing all kinds of aesthetic responses to the turbulence of modernity.

At this moment, the concept of modernism appears to be losing its cohesive force. If it is neither a tradition nor a delimited set of aesthetic practices, then what is it? If the works that it seeks to describe can now be differently constellated around a growing array of critical magnets, then does it even make sense to use the term to describe a fixed historical period or a canon of works? Chapter 4, "Networks," looks at the way modernism's coherence around novelty and difficulty has aligned it with an array of professional practices that now govern the intellectual life of the university. Seen in this way, modernism becomes not a single thing to be discovered or finally resolved, but the product of some dynamic institutional practices that still remain entangled in Pound's original charge, "Make it new." Thus, when the field began to redefine itself in the late 1990s, a "New Modernist Studies" emerged that set out explicitly to make modernism new again. Now, nearly two decades later, the "new" in that original title seems suspect even as the desire for new approaches, new texts, and new ways of reading continues to escalate. This chapter analyzes not only the ways in which recent attempts to redefine modernism partake in the movement's own logic, but also the ways in which the concept creates new interdisciplinary connections that weave through fields as diverse as law, architecture, and media studies.

Initially conceptualized as a site of resistance to modernity's regulatory and routinizing practices, modernism has become part of an institutional system. And yet, the troubling nature of the term—its relentless reinvention, its slipperiness, and its conceptual dissonance—suggests that it retains the potential to trouble our habits of consumption and disturb our interpretive assumptions. Grappling with a few lines from César Vallejo's *Trilce* (1922), looking even briefly at Picasso's distorted faces, listening to atonal music, reading Mina Loy's "Feminist Manifesto" (1914), or watching Expressionist cinema—these things are still jarring and indicate that the many and varied definitions of modernism this book traces are still inadequate to the works they hope to describe. Thus, this book will end by articulating some of the questions that continue to unsettle modernism while also surveying the other books in this series to which this slim volume, with its glossary and critical bibliographies, is but an introduction. These books include studies on globalism, race, war and violence, print culture, science, new media, environments, law, and gender, all constellated around a fluctuating idea of modernism to which aesthetics, despite itself, remains vital. Perhaps "there is no there there," but as with Stein's writing, what matters might be more the process of trying to make sense of our unsettled and unsettling relation to modernity's complex expression in art and literature than the always insufficient cables of tradition or the shifting patterns we trace in iron filings of a past that may not yet be past.

# 1

# The Emergence of "Modernism"

## Overview

How did a collection of formally experimental writers and artists working in the early twentieth century come to be known as "modernists"? Contrary to a longstanding belief that this term was only applied retroactively, "modernism," it turns out, is a charged, complex word that was claimed, debated, transformed, and promulgated pointedly in the early 1900s as disparate cultural trends and forces converged. Indeed, to glance at the entries in the *Oxford English Dictionary* for "modernism" and "modernist" is to find the familiar senses of the terms—"any of various movements in art, architecture, literature, etc., generally characterized by a deliberate break with classical and traditional forms or methods of expression," and an "adherent or exponent" of such movements—buried amid a half-dozen other definitions from philosophical, theological, and other histories from across centuries ("modernism"; "modernist"). If anything, "modernism" risked meaning *too many* things in the early twentieth century. In this chapter, therefore, we will attempt to discern the ways in which it came to be associated with a particular set of arguments that become ever more pressing at the moment. Here, "modernism" emerged as the name of a nascent aesthetic idea as well a brand name that was contested fiercely by generations of creators and critics. In the space of just a few decades in the first half of the twentieth century, academics narrowed these debates into a more or less coherent tradition—to return to our metaphor, a cable encircling a small archive of works around the term "modernism." As we will see, even as early as 1924, the poet-critic John Crowe Ransom believed that a writer could "escape" neither from "modernism" nor from the critics who judged literature by the tenets its figures delineated ("Future" 2).

Ultimately, our focus in this chapter will be the processes by which "modernism" became a byword in English for a set of formal practices for which T. S. Eliot was often taken to be the paragon of a "movement," if not an "era." This chapter, like most of this book, will proceed more or less chronologically, but that should not give the illusion of a uniform development of a "tradition" of modernism. Over the course of this book, we will touch on the many competing schools of criticism in the interwar and the immediate post–Second World War era—New Critics, American Marxists, the Frankfurt School, Formalists of various stripes, and the New York Intellectuals—and on post-1960s' movements and schools, ranging from gender studies to postcolonialism. But rather than outlining each of them in an orderly or encyclopedic way, we will focus on the enduring tensions among them that have distilled and dissolved a sense of "modernism" that still remains dynamic, unruly, and urgent. The reality is that a group of aesthetic products was segregated from the vast field of culture, and then was successfully joined to a term ("modernist") that still signified many other things, in a collaborative effort among figures who, in some cases, had no knowledge of one another or were openly hostile to one another's analytic precepts.

We'll therefore begin our exploration of the term "modernism" by first tracing the representative moments in which it passed through cultural debates and religious debates before acquiring a strong association with aesthetic innovation in the late nineteenth century. From there, we will examine the attempts by prominent critics and writers to read modernism into a "tradition" of aesthetic and literary history that skirted narrowly between degraded popular forms and anarchic avant-garde radicalism. Modernism became associated with ideas like formal innovation, difficulty, and aesthetic autonomy, and as we will see, that characterization of the ongoing movement pervaded the assumptions of critics on both the left and the right. We will treat some early landmark studies by figures such as Laura Riding and Robert Graves and Edmund Wilson before turning to the rise of New Criticism. The New Critics developed a kind of scientific formalism capable of dissecting aesthetic objects into discrete units of meaning that could then be analyzed and tested. The academic study of modernism in the United States largely began with them and occurred roughly in parallel with the rise of figures in England such as F. R. and Q. D. Leavis. (Indeed, when R. P. Blackmur looked back on the New Criticism he helped create, he called it "the kind of formal criticism and the kind of technical criticism that was best suited to understand the characteristic poetry written in English both in England and in America in the period between the two great wars" (*New* 1)). But the effects of this critical movement and its symbiosis with contemporary literary production were also limiting. New Criticism and those who came to be known as the practical critics in the United Kingdom both sought to articulate a clear set of conditions for valorizing certain works, and they did so by connecting modernism to other great works. In fact, in 1948, F. R. Leavis published an influential book called *The Great Tradition* that drew a line directly from Jane Austen to Henry James and Joseph Conrad even while excluding James Joyce and Virginia Woolf.

As Blackmur's lament suggests, however, New Criticism's victory proved Pyrrhic when it was taken starkly to task by succeeding generations for drawing the cable of tradition so tightly around a handful of texts—and excluding everything from cinema to manifestos—that it choked the life from them and obscured the wealth of contexts that produced them. Tacking back and forth between creators and critics, including figures like T. E. Hulme, Theodor Adorno, and Clement Greenberg, we'll thus conclude by looking at how the New Criticism managed to weave a set of aesthetic arguments by and about poets into a powerful program of academic and interpretive practices that became both professionalized and routinized after the Second World War. From the many threads and loose ends of the early twentieth century's explosive creativity, there gradually developed a much narrower and tighter cable of tradition that established a modernist canon and moved it from bohemian garrets and ateliers into college classrooms and student anthologies.

# "Modernism" and new forms

Deriving from the Latin *modernus* (*modo*, "just now"), the term "modernist" in English appears in various contexts dating back at least to the Renaissance. It became particularly charged on the heels of the French Quarrel of the Ancients and the Moderns, a seventeenth-century debate over the relative merits of the traditions of the ancient world versus the inventions of modern life. Jonathan Swift, for instance, satirized the "modernist" camp in his *Battle of the Books* and *Tale of the Tub* (1704), and after him, other writers across the eighteenth century generally used it pejoratively to describe an allegedly blind and ahistorical faith in contemporary progress. In the 1760s, Jean-Jacques Rousseau employed the term in a way that, Marshall Berman has argued, is the first instance of "modernist" that is tied to an understanding of European modernity—that is, the rapid, widespread changes brought about by massive urbanization and industrialism (17). By the time of the bohemian circles of Paris in the 1850s and 1860s, it was applied to someone who chased after fads, often those produced by a new commercial culture; thus it began to see increased usage as an in-joke and to be appropriated as a badge of honor by nonconformist artists. In 1866, the word "modernism" appeared in an English-French dictionary, for example, as a "*neologisme*" from the world of letters ("modernism"). Over the course of the 1870s, French dictionaries note the association of *modernisme* with an "obsession with the modern" and recognize *moderniste* as "a painter who aims to innovate" formally ("moderne" 2:1258).

By the 1880s and 1890s, as these mostly French artistic cultures gained more prominence, the attachment of "modernism" to certain aesthetic doctrines became more frequent and respected. For example, a new journal founded by Victor André and Guillaume Bernard, called *La Revue moderniste: littéraire et artistique*, appeared in 1884 (the subtitle distinguishing it from theological associations). During its run of just over two years, it published an astounding range of figures, from Émile Zola to Jean Richepin, from Joris-Karl Huysmans to Édouard Dujardin. Its first issue declares a belief in the autonomy of art, adopting an attitude from Flaubert that is revised with Aestheticism, and yet it includes articles on Stendhal and Honoré de Balzac, among others. Dandies, decadents, and provocateurs also fill its pages. Shortly after the journal's demise, Huysmans spoke extensively of *modernisme* in his essay collection *L'art moderne* (1889), in which he ranked various French painters based on their ability to incorporate and exemplify the modern life of Paris. In the United States, too, the painter and critic William Merritt Chase spoke in 1896 of the "extreme modernism" of Diego

Velázquez's works, which he took to be the formal foundation of Impressionism and contemporary art, regardless of the fact that the Spanish painter lived over two centuries prior to him (4).

At almost the same time, a literary movement that held many similar aesthetic ideals was forming in Spanish America. In 1890, the Nicaraguan expatriate writer and journalist Rubén Darío (who claimed that he had "Gallicized" himself by absorbing French literature) gave it a name: *modernismo*. When invoking this term, he was repurposing all of its sensibilities, including—indeed, especially—those that had been dismissed or attacked by the national academy in Spain: irreverence toward tradition, an infatuation with contemporary fads, an assertion of the primacy of the aesthetic over content, and even a hint of religious rebellion. As he waged a cultural attack from the former colonial periphery against Spain, Darío carried to Madrid in the early 1900s the first movement to be called self-consciously "modernist." The *modernista* movement triumphed in Spain, too, and lasted roughly from the early 1880s to the mid-1910s; while its achievements were important for aesthetic and philological history, its effects on literatures beyond the Spanish-speaking world were limited.[1]

Instead, a particular crisis within Catholic theology that culminated in the early 1900s provided an alternative but interrelated sense of "modernism" that was eventually merged with various aesthetic provocations and adapted by authors and critics across multiple languages. A treatise by the French priest Alfred Loisy in 1903 summarized the reformative thought that he, George Tyrrell, Ernesto Buonaiuti, Maude Petre, and Pierre Batiffol had been circulating. The Modernists, as the church hierarchy described them, drew on secular rationalism and interpretive practices, Enlightenment-inspired Kantianism, and the writings of Henri Bergson to argue that church dogma was subject to change over time. Building on Pope Pius IX's caustic attacks on "liberalism" and "modern civilization" in 1864, Pope Pius X reacted harshly in 1907: he first issued a syllabus ("Lamentabili sane exitu") that refuted 65 of the movement's propositions concerning science, history, nature, perception, agnosticism, and the evolution of dogma, then followed with an encyclical ("Pascendi dominici gregis") that condemned the modernists. He called "Modernism," with its *blind and unchecked passion for novelty*," the "synthesis of all heresies" and mandated in 1910 that all clergy and church officials swear an "Oath Against

Modernism" ("Pascendi"; italics in the original; see also Sabatier). Loisy and Buonaiuti were excommunicated; Tyrrell was expelled from the Jesuits; and Petre was ostracized and denied sacraments. This wide-ranging controversy captured dramatically some of the conflicts that now beset Western societies where religious, economic, political, social, aesthetic, legal, and scientific authorities all began to reorganize the ways by which people understood and managed the world. And the once obscure word "modernism" suddenly entered into vastly greater circulation as a shared if constantly mutating term to describe this experience across a myriad of social, artistic, and intellectual domains.[2]

As the various senses of "modernism" as an antitraditional, rebellious mind-set began to blend more often, the term "modern" began to take on more positive connotations in the arts, where it was filtered through a new attentiveness to the technical elements of aesthetic form. Thus, Romanticism and Realism both seemed increasingly unstructured, chaotic, and out of date. A number of anthologies from the past fifty years have traced these new debates around the issue of form; we'll mention here only a few touchstone statements that inextricably linked form and modernism. In 1871, the French poet Arthur Rimbaud, famous for his declaration "One must be absolutely modern!", stated that we must "ask the *poet* for the *new*—ideas and forms" in a universal language (111; italics in the original). Novelists took up the same concerns: Gustave Flaubert insisted in 1846 that "art is nothing without form," and that the "illusion" of truth in *Madame Bovary* (1856) comes not from its fidelity to life—it was a "totally invented story," he claimed—but from "the *impersonality* of the work" (60, translation modified; 229–30; italics in the original). For Flaubert, the author was to be "invisible"; technique alone defined art, and he decried such things as the "preoccupation with morality [that] makes every work of imagination so false and boring" (207). The American Henry James, in "The Art of Fiction" (1884), prompted an inward turn to form, while Samuel Beckett registered one extreme of this trend in his defense of Joyce's *Finnegans Wake*: "form *is* content, content *is* form," he writes. Joyce's "writing is not *about* something, *it is that something itself*" (14; italics in the original). The ties to modernity were clear when Joseph Conrad defended his slow pace of composition in 1902 by stating to his publisher that "I am *modern*" and by aligning himself with figures such as the American

painter James McNeill Whistler who "had to suffer for being 'new'"
(qtd. in Karl xi; italics in the original). In drama, too, the Swedish
playwright August Strindberg wrote in his preface to *Miss Julie*
(1888), "I have not tried to accomplish anything new, for that is
impossible, but merely to modernize the form according to what I
believe are the demands a contemporary audience would make of
this art" (56). All of this was yoked to what the decadent French
poet Charles Baudelaire had called for: an attention in painting
to "modernity,", by which he meant a focus on the "*transient, the
fleeting, the contingent*" (107; italics in the original).

Visual artists and their critics developed similar modes of analysis.
Oscar Wilde's brand of Aestheticism, which valued "art for art's
sake," elevated purely formal criteria for judging modern art in a
manner indebted to the German philosopher Immanuel Kant. For
Clive Bell, art was a combination of lines and colors that constituted
"Significant Form," and content was hardly important; for his
Bloomsbury colleague Roger Fry, it was a retreat from emotion-
laden "popular, commercial, or impure art" (Bell 8; Fry 356). For
the theorist Victor Shklovskii, art was "technique" and "the making
of symbols" in order to give the viewer "*a way of experiencing
the artfulness of an object; the object is not that important*" (217,
219; italics in the original). As the avant-garde movements of the
early twentieth century burst forth across Europe, the theorists
and practitioners of Russian Formalism, German Expressionism,
Constructivism, even Dada and Surrealism argued insistently that
form, novelty, and modern life were inseparable. No movement was
more ruthless in its attacks on everything that was not "new" and
"now" than Italian Futurism, launched by F. T. Marinetti in 1909.
With a virulent, misogynistic call to destroy the museums, libraries,
and all preexisting organic forms of art that he associated with
femininity, Marinetti called for a poetry of "courage, boldness, and
rebellion," one that praised machines, war, violence, and "struggle."
"A roaring motorcar, which seems to race on like machine-gun
fire," he claimed, "is more beautiful than the Winged Victory of
Samothrace" (13). Dozens of examples could be adduced; Jed
Rasula has cataloged references to "the new" in the late nineteenth
and early twentieth centuries, capturing the belief that "the new
spirit, the new form, the new reality, the new object, . . . [a] new
culture or civilization, new era or epoch, new time and new age . . .
would give rise, naturally, to a new aesthetics, a new beauty—a new

realism and a new archaism, enforced by a new rhythm—arising from new means and new methods [in language, art, and more]" (714). This is not to classify all of these figures (or their calls for "the new") as formal*ists*, but to see them as privileging form as a filter for creating modern art. In his dream of a new literary tongue in his "Proclamation" for a planned "Revolution of the Word" in 1929, Eugene Jolas asserts that "the writer expresses. He does not communicate," that "the plain reader be damned" ("Proclamation" 111). The "literary creator has the right" to disregard syntax and convention, he exhorts, in order "to disintegrate the primal matter of words imposed on him by the text-books and dictionaries"—to make a *literary* language that would be a "super-tongue for intercontinental expression" ("Proclamation" 112; *Man* 2).

# Creating modern movements

Even as the word found purchase in the arts, especially in painting, "modernism" increasingly began to point to a certain group of mostly literary English-language texts that shared qualities of formal experimentation, though the word also found purchase in the arts more broadly and especially in painting. We find, for example, that the critic R. A. Scott-James published his study *Modernism and Romance* in 1908, the year after the papal encyclical. Scott-James treats "modernism" as a dangerous, decadent tendency, found in the works of James, Conrad, and Thomas Hardy, that could potentially ruin contemporary literature. (Hardy, for instance, writes the protagonist of his novel, *Tess of the d'Urbervilles* [1891], feels the "ache of modernism" that characterizes "the age" in her desire for feminist reforms [139].) As it did for the Catholic church, modernism still has, for Scott-James, a bleak, antitraditional quality that does not respect the canon or any orthodoxy. Of Robert Hichens's now-forgotten novel *Garden of Allah* (1904), he writes with concern that its fascination with the "extremes of psychological analysis" in its development of characters is "'modernism' with a vengeance" (109).

But where Scott-James objected to what he called modernism in literature, the poet and essayist T. E. Hulme embraced it and, marking a course for English-language critical history, read it as *the* new formal movement in literature and art. In his "Lecture on Modern Poetry" delivered in 1908 to the Poets' Club in London, he urged that "we are a number of modern people, and verse must be justified as a means of expression for us" (50). Declaring that he has "no reverence for tradition," he spoke "from [a] standpoint of extreme modernism" (50, 54). Hulme was the first poet-critic to begin sketching what modernism might mean as a formal concept or movement in English-language literature, though he did not expound upon the term itself greatly. (He had no patience for modernism in religion and did not allude to the debate in the Catholic church, but rather was referring to a cultural climate in which elite or advanced modern verse and art were being produced.) In his lecture "Romanticism and Classicism" (1911), he "prophes[ies] that a period of dry, hard, classical verse is coming. . . . The period of exhaustion seems to me to have been reached in romanticism," whose effusive style he scorned (69). Hulme thus advocated "the complete destruction of all verse more than twenty years old"; the old would be replaced by a "distinct new art which is gradually separating itself from the older one and becoming independent" ("Lecture" 50, 54).

Hulme looked suspiciously on the idea of single tradition and instead laid out a program for "new art" that would fuse images into one "chord" while avoiding regular meter and syllable patterns (54). As we'll see, his theory shared with the New Criticism a scientistic quality rooted in the precision of mathematics. By reading Wilhelm Worringer and Henri Bergson alongside his studies of Egyptian and Byzantine art, Hulme foresaw "re-emergence of geometrical art at the present day" as "the precursor of the re-emergence of the corresponding attitude towards the world, and so, of the break up of the Renaissance humanistic attitude" ("Modern" 286). In this sense, then, he ends up finally constructing a cable of his own—one that neatly cuts out the last 400 years of history in a paradoxical attempt to connect his own "modern" mode of expression to that of the classical world. Hulme relied on such *discontinuities* precisely because he believed that the notion of "continuity" itself was one of the most pernicious legacies of nineteenth-century thought. His attempt to express the modern condition thus led him to an art that was alienated and estranged from the human world and to a poetics that replaced "sentimental" thought (often equated with women's writing) with "virile" imagery. Hard angles, jagged and unexpected juxtapositions, and the collision of past and present would govern the free verse. Difficulty, obscurity, and misdirection would replace objective coherence in time and space: the poetic text could arrange a world and its many divergent histories primarily through its form—*now*. This—not mere replication of human experience—would give ideas form and life, Hulme held, before they were attenuated and exhausted by the English of newspapers and mass media.

In a 1909 review, F. S. Flint linked Hulme's poetry to the French aesthetic movement called Symbolism through a shared emphasis on the "Image," thus helping to launch a new English-language movement called Imagism. In a later attempt to fashion a cable carefully enclosing his own conception of modernism, Eliot called this movement "the starting point of modern poetry" and named Hulme "the forerunner of a new attitude of mind" (*Criticize* 58; "Commentary" 231). It took shape when Pound, after discussions with Hulme, outlined a new "ideogrammatic method" influenced by his (dubious) understandings of Chinese writing and a theory of composition in which the image would "present . . . an intellectual and emotional complex in an instant of time" ("Retrospect" 4). This fixed, static arrangement would articulate poetically Pound's assertion that "all ages are contemporaneous"—that chronological time was rearranged by formal experiment (*Spirit* 8). Ornament would have no place, nor would "rhetoric"; a poem was first and foremost "poetic" by way of its formal properties. Imagist poetry would, Amy Lowell further argued, "create new rhythms" with a belief "in the artistic value of modern life" (Lowell vi). Here, once again, a strict concern with form is conjoined with a focus on objects and experiences drawn clearly from the experience of modern, often urban, life. Perhaps the most iconic Imagist poem, Pound's "In a Station of the Metro" (1913) illustrates this. Designed for maximum compression of meaning, the poem can be quoted in full:

The apparition   of these faces   in the crowd :
Petals   on a wet, black   bough .

Here the subway and its crowds become the object of a poem that seeks to distill an everyday experience into a single, carefully crafted image.

Among the first of many -isms in English-language literature in the new century, Imagism both drew upon and denied previous literary and cultural movements. From Symbolism, it took an immersion in the instant as a means of capturing slices of modernity, as Baudelaire urged. From Impressionism, it took the inward turn on the artist's medium (in this case, language). From Aestheticism, it took an anti-utilitarian and anti-commercial ethos invested in the autonomy of the art-object divorced from the conditions of its production and to be judged on its own terms. But it added to all of these a layer of "difficulty" that helped Pound argue for the novelty of *his* -ism:

> Imagisme is not symbolism. The symbolists dealt in "association," that is, in a sort of allusion, almost of allegory. They degraded the symbol to the status of a word. . . . The Image is the poet's pigment. . . . The point of Imagisme is that it does not use images as *ornaments*. The image is itself the speech. (*Gaudier-Brzeska* 84, 86, 89)

Imagism quickly gave way to Vorticism, a short-lived movement gathered around a journal called *BLAST* (1914–15), edited by the novelist and painter Wyndham Lewis. The magazine published the work of Eliot and Pound and looked forward to an even colder and more angular aesthetic—one that would quickly be adapted to representing the machine-driven brutality of the First World War. Along the way, it "hurled manifestos and curses, all in enormous black-and-red type, at each and every offender against modernism," Harriet Monroe wrote (216). Looking back at this moment in a 1937 memoir, Lewis told readers that they would be "astonished to find out how like art is to war, I mean 'modernist' art. They talk a lot about how a war just-finished effects [*sic*] art. But you will learn here how a war *about to start* can do the same thing" (4; italics in the original).

In this book, Lewis created what would become one of the most durable cables to encircle "modernism" by dubbing himself and a group of friends that included Eliot, Pound, and Joyce the "Men of 1914."[3] This "literary band, or group," he wrote, "comprised within the critical fold of Ezra Pound—the young, the 'New', group of writers assembled in Miss [Harriet] Weaver's [journal] *Egoist* just before and during the war" and who were Hulme's true heirs (292). Their success was evident when Ford Madox Ford wrote that Eliot and Pound had convinced "a usually unmoved but very large section of the public" to look "not in the stuff but in the methods of Art" (137). Pound meanwhile created genealogies for himself and his circle, placing Joyce, for example, outside of Irish traditions and in the line of Flaubert's innovations. Pound and his camp thus were not simply "new"; as he wrote, "Literature is news that STAYS news," outdoing and outlasting the newness of daily print culture in a state of what Lewis called "permanent novelty" (*ABC* 29; *Time* 126).These amorphous and shifting groupings converged and quickly broke apart, but all shared a basic set of impulses that persisted in critical history:

1   To erase the pejorative sense of the word "modernist" by valorizing art that seeks to break free from the past and its aesthic dictates;

2   To emphasize the importance of form to genuinely artistic expression;

3   To brand their work as distinctive yet still embedded within some deeper, modified sense of tradition and inheritance.

Symbolism, Imagism, Vorticism, and other movements all sought to redefine the modern and thus to make their modern-*ism* a new mode of artistic production that reshaped the conditions of its moment.

The effects of these claims were felt quickly, but need to be qualified: Hulme, Pound, Eliot, and others remained several voices (albeit powerful ones quickly gaining a larger and more influential audience) among many who pronounced on "modernism." Despite its growing appeal, both the brand and the concept of "modernism" continued to gather powerful detractors across the cultural and political spectrum whose critiques also helped shape the term's still-nascent meanings. It could refer to naive progressives grouped together with "birth-controllers, anti-child-laborites, [and] pacifists" (in the journal *American Mercury* in 1925) or to allegedly inarticulate artists who "have attained nothing of the coherence or authority of a school" (in a *History of Modern Painting* in 1927) ("modernist"). "Modernist poetry" was not an uncommon epithet for Jewish, Russian, or Spanish writing, and there were "modernist novels" called *The Priest* and *The Saint* about religion (and book called *The Modernist* in 1913, in a series called *Studies in Modernism* on theology). More pointedly, many critics sought to exclude work that seemed needlessly difficult or too deeply connected to modernity from the larger traditions of Western art and culture. Reginald Blomfeld, for example, condemned the movement in his *Modernismus* in 1934, calling it a "step downhill which, if unchecked, will end in the bankruptcy of Literature and the Arts" (v). His book's title, he notes, aims to capture the unsavory Germanic origins of the movement, which he sees as a product of the war Germany created. John Sparrow's *Sense and Poetry* (1936) was profoundly antimodernist, too. In 1937, longtime vocal opponent W. R. Inge began his presidential address to the English Association in London with a question: "What is 'Modernism'?" The literary modernists, he writes, show "an affinity both with the naïve artistic attempts of savages, and with the newest proletarianism in Russia," and their weird lines, color, shapes, and words are "clearly pathological. . . . [Their] gross want of taste comes very near to blasphemy against human nature. And this . . . is the great sin of Modernism" (33, 38). Even Lenin dismissed experimental and abstract art as an "infantile disorder of Leftism" (qtd. in Sollors 208). For these critics, "modernism" remained inchoate and unstable, but many of them saw the fascination with both novelty and form as a contaminant that had to be excluded or cut out before it took hold.

The content of the tradition and thus the formal expression of what got to be called "modernism" also remained contested. Indeed, almost no one yet thought of him or herself explicitly as a "modernist," and the proliferation of -isms indicates that various writers and artists sought to differentiate themselves rather than join some larger movement. These tensions played out, for example, in the pages of the *New Age*—whose very title signals its desire to embrace the "modern"—as the journal published a series of images titled "Modern Drawings." Over a series of months, the idea of the "modern" was visually represented on the magazine's pages, with realist works by Walter Sickert posted against more abstract paintings by Pablo Picasso. For a reader in 1910, it was still not clear which of these might be more "modern" than the other: the pitiless realist drawing of a prostitute or the abstract rendition of two boxers? In 1919 appeared a short-lived magazine, *The Modernist: A Monthly Magazine of Modern Arts and Letters*, and it included works by G. B. Shaw, Theodore Dreiser, and Hart Crane. But like the *New Age*, this periodical was more about politics than literature and aimed to promulgate the socialist vision of its editor James Waldo Fawcett, a pro-Russian and futuristic figure (see Călinescu 81). In an effort to cut through this confusion, the magazine *Poetry* featured, across the 1910s and throughout the following decades, frequent discussions of "modernism" in literature, including articles on how to distinguish modernist works from the others beside them on bookshelves—or even in the same anthology. The critic Holbrook Jackson meanwhile wrote in the journal *Rhythm* (1911–13) of a transnational "modernist art movement" in painting, while many others described a variety of constellating trends in music, sculpture, and architecture especially (9).

In short, far from a concept monopolized by Hulme and his associates, "modernism" had become a term that was at once specific and loose, cornering and mobile, all the while heard increasingly in all parts. Beyond the world of art, claims of "modernism" were a pervasive part of a new consumer-driven economy in the West where variations on the word "modern" became ubiquitous in advertisements for everything from razors and light bulbs to bricks and insurance policies. An ad in *Cosmopolitan* in 1911, for instance, called Rubdry Towels "a sign of modernism and true refinement," while the new Edison-Dick mimeograph was advertised in *Life* in 1929 under the large, bold heading "MODERNISM" (qtd. in Cuddy-Keane et al. 40; "Mimeograph"). Figures ranging from Rimbaud to Pound were thus entangled in this larger revaluation of the meaning and value of the modern; they helped fashion one of the earliest definitions of modernism by proclaiming first that form was *the* defining feature of an art-object or text, and second, that this new formalism was supremely "modern." Elevating themselves to the realm of Shelleyan prophets of culture—an intellectual and creative vanguard that saw and captured "the modern" spirit better than the mass of capital's products could—these figures especially worked to "brand" their own interpretation of modernity through innovative forms. In this way, they participated in the very elements of culture as a whole that they sought to relegate to the realm of the nonaesthetic. As we'll see, it became the task of critics—many of whom were also writers or artists working within the precepts that Hulme, Pound, Eliot, and others laid out—to give some structure to the term, to define its "newness" within a tradition, and confer on it a retroactive sense of history.

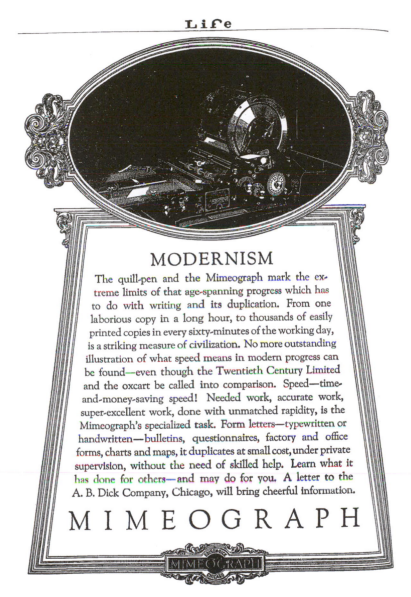

*Advertisement for the Edison-Dick Mimeograph in* Life *magazine, 1929.*

# Grasping the "New"

Defining the "modern" meant not just privileging novelty and form, but also trying to establish the *terms* by which aesthetic newness would be understood. Was modernism an emergent phase of an ongoing historical project with a coherent history and past of its own? Or was it a revolutionary break with the past expressed within a set of completely new formal strategies? Did the logic of being "new" and "modern" replicate and extend the logic of capitalism, or the logic of an alternative revolution? In answering these questions, various schools of critical thought, even diametrically opposed ones like New Criticism and American Marxism, had to wrestle with the questions of whether literature *represented* the alienated, massified conditions of modernity—and if so, perhaps further accentuated them—or offered a bulwark against their ill-effects by creating objects of eternal structure and order. The answers posited were many and varied, with critics laboring diligently to explain the new forms that artists and writers were creating in every field.

This debate now starkly defines our ongoing attempts to define modernism, but in the early twentieth century its terms and stakes remained unclear. For writers and thinkers in the period, the "modern" was a seemingly infinite term that had to be given shape, meaning, and value. Virginia Woolf, for example, looked backward, seeking to link "modern" art to French Impressionism, and more specifically to Post-Impressionism—a movement that emphasized the value of the artist's perception, even at the expense of the object being painted or described. In "Modern Fiction" (1925), Woolf calls Arnold Bennett, H. G. Wells, and John Galsworthy "materialists" because "they write of unimportant things; . . . they spend immense skill and immense industry making the trivial and the transitory appear the true and the enduring" (2:105).[4] She asks, "Is life like this? Must novels be like this?," then argues (in terms echoing Baudelaire) that the modern novelist must be suspicious of such materialism and seek, instead, to capture the "myriad impressions—trivial, fantastic, evanescent, or engraved with the sharpness of steel." This "incessant shower of innumerable atoms" composes a "varying, . . . unknown and uncircumscribed spirit" that the modern novelist will convey (2:106). For Woolf, the shower of impressions becomes a form of its own, manifested in the stream of consciousness or in the long, exploratory sentences of Walter Pater or Joseph Conrad.

This form separates certain works of contemporary literature from those that focus on the material, "real" world. And this literature, she asserts, is quintessentially "modern" in its spirit, cut as it is from the same cloth being woven by Bergson and by Sigmund Freud. Against the materialists, she offers as her ideal practitioner Joyce, who is "spiritual" and "modern" because he "is concerned at all costs to reveal the flickerings of that innermost flame which flashes its messages through the brain, and . . . disregards . . . [the] signposts which for generations have served to support the imagination of a reader" (2:107). In "Mr. Bennett and Mrs. Brown" (1925), she further categorizes contemporary writers by distinguishing between the Edwardians (Wells, Bennett, Galsworthy—her "materialists") and the Georgians (Forster, Lawrence, Strachey, Joyce, Eliot—her "spiritualists") in order to claim that "we are trembling on the verge of one of the great ages of English literature" (1:337). This new age, she imagined, drew on the past but nevertheless offered a revolutionary way to break free from moral and ethical constraints of a realism that had exhausted itself.

Woolf's account is now the most prominent, but she was only one of several critics trying to sort out the newest forms of fiction by trying to differentiate them from a dwindling mode of Victorian Realism. W. L. George, for example, sees British writers as "Neo-Victorians" (Wells, Galsworthy, Arnold, and Conrad), "Edwardians" (Lawrence, Walpole, Forster), and "Neo-Georgians" (Joyce, Lewis, Woolf, Richardson, Sinclair, and the forgotten Romer Wilson). The final group, he writes, "can be described as painters rather than as writers. . . . *The modern novel is becoming a painter's literature*" (1:147; italics in the original). Like Woolf and George, Edith Sitwell, in her *Aspects of Modern Poetry* (1934), pushes the advent of the "new" even deeper into the twentieth century, arguing that a "new reign" in poetry began in 1917 with Eliot's *Prufrock and Other Observations* (99; see also Lowell, *Tendencies*). John Rodker, a poet-critic who introduced and defended Marinetti's Futurism as a source of "The 'New' Movement in Art," divided contemporary writing into one camp notable for its debt to the "cerebral" elements of Symbolism, and another for its debt to the sublime primordialism of Russian novels since Dostoevsky (see "New"; *Future*). Others looked back into the earliest decades of the nineteenth century. Janko Lavrin's *Aspects of Modernism: From Wilde to Pirandello* (1935), which begins by claiming polemically that "nothing is more hackneyed and yet more vague than the words 'modern' and 'modernism'," traces the "new" and "advanced type" of "European sensibility" explicitly back to Romanticism (9). In a broadly international survey focused primarily on his authors' subject matter, he claims that the "brutal" and misogynistic features of Futurism, for instance, were a misguided and childish response to the fact that art since Romanticism had been "largely dominated . . . by the 'feminine' impulse" (186). Herbert Read's *Art Now* (1933), on the other hand, sees a tautology in the term "modern art"—"Modern art is inevitably modern," he writes—but claims that a certain spirit separates some new art whose "modernity is expressed in terms which are strictly artistic," a line he traces from Symbolism, German Expressionism, Cubism and Abstraction, and more (11).

     In one of the first attempts to mark out a purely American tradition, Alfred Kazin, a New York Intellectual, claimed in his landmark study *On Native Grounds: An Interpretation of Modern American Prose Literature* (1942) that the country's "'modernism' grew principally out of its surprise before the forces making a new world" of anti-Puritanism, populism, and disillusion with Realism. This led, he argues, to "our writers' absorption in every last detail of their American world together with their deep and subtle alienation from it," an "estrangement" and defamiliarization that he traces from Edith Wharton and Theodore Dreiser through Sherwood Anderson and Sinclair Lewis, from Willa Cather and the Lost Generation to the return of Naturalism in the 1930s (ix). Like Edmund Wilson and Irving Howe, Kazin was ambivalent about the effects of modernist literature, but saw its project as having a parallel course yet an exceptional lineage that separated it from Europe and grounded it clearly in national experience. John Crowe Ransom, meanwhile, argued that E. A. Robinson, Robert Frost, W. B. Yeats, and Gerard Manley Hopkins represented "traditional" poetry, while Pound, Eliot, Allen Tate, Wallace Stevens, and W. H. Auden were the figureheads of "our modernist poetry" ("Wanted" 177). Here we see clearly the surprising instability of the concept, since some of the very figures that his colleagues promoted as "modern" were, in this account, not at all. Ransom's modernist writers are "end products" of tradition, no longer within its vein, and are, in fact, "posttraditional: they are only the heirs of a tradition." But they have gone too far: they create brilliant images, but have no sense of prosody in composition. Thus, "the dense and brilliant yet obscure world of the modern poets may reflect a certain initial ontological sense," a very skeptical sense, in fact; but while "modernist poetry" is "entitled to its day," it nevertheless lacks a "systematic" approach to art and finally fails to justify its difficulty (179). According to Ransom, modernism, though rooted in a clear tradition, had cut itself off from some essential aesthetic force and was thus dead on arrival.

Despite their suspicions and disagreements, Woolf, Read, Kazin, and Ransom all clearly believed that modernism must be understood as part of a tradition; however radical its aesthetic experiments, it nevertheless cohered as a single movement, a presiding spirit, with a historical trajectory of its own. The culmination of this mode of thinking can be seen in two very different figures: Edmund Wilson and F. R. Leavis. Prior to Wilson, Arthur Symons in his *The Symbolist Movement in Literature* (1899) had introduced Anglophone readers to the French tradition that many writers who sought to identify themselves as modern or modernist claimed to have inherited. Yeats, Pound, and Eliot all read and appreciated the book greatly. Symons pointed to a "revolt against exteriority, against rhetoric, against a materialistic tradition" in French Symbolism, which he claimed had led to the liberation and autonomy of "literature" by way of its attaining its "authentic speech" (8–9). "Without symbolism," he declared boldly, "there can be no literature; indeed, not even language" (1). Extending and deepening this French-English connection, one of the first literary-historical studies of Anglophone modernist authors was Wilson's still lively and accessible book, *Axel's Castle* (1931). Wilson argued that Yeats, Joyce, Eliot, Stein, Marcel Proust, and Paul Valéry were all part of a tradition derived from French Symbolism. These English-language authors were indeed, for Wilson, carrying on a "literary revolution which occurred outside English literature" and representing "the culmination of a self-conscious . . . literary movement" (1, 23). But he believed that literary historians who attempted to understand them through the lens of national histories found little success.

The literary history of "our time," Wilson writes, is "to a great extent that of the development of Symbolism and of its fusion or conflict with Naturalism" in the French and English languages (25). Symbolism was, for Wilson, a "second flood of the same tide" of Romanticism, and as Romanticism's counterpart, the Symbolists and modernists broke the rules of meter, logic, imagination, intelligibility, and transhistorical reference (2). Their antiscientific, aestheticized work was carried to English by Yeats, who identified the mythical workings of Symbolist poetry by looking beyond Irish and English literature; by Joyce, who exiled himself personally and literarily; and by expatriates such as Eliot and Stein. But for Wilson, a Marxist reader, Eliot and Valéry failed by attempting to be ahistorical and purely aesthetic. *The Waste Land*, for him, was little more than despair and disillusion that neglected the importance of politics and ideology. Like the writers for the *New Age*, Wilson imagined that the political energies building around democratic socialism blended with the aesthetic innovations that flowed from France into England, Ireland, and the United States. By linking these two forces, furthermore, Wilson sought to fashion a tradition that could exclude commercialized, mass, and popular culture, all in a book that he hoped would make elite arts intelligible to average readers. In his mind, Joyce's recovery of Naturalism and union of it with Symbolism was the best hope for a future literature that could survive the economic and political wreckage of the First World War.

Far away from Wilson's work, Leavis, the immensely influential Cambridge scholar, was attempting to define a different tradition— one that could encompass the modern without being displaced by it. While appreciating Eliot, Leavis did not see modernism as cosmopolitan, international, or invested in autonomy, and he had no patience for Pound, Lewis, or the Joyce of *Finnegans Wake*. Furthermore, Leavis opposed the critical methods of his circle to those of the Bloomsbury Group, whom he characterized as detached elitists. He edited the journal *Scrutiny* (1932–53) with his wife Q. D. (Queenie) Leavis and alongside Eliot's *Criterion* (1922–39), the *Kenyon Review* (1939–), and the *Sewanee Review* (1892–), it became the site of important early readings of modern texts. Believing that criticism and pedagogy—especially pedagogy directed toward students not well versed in literary history—must work symbiotically, Leavis cultivated a rigorous program for reading that could link the classics to contemporary literature. Indeed, he was famously investigated by the Home Office for having sought to import a copy of *Ulysses* to teach to undergraduates while the novel was still banned. With a focus on the text rather than on the author, he also explicated literature through cultural conditions and the reformation of broader trends of "traditions," having students analyze popular fiction and advertisements alongside Eliot in order to learn to distinguish types of literariness. For Leavis, literature must be part of a growing organic community, and he believed that "imaginative literature has a unique and crucial significance within a larger conception of human creativity in language" (Bell 405). Thus, it must be neither something non-vernacular like Milton's poetry, nor something excessively rhetorical like Tennyson's. Unlike Wilson, Leavis sought to ground literature in a specific set of national traditions, believing it was only genuinely creative when it recovered and employed living modes of expression; for this reason, he looked, instead, to the neglected Gerard Manley Hopkins. Criticism could discover those values, too, in ways that were invisible to other modes of inquiry, and could thus reveal a cable named by Leavis's notion of "tradition" that united a present community by way of its formal engagement with a vital force.

This leads Leavis, as Michael Bell explains, to emphasize the creative power of a critic who must be equal to the art itself and be able to recreate the "struggle of its production" by producing criticism that is neither overly academic nor interested in abstract symbols (412). As a reader and critic, he believed that a poem came into being when it was apprehended by an attuned, historical mind. The process of comprehending and explicating the poem then revises it as two minds must collaborate in a shared third place to arrive at an understanding. The poet and critic alike, however, both speak for a minority, and Leavis entered into the contest over the idea of modernism by rejecting the "line" of poetic history "running from the Romantics through Tennyson, Swinburne, *A Shropshire Lad*, and Rupert Brooke" (*New Bearings* 25–6). In place of these often popular writers, he praised the work of Eliot, whose poetry "expresses freely a modern sensibility, the ways of feeling, the modes of experience, of one fully alive in his own age" (76). His work embodies "life" because it "reflect[s] the present state of civilization" in its disorder, by which *The Waste Land* is "an effort to focus an inclusive human consciousness" (91, 95). Like Wilson, Leavis sought to locate modernism within a clear tradition, which meant selecting a canon of works that could be woven into a cable stretching from the deep past into the present moment. But in the work of these two thinkers, two different kinds of cables cross—cables that still play a key role in debates over the meaning and history of modernism. On the one hand, there is an ongoing attempt to lodge modernism

within national and linguistic traditions—to use it to encircle the
political borders that would play so vital and so bloody a role in
the world wars and anticolonial conflicts of the twentieth century.
On the other hand, for critics like Wilson, this new movement in
the arts had developed a cable of aesthetic language that necessarily
crossed national and cultural boundaries.

## Novelty and tradition

When looking back from the present moment and judging how the
term "modernism" was invented, claimed, and winnowed into a
canon in this era, the most important early voice, both creatively
and critically, was that of T. S. Eliot. Because of the way his writings
were adopted and fashioned into an ethos and a critical position,
then into reading practices, Eliot is both difficult to overestimate and
difficult to grasp in his role as a linchpin figure. He deftly combined
avant-garde and rear-guard impulses, and he assembled Symbolist
and Imagist poetics and critical practices alike; it was Eliot himself,
after all, who published the first set of explanatory footnotes to
*The Waste Land*, against Pound's advice to remain more difficult. In
his groundbreaking collection of essays *The Sacred Wood* (1920),
Eliot built on the arguments of figures like the Aestheticists and
Hulme and Pound to argue for reading and analyzing poetry first
and foremost *as* poetry, asserting that "a poem, in some sense, has its
own life" (x). He captured the impulse to characterize the interplay
of form and content as the defining feature of this new writing and
art, and he claimed straightforwardly in 1923 that "I have assumed
as axiomatic that a creation, a work of art, is autotelic" ("Function"
73–4). Influenced by Stéphane Mallarmé, Jules Laforgue, and Valéry,
he maintained (controversially, in 1910s London) that we must read
literature "beyond time" in order "to see the best work of our time
and the best work of twenty-five hundred years ago with the same
eyes" (*Sacred* xvi). Like Leavis, he also sought to remove criticism
from the realms of belletristic impression and thereby to elevate it
to a serious, modern practice on a par with creative work.

Eliot's "Tradition and the Individual Talent" (1919) is not an
argument for the autonomy of the art-object per se, but for what
he calls his "Impersonal theory of poetry." He asserts that "no
poet . . . has his complete meaning alone," nor does any national

literary tradition flourish without the cooperative nourishment of its European neighbors. Eliot believes that the mature poet's mind must be

> aware that the mind of Europe—the mind of his own country—a mind which he learns in time to be much more important than his own private mind—is a mind which changes, and that this change is a development which abandons nothing *en route*, which does not superannuate either Shakespeare, or Homer, or the rock drawing of the Magdalenian draughtsmen. (38)

The poet—and thus the critic—can only uncover this awareness and "historical sense" by way of "depersonalization," according to which the expression of a poet's personality is to be avoided in favor of a catalytic process. Eliot compares the mind of the poet to a piece of "filiated platinum . . . introduced into a chamber containing oxygen and sulphur dioxide"; the resulting product, sulfurous acid, is formed only in the presence of the platinum and yet does not alter the platinum at all (40, 41). Thus, Eliot holds, "the emotion of art is impersonal," and "the poet cannot reach this impersonality" without transforming his own emotions and "surrendering himself wholly to the work to be done" (43). *The Waste Land* was seen as a demonstration par excellence of his theory, one that lifted a cable from the mass of literary history's sedimentary fragments and used it to realign all that came before it. This same cable, of course, was also used to exclude many forms of writing and creation that could be dismissed as too personal, too popular, and too distant from the mind of Europe.

This notion formed the kernel of Eliot's attack on Romantic theories of poetry, especially those of Wordsworth, against whom he claims that "poetry is not a turning loose of emotion," but rather "an escape from emotion" (43). Freed from the inhibiting limits of one's own emotional life, the "truly great" poet's task is to gain

> a perception, not only of the pastness of the past, but of its presence; the historical sense compels a man to write not merely with his own generation in his bones, but with a feeling that the whole of the literature of Europe from Homer and within it the whole of the literature of his own country has a simultaneous existence and composes a simultaneous order. (38)

William Blake, for instance, was too eccentric and ahistorical, while Dante renovated a strong religious tradition formed by Latinate vernaculars. Eliot thus implies that to be traditional *is* to be novel and original, not derivative or imitative, because the poet must draw upon and reorder a host of literary monuments into "organic wholes," far beyond the workings of his own mind ("Function" 68). The poem, as art-object, thus gains its autonomy by being set free from the control or interference of the poetic ego and by operating outside of the temporal constraints of everyday life.

Eliot here does something surprising with the meaning of "tradition," using it in a way that becomes important to a number of subsequent critics. First, he rejects—as Hulme did—a commonplace sense of "tradition" as something like "the reigning modes and canons of writing in English since the eras of Romanticism and Realism," including both the then respected Georgian school of poets and the popular realism of genre and commercial fictions. Rather than treating tradition as an *inheritance* from one's immediate predecessors, Eliot envisions it as an *assembly* of one's own predecessors from across the deep time of an aesthetic history that reaches back to the origins of Western culture and sometimes across Byzantine, African, Egyptian, and other sources. Tradition for Eliot thus means having a strong "historical sense" of one's self-appointed literary predecessors, and then often aligning them into a new canon to fit one's own creative project. In the jumble of quotations and citations at the end of *The Waste Land*, the poet bears this out by collapsing time and reordering it by way of form, so that Gerard de Nérval, Thomas Kyd, and the Upanishads all touch hands. This renovated sense of "tradition" produces numerous effects: it allows aesthetic history to operate autonomously from politics and science; it allows the poet to distance himself from the more radical or iconoclastic avant-gardes of the era, such as Dada and Surrealism, which seemed intent on destroying the very idea of tradition; and it allows Eliot and other critics to impose both order and continuity on the incredible diversity of human creativity.

Eliot used this new sense of tradition to extend this theory of poetry into a reading and evaluation of English-language literary history. In "The Metaphysical Poets" (1921), he argues that since Milton, a "dissociation of sensibility set in, from which [English poets] have never recovered," wherein thought and feeling became separated. This dissociation was most evident in the Romantic exaltation of emotion over intellect. The problem becomes acute in the time of Tennyson and Browning, who "do not feel their thought as immediately as the odour of a rose. A thought to Donne was an experience; it modified his sensibility. When a poet's mind is perfectly equipped for its work, it is constantly amalgamating disparate experience." The metaphysical poets, Eliot writes, had minds that were capable of "devouring any kind of experience" because no misguided poetic ego stood in the way (64). In an often-cited passage, he argues that

> it appears likely that poets in our civilization, as it exists at present, must be *difficult*. Our civilization comprehends great variety and complexity, and this variety and complexity, playing upon a refined sensibility, must produce various and complex results. The poet must become more and more comprehensive, more allusive, more indirect, in order to force, to dislocate if necessary, language into his meaning. . . . Hence we get something which looks very much like the conceit—we get, in fact, a method curiously similar to that of the 'metaphysical poets', similar also in its use of obscure words and of simple phrasing. (65; italics in the original)

Like many of the other early thinkers trying to define something called "modernism," Eliot too emphasizes the importance of difficulty—of the idea that art itself must resist the reader's efforts at immediate comprehension since it occupies a special place outside of an increasingly fractured world of sensation. Rather than imagining, as the Romantics did, that the poet should attempt to convey the immediacy of this experience or discover in it some mystical set of symbols, Eliot insisted on the importance of poetic history as a resource for controlling and ordering the process of representation. The cables of tradition he fashions thus neatly cut out much of the eighteenth and nineteenth centuries, paradoxically linking the novelty and difficulty of modernism to much older practices and forms.

Eliot's ideas about tradition and order converged as he struggled with Joyce's *Ulysses*—one of a handful of works that became (and remain) the touchstones for the idea of modernism. In "*Ulysses*, Order and Myth" (1923), Eliot finds that difficulty, alienation, autonomy, and tradition converge in what he calls Joyce's "mythical method" (178). He claimed that Joyce's use of the *Odyssey* "has the importance of a scientific discovery. No one else has built a novel upon such a foundation before: it has never before been necessary." It relies on myth, on "manipulating a continuous parallel between contemporaneity and antiquity" that "others must pursue after [Joyce]." Joyce introduces "a way of controlling, of ordering, of giving a shape and a significance to the immense panorama of futility and anarchy which is contemporary history" (177). Eliot's notion here, which has clear resonance with *The Waste Land*, is again indebted to Hulme, but with the idea that order—like myth—preexists the artist's present moment. Joyce's is not a "narrative method," but an atemporal "mythical" one that is "a step toward making the modern world possible for art, toward . . . order and form" (178). Eliot believes that the great novel of the present moment, like his own poetic masterpiece and like Pound's *Cantos* (1917–69), uses myth as a means of structuring a disordered postwar world, and this became a governing truth about modernist literature. His essay famously ignores much of what also made *Ulysses* modernist to other critics, most notably its sexual frankness, its loving descriptions of urban life, and its Irish context. These elements presumably belong to the "anarchy" of "contemporary history," which autonomy, difficulty, and tradition sought to control. Eliot thereby lays the groundwork for a new mode of studying literature that would, in turn, characterize the texts from which it seemed to spring forth— texts that were increasingly described as "modernist." Indeed, in a note published alongside the American debut of *The Waste Land* in the *Dial*, the critic Gilbert Seldes linked Eliot's poem and *Ulysses*, as many have for almost a century now, by writing that they were the "complete expression of the spirit which will be 'modern' for the next generation"; in other words, their "modernism" itself would survive the passage of time (577).

# New criticism, Eliot, and modernism

As we've seen, Eliot, by ingeniously linking aesthetic practice to criticism and explication, argued for the importance of difficulty, allusion, and tradition to creating the fragmented wholes of modern art—and thus also implicitly argued that such works required critics and teachers that could successfully explain their complexity.

So alongside the new writing of the 1920s, there arose a new criticism (indeed, it would soon be labeled the "New Criticism"), a loosely configured movement whose modes of interpretation and pedagogy remained preeminent through the 1950s. These New Critics, for whom Eliot was a key arbiter of values and aesthetic criteria, synthesized some of the early impulses in modernist criticism into a more systematic theory of literature and how to read it, interpret it, and teach it. They did not set out to define "modernism" (or any other literary period), but they circulated the term extensively. More important, they prescribed parameters for reading and analyzing texts that valorized the difficulty, allusion, and autonomy that they saw in modernist texts. For these figures, the poem was a self-sufficient entity, a pattern of words referring to one another with only an analogical (not mimetic) relationship to reality; it was ontologically knowable and explicable through precise study that situated it in an organic history of poetic forms. With a dual focus on the art-object and on readerly apprehension, they looked for things like irony, paradox, ambiguity, formal unity, complexity, and the necessity for professional instruction in order to understand literature on its own terms.

The segue from Eliot's essays into this new program was not simple, but was efficient, as New Critics cordoned off the study of vast swaths of literary history which they saw as too emotional, explicitly political, or reflecting a degraded mass culture that compromised the integrity of art. And, unlike previous generations of scholars, these critics saw themselves as rigorously trained experts (rather than simply people of taste) who performed their work primarily in universities. The professional study of contemporary literature began to rise in the late 1800s as universities increasingly opened their doors to studying languages other than Latin or Greek and to the analysis of texts by modern authors. (Thus, Joyce remarked that his work would keep the scholars busy for centuries in a way that Dickens would not have imagined of his own.) The New Critics, Mark Jancovich explains, ultimately "shifted the dominant forms of academic study from philology, source-hunting, and literary biography to textual analysis, literary theory, and what is now understood as 'literary analysis'" (200). They sought to avoid questions about morality and ideology by developing specific protocols for identifying and then analyzing the same kinds of difficulty that Eliot had linked to his own understanding of modern poetry. They advocated a set of protocols that required both dense texts and relatively consistent modes of teaching and writing that could be shared across an expanding system of higher education whose disciplines were increasingly partitioned into monolingual, national literary traditions.

When a young, idealistic British scholar and rhetorician, I. A. Richards, propagated his new readings of Eliot, he began to elaborate an influential version of what would become the New Criticism—or "practical criticism," as he called it—in which form was even further separated from content. In his *Principles of Literary Criticism* (1924), Richards detailed an expansive set of over thirty modes of analyzing literature that Raymond Williams later noted "contained a programme of critical work for a generation" (*Culture* 244). Richards asserted that poetry makes "pseudo-statements," which are statements about attitudes or worldviews that are not empirically verifiable but are, nonetheless, fundamental to humanity. Poetry—and literature in general—was a special form of communication that revealed essential truths, and it did so in forms that were inseparable from the pseudo-statements themselves. Thus, one could not "translate" a sonnet into plain prose "facts." "Words," he believed, "are the meeting points at which regions of experience which can never combine in sensation or intuition, come together. . . . [Language] is no mere signaling system" (*Philosophy* 131). Having elevated language to this position and simultaneously cut it off from the marketplace and the public square, Richards could then argue that poetry is a specially privileged form of speech in the modern world. Thus, he famously claimed, "poetry is capable of saving us" from the dispiriting chaos and miscommunications of contemporary life, but only if it remains isolated from questions of morality, politics, identity, and economics (qtd. in Fry 182).

Richards argued that Eliot had crucially "effected a complete severance between his poetry and all beliefs" (*Poetries* 64n. 3). In an appendix to his *Principles of Literary Criticism*, he rebuts those who attempt to find an ideology or force a doctrine out of *The Waste Land*. Rather, Eliot's poetry, like Shakespeare's works, causes the mind to grow—Richards was deeply interested in the science of poetry's function—because of its confrontation with obscurity, difficulty, and ambiguity, which were the exact properties, as we have seen, around which a conception of modernism was forming. Richards celebrates the fact that Eliot's epic "as a whole may elude us while every fragment, as a fragment, comes victoriously home" through study, investigation, and analysis (*Principles* 277). Eliot himself, with his own critical ideals shifting, would rebut these ideas, but Richards's style of reading had become part of an increasingly pervasive mode of reading and teaching that depended, in part, on the idea that good art was difficult art.

Richards had a profound influence on leading critics such as William Empson (his own student) and Yvor Winters. Empson's *Seven Types of Ambiguity* (1930) aims to uncover the various forms of ambiguity, irony, allegory, apparent contradiction, and subtle suggestion by which poetry works metaphorically to posit an "otherwise" scenario. That is, poetry manipulates ordinary language to offer the possibility of multiple readings, multiple interpretations, and multiple understandings. An eccentric figure who later disagreed with other New Critics and favored biographical criticism, Empson, nonetheless, wrote on Eliot that his use of ambiguous syntax in *The Waste Land* was ideal, for in it we are unable to distinguish parts of speech and subject/verb pairings. The best kind of poetry, that is, did not describe the world, but revealed the impossibility of representing it transparently. Likewise, Winters, a poet-critic who championed Imagistic precision over longer narrative-style poetry, urged that a poem should *be* a new experience. That is, following Eliot, he attacked the idea that a poem should be merely expressive and instead sought to privilege form as itself the meaning and content of aesthetic expression. Thus, he argues, "poetic morality and poetic feeling are inseparable; feeling and technique, or structure, are inseparable. Technique has laws which govern poetic (and perhaps more general) morality more widely than is commonly recognized" (14). For all of these critics, great literature was antiexpressive and thus complex, resistant to easy or familiar interpretation, and often lodged in a long literary tradition that had been obscured in the nineteenth century. These early attempts to devise a new criticism bound together a new kind of authentically modern writing— most often poetry—and thus helped institutionalize the canon of modernist works that would be taught in colleges and universities for decades after the Second World War.

Working simultaneously—sometimes sharing ideas, sometimes independently—were a group of writers who came to be known as the Southern New Critics because of their origins in the American South. John Crowe Ransom, Allen Tate, Robert Penn

Warren, Cleanth Brooks, Donald Davidson, and others originally congregated at Vanderbilt University in Nashville, Tennessee, around their short-lived journal the *Fugitive* (1922–25), and many of them later became known as the Agrarians with their collective manifesto *I'll Take My Stand* (1930). Brooks claimed that the *Fugitive* poet-critics were, in fact, modernists in the same vein as Yeats and Eliot. Stan Smith notes that the term "modernism" had been used in correspondence among *Fugitive* editors, especially when referring to Eliot, since the early 1920s (see *Origins*). By the late 1920s, Tate "took to describing himself as Modernism's gift to the Old South," and he used the term to name the movement that he saw flourishing, centered on Eliot and Pound.[5]

The American New Critics were deeply committed to literary form in their works and their criticism, and like their British peers, they objected to interpretive practices that seemed overtly moralistic, political, or impressionistic. All such readings—all such approaches to literature—were premised on what they called "abstraction," which they took to be at the root of many contemporary intellectual, economic, and social problems. This made them hostile to science and to mass culture alike since both, they believed, relied on models and typologies, which literature resisted to the end. Like Richards, Tate argued that art offered a particular way of knowing about the world—that a poem is not "about" something, but *is* that knowledge and cannot be reduced to statements or positions. It cannot be subjected, that is, to what Brooks would famously call "the heresy of paraphrase" (see "Heresy"). Emphasizing once again the importance of difficulty as a constitutive part of aesthetic form, Tate argued that a text's "inter-relations were so complex that it was quite literally a process of productivity, and hence could never be resolved into a simple paraphrasable meaning" (Jancovich 206). The text, instead, was a luminous object, its form and texture unique to the subject or emotion described. Emphasizing the religious sense of transcendence underlying this kind of thought, W. K. Wimsatt called the poem a "verbal icon"—something made of language that nevertheless pointed beyond its mere expressive or representational capacities (see *Verbal*). When these linguistic qualities were exhibited in poetry that was "tortured, . . . not facile, [that] does not worry so much about success in communication, . . . [and that eschewed the] predictable and easy," it was essentially "modernist" poetry (Ransom, "Making" 864, 868).

Ransom, himself a poet, was the de facto editor of the *Fugitive* and a major figure in the movement; he actually coined its name, the "New Criticism," in 1941. His essay "The Future of Poetry" (1924) argues that "the arts generally have had to recognize Modernism," but that this has created a predicament: "How should poetry escape? And yet what is Modernism? It is undefined. . . . In poetry the Imagists, in our time and place, made a valiant effort to formulate their program. Their modernist manifestoes were exciting, their practice was crude, as was becoming to pioneers, and instructive in more ways than they had intended" (2). Ransom sees that Imagism— which he takes to be the clearest articulation of modernism—had demanded "accuracy of expression" and "newness of matter," but that had led to a "free verse [which had] no form at all, yet it made history" (2). Herein lies the problem for Ransom, who mixed respect and reservation when regarding modernism: critics demand form so that poetry can be analyzed thoroughly, yet the greatest poetic movement of the day had no respect for the traditions of form. What kind of legacy is this for modernism as poetry and criticism alike move further into the academy? And, "how can poetry stand up against its new conditions?" Ransom questions whether "the future of poetry is immense? One is not so sure in these days, since it has felt the fatal irritant of Modernism. Too much is demanded by the critic, attempted by the poet" (3). Here we see that Ransom equates Imagism and "Modernism," which is a victory for the Pound/ Hulme camp, and, forecasting much of the New Criticism, he sees that victory as one that determines the ascent of form in critical discussions and necessitates a new brand of analysis.

Ransom's "Criticism, Inc." (1937) makes explicit the importance of professionalism and exacting training by asking about the "proper business of criticism" (93). The essay lays out a program for making it "more scientific, or precise and systematic," so that "the critic [may] regard the poem as nothing short of a desperate ontological or metaphysical manœuvre" (94, 105). Ransom developed this line of formalism further in "Wanted: An Ontological Critic" (1941), in which he proposes that a poem differentiates itself from prose and from ordinary speech not by moral, emotion, or expression, but by structure (147). "Poetry," he claims, "intends to recover the denser and more refractory original world which we know loosely through our perceptions and memories. By this supposition it is a kind of knowledge which is radically or ontologically distinct," and thus itself a proper object of serious academic study alongside science and philosophy (148). Along the way, Ransom himself feared in 1935 that "modernism" had become understood as "nothing but a new technique," and he stressed, instead, that the "substance of modernism is . . . an attitude" toward "decay" in the contemporary world ("Modern" 184, 185). Extending Eliot's claims, he thus saw a line of "modernism" that extended back to the work of Donne. The "wear[y]" and "cynic[al]" response to this world that we find in interwar modernist poetry, he holds, resists easy interpretation because of the formal complexity that enfolds it; it is often neglected, furthermore, by other critics and scholars ("Modern"). It looked, in other words, a lot like the works that would later be constellated around Eliot's *The Waste Land* to become modernism.

The intrinsic and untranslatable character of great poetry was paramount for Brooks, who wrote the great synthetic "apologia for modernism," as Ransom called it, in his *Modern Poetry and the Tradition* (1939) (see "Apologia"). He too proposed aesthetic categories such as irony, paradox, and ambiguity for reading literature, arguing that meaning is only intelligible through form and rhetorical figures that resist explanation. Stringently removing extrinsic judgment from the field of critique, he asserts that only form, not content, provides meaning. Brooks's exemplary New Critical exegesis of Eliot, "*The Waste Land*: Critique of the Myth" (1939), therefore provided an account grounded in the many symbolic layers of the poem. The central paradox of the poem, he argues, is that "life devoid of meaning is death; sacrifice, even the sacrificial death, may be life-giving, an awakening to life" (*Modern* 137). From here, he explains Eliot's allusions to Tristan and Isolde, to Madame Sosotris, to Philomela, and to many other figures, so that Eliot collapses history and literature into one form: "It is plain that Eliot in having the protagonist address the friend in a London street as one who was with him in the Punic War rather than as one who was with him in the World War is making the point that all the wars are one war; all experience, one experience" (145). But perhaps Brooks's disclaimers about his own readings tell us the most about his understanding of a poem that was quickly coming to stand for what would become modernism as a whole:

> The foregoing account of *The Waste Land* is, of course, not to be substituted for the poem itself. Moreover, it certainly is

not to be considered as representing *the method by which the poem was composed.* . . . The account given above is a statement merely of the "prose meaning" [of the poem]. (165–6; italics in the original)

This is to say that, for Brooks, the essence of Eliot's poem is not its commentary on the decline of civilization or its depiction of the aftermath of the First World War, though those elements are present. It is not an allegory or a symptom of its time, but rather, merely and miraculously, a literary object. As Harriet Davidson summarizes of the New Critical approach to *The Waste Land*, for these critics Eliot represented the ideal poet who "powerfully depicts and rejects modern life, valorizing myth over history, spatial form over time, an orderly past over a chaotic present, and the transcendence of art over the pain of life" (123). Such readings of Eliot especially were extended by figures like the American critic F. O. Matthiessen, who was not a New Critic but nevertheless shared the growing emphasis on the overriding importance of form. He makes this point directly in *The Achievement of T. S. Eliot* (1935), in which he argues that *The Waste Land* was "in danger of being obscured by the increasing tendency to treat poetry as a social document and forget that it is an art" (vii). By 1941, Winters would use similar terms to speak of Eliot's "modernist followers" in contemporary poetic history ("T. S. Eliot" 239).

Thanks to the efforts of these critics, the New Criticism established itself as the dominant mode of professional literary discourse in American universities. By 1932, Pound himself acknowledged that

> a new level of criticism has, within the last few years, been attained in America. This is not a matter of there being one intelligent critic with an enlightened view. It is very nearly an impersonal criticism, and comes from the sharpened perception and greater desire for, or even insistence on, greater accuracy of expression, which is shared by more than a half-dozen writers. ("Manifesto" 40–1)

Soon, the New Critics set out establishing an implicit yet highly influential canon of modernist texts—works, not surprisingly, that foregrounded their formal experimentation and difficulty. Brooks and Warren's *Understanding Poetry* (1938), for example, was both a textbook and anthology which trained generations of students—not to mention professors and teachers—to read both traditional and contemporary literature alike. The collection divides literature into categories such as narrative poems, descriptive poems, metrics, tone, imagery, theme, and "poems for study" with accounts of how certain poems changed in revision. It included works like Pound's "In a Station of the Metro," H. D.'s "Heat" (1915), E. E. Cummings's "Portrait" (1920), and Eliot's "The Love Song of J. Alfred Prufrock" (1915). The importance of these poems as canon-worthy contemporary works is emphasized by the company they keep, including poems by Shakespeare, Pope, and Keats. In their companion *Understanding Fiction* (1943), Brooks and Warren urge teachers to eschew plot summary and narrative content, biographical materials, or didactic readings of literature. And here again they not only assemble but also institutionalize one of the first canons of modernist prose writing with work by Lawrence, Kafka, Faulkner, Conrad, and Joyce. Unlike the Imagist anthologies and other earlier attempts by artists and writers to assemble contemporary movements that are still unfolding or collapsing, Brooks and Warren retroactively align and embed these works within a now closed period of literary history.

This new canon, however, was not outlined entirely in the works of the New Critics. The first book-length study to diffuse the term "modernism" as an increasingly coherent way of describing this new mode of writing and critique was Laura Riding and Robert Graves's *A Survey of Modernist Poetry* (1927). This text marked a pivotal moment in the development of modernism as a distinctive aesthetic movement read against various strands of cultural history. Both authors were practicing poets and Riding was a protégée of Allen Tate, who encouraged her use of the term "modernism." Their guide had a simple aim: to explain to common readers what "modernist" poetry was and why it was so "difficult," similar to the premise of the Spanish philosopher José Ortega y Gasset's famous essay *The Dehumanization of Art* (1925). They explain, in other words, "the divorce of advanced contemporary poetry from the common-sense standards of ordinary intelligence," without seeing that poetry—as many charged—as an insult to public intelligence (9). The difficulty of contemporary poetry has scared off the "plain reader," they argue, and made his tastes more conservative. They trace the historical reasons for this, arguing that what they call "modernist" poets are reacting against "rules made by the reading public" of the late nineteenth century (83). The Victorian-era "domesticated" poetry, they hold, and allowed the marketplace to dictate which poets were successful; these were poets whose works were readily consumable, quotable, simple, and short, allowing for paraphrase into sentimental platitudes and never "frighten[ing]" a reader (110). Since these conditions made bad poets well known and indeed treasured, "modernist poetry, if nothing else, is an ironic criticism of false literary survivals" (111).

Riding and Graves offer a conception of the modernist poem as art-object that is New Critical in spirit and draws explicitly on the idea of the artwork's fundamental autonomy from politics, morality, and impression. For them, above all, "modernist poetry is a declaration of the independence of the poem" (124). Thus we find poems that are "irregular" and even "freakish" as poets allow the poem to "find its own natural size in spite of the demands put upon poetry by critics, booksellers and the general reading public" (58). In justifying this "new" poetry, they reject the idea that modernism is simply a faddish attempt at novelty within a declining civilization. This new kind of poet is an "original individual" who is "something more than a mere servant and interpreter of civilization. . . . *Modernist*, indeed, should describe a quality in poetry which has nothing to do with the date or with responding to civilization" (163, 178; italics in the original).

Working in some ways against the aspiring professionalism of the New Criticism, Riding and Graves make their case by invoking an ideal average reader who uses the name "modernist" for "the contemporary poetry that perplexes him and that he is obliged to take seriously without knowing whether it is to be accepted or not" (102). They furthermore connect this situation explicitly to the battles over orthodoxy and heterodoxy in the modernism debates in the church and the ways in which they have affected lay believers. This situation increases the importance of the role of the literary critic as mediator, one who can explain why a public that tolerates experimental modern music should be equally open to modern experiments in letters. Like the American and British New Critics, Riding and Graves—though they discuss Cummings extensively and many other figures in passing—ultimately see Eliot's *The Waste Land* as the most significant example of their modernism. They describe it as a poem that has to be read "as a

unified whole" and they praise its "well-controlled irregularity," yet
*The Waste Land* is finally a failure for them as they conclude that
"the most serious flaw in poetic modernism has been its attachment
to originality" (51, 277). This endless emphasis on novelty is too
often purchased through an excess of irony and self-mockery;
likewise, Eliot's and Pound's uses of foreign languages border on
gimmicky. In their readings, Riding and Graves thus affirm the
idea of aesthetic autonomy so essential to the emergent definition
of the modernist canon. They look less to give modernism a
literary-historical tradition—though they do cite its precedents in
Impressionism and in French Symbolism—and more to validate
its experiments in the moment and to separate "modernism" from
its connotations of nihilistic celebrations of contemporary decay.
Indeed, by 1934, Leavis saw the tide turning: he believed that the
"poetic taste" of England now showed a "general readiness, even
among the respectable and conservative, to recognize that there is
(corresponding to 'modernism' in music, painting, sculpture and,
some would add, scientific theory) an advanced poetry that ought
to be encouraged even if one does not really expect to understand
it" ("English" 98–9). This occurred, he posits, in part because of
"how completely Eliot has won to academic respectability" and
the "extraordinary authority he now enjoys," and it has opened
the door for other "new and difficult" poets like Stephen Spender
and W. H. Auden to earn greater respect (99, 100). Spender, Auden,
and their peers like Louis MacNeice and Geoffrey Grigson also
became key figures in disseminating this sense of "modernism"
in their attempts to reconfigure their own literary heritage in the
late 1930s. As we'll see, however, the fixation on poetic autonomy,
professional critique, and the construction of a canon worked also
to end the idea of modernism as an active practice. The first cables
have been cast around an increasingly stable collection of texts
embodying a modernism that could be isolated, mapped, defined,
and lodged in textbooks and anthologies.

# Form across fields

The idea of modernism as a unified movement developed at the
intersection of two trends: the attempt to adumbrate a new
aesthetic tradition—as we saw in Woolf, Leavis, and Wilson—and

a new attention to the autonomy of form as the supreme marker of modernist art, as the New Critics and their associates had posited. As modernism's development in literary and visual arts experiments was theorized anew, one of the major early figures to interpret and consolidate these intersecting trends found his platform in the mid-1930s. The art critic and historian Alfred Barr, who was among the first university professors to teach contemporary art in the 1920s before becoming the founding director of the Museum of Modern Art (MoMA) in New York in 1929, created a diagram that he titled "Cubism and Abstract Art" (1935) [revised as "The Development of Abstract Art," 1936] in order to trace patterns in the visual arts from roughly 1890 to 1935. He read "non-geometrical abstract art" back through Surrealism, Dada, Expressionism, Fauvism, and more, while "geometrical abstract art" came from Bauhaus, Constructivism, Cubism, and Neo-Impressionism. Movements such as Futurism and characteristics such as the "machine esthetic" made links between the two columns. Barr's formalist diagram offered a stark visual representation of modernism as a clearly visible cable binding together what initially appears to be a whole collection of disparate, even antagonistic forms, movements, and artists. Although its many critics were able to revise it in provocative ways (and Barr himself did too), it nevertheless worked effectively to cut across an array of artistic practices ranging from magazine illustration to cartoons and commercial art. Like the anthologies published by Brooks and Warren, it created what became a canon of modernist art through both inclusion and exclusion—and Barr himself could put these ideas into practice through MoMA in the same way the literary scholars did from their posts in colleges and universities.

That is, some of modernism's earliest theorists, including figures like Hulme and Lewis, attended closely to the development of modernism as a concept that could work across the arts, linking fiction, poetry, painting, music, and dance. Now, even as literary criticism became increasingly professionalized and often focused intensely on poetry in this period, this urge to make modernism into a super-movement persisted. Building on the work of critics such as Percy Lubbock, Joseph Warren Beach noted, for example, that criticism has been concerned with technique, rather than about fidelity to nature or humanity, since 1920. Borrowing language from the visual arts, he writes that "in applying terms like 'expressionism' and 'impressionism' . . . [or sometimes 'post-impressionistic,'] to

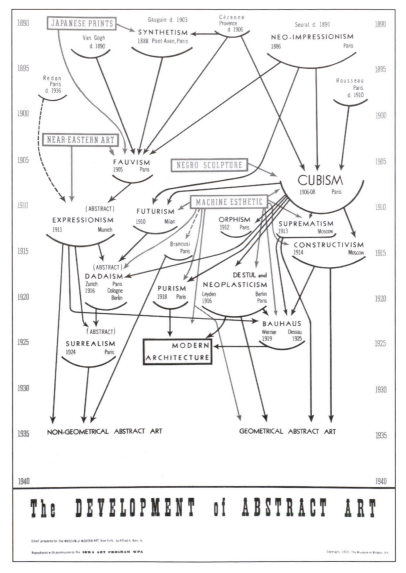

*Alfred Barr, "The Development of Abstract Art" (1936). Copyright Museum of Modern Art, New York.*

works of fiction, I wish to suggest the roughly parallel development in our time of the several arts . . . I have particularly in mind the notion of abstract composition derived from painting" (9). His account studies the transitional "modernists" Conrad, Lawrence, and Dorothy Richardson alongside "expressionists" like Joyce by contrasting them with the impressionist Henry James, their nonetheless important precursor (332). They use what Beach calls *"deformalization"*—a process that values an overarching lyricism to the novel's prose and, in turn, allows for discontinuities and irregularities in plot, all in rebellion against the nineteenth century's alleged rationalization of literary styles (334; italics in the original). These writers are, for Beach, the last in a line from "Fielding to Ford" whose works exhibit the greatest feature to develop across modern literature: the "disappearance of the author" (14). Charles Feidelson, meanwhile, traced a Symbolist tradition in American literary history not through Wilson's notion of the movement, but through an understanding of Symbolism as a movement fully divorced from Romanticism, thriving on paradox and incongruity— in other words, what was being called "modernism". This emphasis on Romanticism across the arts allowed Feidelson to expand the concept of modernism in a way that made New Critical reading modes and modernist writing interrelated: "Empson's *Seven Types of Ambiguity* and Joyce's *Finnegans Wake* suggest at once a new departure in taste and a close kinship of theory with practice" (44). The turn inward on language itself as a medium, giving language a "kind of autonomy" that is "distinct from the personality of its author and from any world of pure objects, and creative in the sense that it brings into existence its own meaning," is for Feidelson the "intellectual genesis of this modern taste" for new literature (45, 49).

Perhaps the most important mid-century attempt to link literature and the arts around a generalized conception of modernism, however, was Joseph Frank's groundbreaking essay "Spatial Form in Modern Literature" (1945). Building on the radical shifts in perspective so essential to modern painting, this still widely cited article argues that in modernist writing—and especially in novels—space had overtaken time as the primary way of organizing narrative, consciousness, and form itself. This argument is similar to Brooks's assertion that *The Waste Land* too could not be understood as a temporal or historical document.

The triumph of space moves art away from time and thus politics, into a potentially ahistorical autonomy. Drawing heavily on the thought of Albert Einstein and of Henri Bergson, Frank contends that narrative in modernist works occurs without the passage of chronological (external) time. Frank sees important origins for this technique in Worringer's *Abstraction and Empathy* (1908) and in Hulme, and he believes that both plastic and literary arts "have moved to overcome, so far as possible, the time-elements involved in their perception" (651). Past, present, and future instead are "fused in one comprehensive view" in which "the distinctive quality of a poetic sensibility is its capacity to form new wholes, to fuse seemingly disparate experiences into an organic unity" (652). This is "modern" literature; it undermines the "inherent consecutiveness of language," then suspends the "process of individual reference" in favor of a pattern of internal reference that puts both the past and the present into a "timeless unity" (224, 230). For Frank, now that linear narrative has given way to spatialized form, modernism asks readers not to look for a plot or story, but for a pattern, and its authors—he discusses Djuna Barnes at length as a peer to Eliot—"ideally intend the reader to apprehend their work spatially, in a moment of time, rather than as a sequence" (225).

In a related vein, Mark Schorer's "Technique as Discovery" (1948) extended these arguments and asserted that "technique alone objectifies the materials of art; hence technique alone evaluates those materials." James, Conrad, and Joyce thus "discover new subject matter" through their technical innovations, using revision as a way of re-seeing and enlarging the intrinsic development of his text; H. G. Wells, on the other hand, cannot do this (73). For Schorer, the novel changes when technique not only "*contains* intellectual and moral implications, but [also] *discovers* them" (74; italics in the original). Thus, where Naturalists struggled to find a style that replicated a preexisting reality, modernists *are* their styles; and therefore, a text that does not fit this formal criterion is not modernist. Here, in the triumph of style, form, space, and autonomy as the defining elements of modernism, we find the powerful intellectual cables that will draw together a diverse collection of works into a relatively stable canon. These concepts, in fact, remain important touchstones even amid the changing definitions of modernism, which we'll explore in later chapters. Before looking at those changes, however, we first need to look at the way critics with explicit political agendas sought to construct their own definition of modernism using many of these same works and ideas.

# Autonomy and the left

In a different and very influential tradition of thought, European Marxist critics were never willing to see form as a neutral element or a purely aesthetic category. Rather, they looked to the convergence of social, economic, political, and ideological forces that *produced* form. For them, nothing is ideologically empty; what Ransom called aesthetic "ontology" can only be constructed as beautiful or artistic within certain conditions. The stream of consciousness, for instance, elevated individual subjectivity and interiority as an escape from a socially constructed reality that Marxist thinkers found stultifying and repressive. Formal and stylistic difficulty, furthermore, appeared to shatter aspects of that social reality by representing the world in new, disorienting, and even alienating, ways. But, these critics asked, did this modernism *reflect* alienation or *induce* it? In other words, the debates over "modernism" were not simply disagreements about themes and form in literature, but about the fundamental nature of what "literature" should be, especially in a particular interwar moment in which both communist and fascist states were rising. The pointed arguments among the Frankfurt School theorist Theodor Adorno, the German dramatist-critic Bertolt Brecht, and the Hungarian thinker György Lukács, illustrate both the expanse of modernism's provocations and the continuity among the patterns by which critics across England, the United States, and Europe read them.[6] Put simply, Adorno and Brecht saw progressive *potential* in the new experimental forms, depending on how those forms interpreted social realities and structures of labor, while Lukács grew to see this new art as dangerously corrosive. Taken as a whole, the debates among these critics set the terms for a politically engaged definition of modernism that sought to locate it within and against capitalist ideology. Despite their obvious political and philosophic disagreements with the New Critics and other formalists, they nevertheless shared (and helped promulgate) a general understanding of a modernist canon that was defined primarily by style, difficulty, autonomy, and a reinterpretation of tradition. And they may have differed widely about the meaning of modernism, but they agreed on its structure and contents, thus elevating a canon of works that looked remarkably similar to that in New Critical textbooks and anthologies.

Like Woolf, Eliot, Riding, and Graves, the experimental playwright Brecht was an artist as well as a critic. He introduced a mode of privileged form over ideological content that has influenced many Marxist discussions of modernism, and of art in general. An ardent defender of experimentation, he rejected the idea that political art should be realist. This set him at odds with Lukács, who maintained a deep faith in classical modes of expression and reception. Rather, Brecht's famous "epic theater" was an open-ended art-world that used formal innovation to inspire a revolutionary re-vision of the bourgeois world. Naturalism in theater was an illusion to be destroyed, which meant interrupting the show, employing montage and defamiliarization, and revealing art to be labor, too. Commodified art should be *experienced* and is useful as such, Brecht believed, for that experience "helps to undermine the myth of art as 'personal expression,' and shows artists their situation as workers and producers" in something akin to what Adorno and Max Horkheimer would later call the "culture industry" (Lunn 126). Form, in other words, had revolutionary potential if it could be enacted in the correct—demystifying, enlightening—manner. And, crucially, it measured its success against other forms of mass culture that could then be safely excluded from modernism.

By contrast, Lukács famously condemned such experimentation as a retreat from "social reality" in his essay "The Ideology of Modernism" (1955). He understood the difficulty and formal experimentation that increasingly defined modernism as a kind of ideological artifice that cut people off from history and politics, leaving them passively adrift, "asocial," and "unable to enter into relationships with other human beings" (20). Modernism's ideology, he asserts, is the same ideology underpinning Symbolism, Naturalism, Futurism, and Constructivism: a "static" view of the world that negates the "fundamental" reality of the moment, which was the struggle between socialism and capitalism, and the possibilities that Lukács saw for change (21). Rejecting the exclusive and "exaggerated concern with formal criteria, with questions of style and literary technique" that had been promulgated by "bourgeois-modernist critics themselves," Lukács holds that style *is* content, and "content determines form" (17, 19). Thus, the attempt to represent the world in new ways does not produce the kind of revolutionary consciousness Brecht imagined; rather, it becomes an abstract and passive dream-world—most hazardously embodied in the work of Joyce, Eliot, Kafka, Gottfried Benn, and Robert Musil. Seen in this way, modernism is "not the enrichment, but the negation of art," in which personality and the world disintegrate together, and "outward reality" itself is negated in favor of formal superficiality (25, 46). Crucially, Lukács shared in the now growing consensus about the canon of writers and works that counted as modernist, but he understood the practices themselves to be disastrous. For him, Joyce uses Dublin, and Kafka and Musil use the Hapsburg monarchy, only as backdrops for their self-absorbed bourgeois artistic innovations, giving no conception of the "normal" against which they places their "distortions" (33). By contrast, realism done correctly, as in Honoré de Balzac or Thomas Mann, could forge a critique that could reveal revolutionary potential that was only further obscured by modernist formalism.

Where Brecht and Lukács looked to a modernism defined primarily by stylistic difficulty and experimentation, Adorno and Benjamin focused on autonomy—on the idea that modernism possessed a certain degree of freedom that allowed it to critique an otherwise degraded yet mystified social world. Drawing on a set of works and ideas similar to the ones developed by Eliot, Adorno defined modernism in opposition to mass culture and industrialism. He held that the commodification of art in advanced capitalist societies transformed it into just another tool of false consciousness and oppression; modernists, however, used obscurity and difficulty to resist this disastrous process of commodification and its imperatives of clarity for easy consumption. Without giving a distinct genealogy of modernism, Adorno saw the late work of Beethoven as a forerunner of the movement and saw modernism as having arisen in the refined division of labor, in modern industry, and under the inhumanity of capitalism and the repression of popular will. He praised Symbolism, but was hostile to Surrealism and to both the French and Russian avant-gardes, preferring instead German and Austrian Expressionism and, later, figures like Proust, Joyce, and Beckett. In Kafka, he saw bizarre manipulations of narrative more than that of content, so that Kafka did not have to address monopoly capitalism directly: form *is* the key to his social content. He appreciated Beckett because his "dramas exemplify the proper relation between the two contradictory desiderata, i.e. successful figuration and adequate social content" (*Aesthetic* 353). His Manichean arguments about a divide between industrialized mass culture and an autonomous modernism took their clearest shape in his music criticism, where he praised Arnold Schoenberg's atonal experiments, but denigrated jazz as a mere excrescence of industrialized cultural production. Even though jazz used improvisation, spontaneity, collective production, atonality and syncopation, and irrational structure, he saw it as masking a reactionary ideology. Adorno is still criticized for an Old World elitism in his response to the New World phenomenon of jazz, but his claims are telling since they emphasize the importance of aesthetic tradition and autonomy rather than formal invention: jazz could not escape to an autonomous sphere because it came *from* the culture industry rather than standing outside it.

The key to modernism's autonomous art-object, for Adorno, lay in its recalcitrant resistance to modernity, which he defined as an ongoing process of rationalization that led from the Enlightenment to the Holocaust. Authentic modernist art, though entangled in this process, nevertheless offered an ideal critical vantage by becoming a kind of anti-art, a negation (not simply a reflection, as Lukács held) of the elements of beauty, reason, and realist representation that underwrote the unfolding disaster of modernity. Adorno wrote that not even the autonomous art-object is free from ideology or uncontaminated by its forces; rather, autonomy is made possible by the rationalizing forces of modernity that divide human experience into realms of experience and expertise. Thus, while modernist art has political content, it is ultimately ineffectual: the autonomy of the art-object within avant-gardism actually *elucidated* its own construction and function, and thus performed an immanent critique in a way that demystified it in the moment that the viewer received it, but it had no revolutionary potential.

Like the New Critics and the other early theorists of modernism we have discussed in this chapter, Adorno wove his theory by linking together a selective group of texts into what would become a shared canon. Although critics like Lukács, Brooks, Eliot, and Riding and Graves all differed radically about what modernism might mean, they shared a general understanding of the works that belonged in this category and why they would persist. Joyce, Eliot,

Stravinsky, Kafka, and Musil were in; Marie Corelli (the best-selling novelist of the early twentieth century), Noel Coward, and Academy painters were out. And these works, furthermore, constituted part of a tradition whose origins could be traced back through Western aesthetic history (and beyond)—just not along the lines that the nineteenth century had dictated. Modernism, understood this way, may have been new, but it was nevertheless continuous with the past—bound up with the cables of tradition that made it a clear, coherent, and knowable aesthetic movement. This way of understanding modernism has proven remarkably durable. In Chapter 3 we'll explore at length the ways in which this model has been contested by those who sought to locate modernism beyond a set of texts and figures defined by their opposition to or autonomy from mass culture.

# Could the center hold?

Autonomy, novelty, difficulty, formalism, fragmentation, anti-orthodoxy, tradition—these are the strands woven together by a diverse array of critics in the first half of the twentieth century to create a fairly fixed conception of modernism. The staggeringly diverse cultural work of the period was ordered into a select, coherent aesthetic project—one closely tied not only to an interpretation of modernity but also to certain aesthetic and cultural precursors. Though these models shared a great deal, tensions, disagreements, and inconsistencies remained. By 1950, Eliot had become what Leavis called a "public institution, a part of the establishment," and though he was indispensable for the New Critics, he disagreed with some of their readings of his work, had little interest in pedagogy, and even retracted or greatly revised several key terms ("dissociation of sensibility," "impersonality," "tradition") around which they structured their conceptions of literary history ("Retrospect" 220). As Michael Edward Kaufmann has pointed out, the New Critics, Richards, and Leavis all relied on Eliot's notes to *The Waste Land*, which themselves were somewhat disingenuous and at times misleading (see "T. S. Eliot's"). Few, if any, paid attention to the references to lowbrow culture in the poem—the bar scenes with working-class London voices, the lines from Irving Berlin and Ted Snyder's popular, mass-produced musical recording "That Mysterious Rag" (1911)—that would seem to counter the project of lifting the poetic object out of daily life. And indeed, some New Critics in the 1940s joined Eliot in turning away from seeing texts as hermetic objects and toward social critique, too. Had modernism's most consistent apologists mischaracterized the movement or misread its achievements?

The ambivalence toward the project that had become associated with "modernism" is best seen in the figure of the New York Intellectual and *Partisan Review* art critic Clement Greenberg, whose landmark essay "Avant-garde and Kitsch" (1939) begins with the famous line, "One and the same civilization produces simultaneously two such different things as a poem by T. S. Eliot and a Tin Pan Alley song, or a painting by Braque and a *Saturday Evening Post* cover" (1:5–6). Here Greenberg hits on a question that continues to shape our debates and definitions of modernism: What had so clearly separated *The Waste Land* from all the rest of the cultural work around it—work that so many critics dismissed out of hand? Greenberg answers the question by historicizing the sudden ruptures produced by the avant-garde within the institutions of art in Western bourgeois culture. Modernism, he held, tried to maintain the aesthetic standards of high art, and thus art's vitality, by linking it to an ongoing appetite for change.

For Greenberg, high art and the values it conveyed used to be the property of the bourgeoisie, but modern industrial mass culture had destabilized their social position in the art-world. At this moment came an avant-garde that offered a critique of modern capitalism and bourgeois culture through an entirely new kind of art:

> Hence it developed that the true and most important function of the avant-garde was not to "experiment," but to find a path along which it would be possible to keep culture *moving* in the midst of ideological confusion and violence [through the autonomy of form. Thus] . . . "Art for art's sake" and "pure poetry" appear, and subject matter or content becomes something to be avoided like a plague. (1:8; italics in the original)

Confronted by historical and cultural confusion, Greenberg argues, art turned inward on its own media and materials—and their limits. Thus, Picasso's interest in paint, color, brush-stroke, and the two-dimensional canvas means he seems to care less and less about the representation of any particular object. Similarly, Joyce's increasingly ambitious experiments with language led to *Finnegans Wake*, a book that many find unreadable. But Cubism was now appropriated for advertising campaigns and Joyce, like Eliot, was already being taught in university classrooms. For Greenberg, this means that "the avant-garde is becoming unsure of the audience it depends on—the rich and the cultivated" (1:11). Some bourgeois patrons would still sponsor the avant-garde, but the roles were now reversed in that it was the duty of the avant-garde to *preserve*, rather than attack, high culture. Modernism, as the heir to the avant-gardes of the past, therefore has a historic purpose—indeed, a mission.

Greenberg juxtaposes this situation with the other end of the high/low spectrum: kitsch, which "is a product of the industrial revolution which urbanized the masses of Western Europe and America and established what is called universal literacy. . . . Kitsch is the epitome of all that is spurious in the life of our times. Kitsch pretends to demand nothing of its customers except their money—not even their time" (1:11–12). What, he asks, could link these two—avant-garde and kitsch? How do they coexist in the same culture? His answer is that the avant-garde "imitates the processes of art," while kitsch "imitates its effects" (1:17). Greenberg's turn here toward reception and consumption as intimately linked to form and medium leads him to analyze the way "art" has become synonymous with mass propaganda in Germany, Italy, and Russia. "Kitsch is the culture of the masses" in these and all countries, he writes, and their dictatorial regimes are not necessarily anti-art (1:20). Rather, they did not know what to do with avant-garde art and could not "inject effective propaganda" into it the way that they could with kitsch, so "kitsch keeps a dictator in closer contact with the 'soul' of the people" (1:20).

In a subsequent essay, "Towards a Newer Laocoon" (1940), Greenberg historicizes how art carved out its medium specificity and why literature dominated art for so long. Painting and sculpture in the seventeenth and eighteenth centuries became servants of Romantic literature, he holds. But Romanticism died in the Revolutions of 1848, and rather than an "about-face towards a new society," it was "an emigration to a Bohemia which was to be art's sanctuary from capitalism. . . . The avant-garde, both child and negation of Romanticism, becomes the embodiment of art's instinct of self-preservation" (1:27, 28). That is, art had to escape capitalism's ongoing penetration into every realm of life, by retreating into and expanding the "expressive resources of the medium"; this led to the destruction of the "realistic pictorial space" and the represented object, which, for Greenberg, also brought about "the travesty that was cubism" (1:30, 35). Greenberg instead saw the Abstract Expressionists as legitimate and logical heirs to modernist traditions in their effort to explore fully the nature and medium of their work, all the way to the level of the flatness of the canvas.

This manner of thinking about modernist art as the formation of autonomy through the exploration of material form led Greenberg eventually to "identify Modernism with the intensification, almost the exacerbation, of this self-critical tendency that began with the philosopher Kant. Because he was the first to criticize the means itself of criticism, I conceive of Kant as, the first real Modernist" ("Modernist" 4:85). Modernism, Greenberg argues, is exemplified by its use of "characteristic methods of a discipline to criticize the discipline itself, not in order to subvert it but in order to entrench it more firmly in its area of competence," just as Kant did with logic (4:85). But whereas Enlightenment thinkers criticized from the outside (or so they thought, Greenberg notes), modernism does so from within, providing an alternative and singular means of experience for the viewer that could not be found elsewhere. And to specify its uniqueness and explore its medium fully, art took on a mode of self-criticism that aimed to purge any elements of its making that were borrowed from other media. Thus, because "flatness was the only condition painting shared with no other art, Modernist painting oriented itself to flatness as it did to nothing else," and this led to abstraction (4:87). For Greenberg, modernism was not a complete "break with the past" but an "evolution" of tradition—not by "theoretical demonstrations" of new techniques, but by "convert[ing] theoretical possibilities into empirical ones" (4:92). But even while placing modernism in this line between Romanticism and Abstract Expressionism, Greenberg noted, with some worry, that modernism had already contained itself and its limits by concentrating solely on formal autonomy as its mark.

Greenberg points to a problem that continues to afflict any attempt to define modernism. Put simply, does modernism have an end? Is it an ongoing movement in the arts, or is it, as he worries, a dead-end street that can now be fully circumscribed and defined? The poet-critic Randall Jarrell's "The End of the Line" (1942), after roughly three decades of discussions and provocations, captures what the term and the movement it described signaled. Jarrell claims that "Modernism As We Knew It—the most successful and influential body of poetry of this century—is dead. Compare a 1940 issue of *Poetry* with a 1930 issue. Who could have believed that modernism would collapse so fast! Only someone who realized that modernism is a limit which it is impossible to exceed" (81). Modernism, in his view, was a nihilistic movement promulgated by Pound, Eliot, Crane, Tate, Stevens, Cummings, and Marianne Moore, and its deep, evolutionary ties to Romanticism have been obscured because critics focus on "breaks" rather than their similarities and continuities. Poems now, he says, are as violent and disorganized as they could be, and while the experimentation of the 1910s and 1920s was linked to a belief in revolution around the corner, that "Manifest Destiny" is now gone and innovation has stopped. Was it the case, then, that "modernism" was a hollow invention, one that migrated from the world of religious rebellion to now define a poetic establishment? Was the fusion of the New Critical focus on form and Greenberg's notions of autonomy a mummification of living texts? Was it, as scholars would later charge, an American critical formation that coincided with the rise of its global power after the Second World War, during which time its academies imported a certain genealogy of "modernism" to Britain and claimed it began there? Had modernism undone itself in its very critical-creative formulation as it struggled to encase a coherent whole from too diverse a range of artists and works, since many other ideas of what "modernism" meant still circulated? Had the very cable the critics wove to embed "modernism" in tradition and cut it off from mass culture and kitsch actually strangled the term's possibilities itself? As we will see in the next chapter, figures like Jarrell became increasingly rare in the second half of the twentieth century as the scene of debate about modernism shifted quickly to colleges and universities. There, aesthetic arguments intersected with professional practices in order to produce a canon of major works that still privileged autonomy, tradition, and difficulty while making modernism itself into a compelling field of study—albeit one beset by increasingly disruptive contradictions.

# Notes

1  For a more detailed history of this period, see Călinescu 13–92.

2  The Google Books Ngram Viewer tool illustrates this spike well: search for "modernism" and "modernist" at https://books.google.com/ngrams/.

3  Lewis had attacked Eliot in *Men Without Art* (1934), but nevertheless grouped him with others he called "modernists."

4  The first version of this essay was "Modern Novels" (1919).

5  See the exchange between Stan Smith and Ian Hamilton in the letters section of the *London Review of Books* 23:10 (May 24, 2001) and 23:11 (June 7, 2001).

6  The German critic Walter Benjamin played an essential role in these debates as well, but his work often led him to a much broader interest in mass culture than was evident in the early Frankfurt School. We'll return to him and to similar Marxist thinkers like Siegfried Kracauer in Chapter 3.

# 2

# Consolidation

## Overview

In looking across a range of approaches to contemporary aesthetics in the first part of the twentieth century, we have seen plenty of disagreements, but also a burgeoning consensus about which figures and traits best represented "modernism." This chapter will explore how a relatively small collection of writers and their works became consolidated into a canon that later critics called "high modernism"—a term used to distinguish it from some of the other competing definitions of modernism that we will discuss in Chapter 3. This first and still deeply influential consensus emerged in the 1950s when the critical, pedagogical, and institutional practices associated when the New Criticism were successfully integrated into the academic establishment. This formalist mode of reading—and its cognate mode of viewing advocated by Clement Greenberg—required difficult objects to teach and interpret in isolation, removed from the tumult of the early twentieth century and the polarized global politics of the Cold War era.

As this chapter shows, however, the transition from New Criticism to the conception of high modernism involved a number of internal and external pressures and influences. On the one hand, the New Critical version of modernism created the core of a canon, and it marginalized or excluded some figures whom later scholars would consider central to the era: there were almost no women writers, writers of color, political writers, playwrights, or writers whose works were not originally in English. The New Critics basically ignored, furthermore, the influence on modern poetics of Walt Whitman, whose expressive free verse and Northern US nationalism were at odds with their literary and cultural politics. Indeed, they rarely discussed political or social issues at all—a decision that helped accommodate this version of modernism to the anticommunist models of study that overtook postwar US classrooms. Their legacy—sealed in masterful works like René Wellek's *History of Modern Criticism* (1955) and Cleanth Brooks and W. K. Wimsatt's *Literary Criticism* (1957)—thus helped place modernism at the apex of a long critical and aesthetic tradition that privileged specific types of difficult, autonomous objects alongside a narrow conception of interpretation as close reading. These values took on special urgency in the post–Second World War moment in which this chapter begins. On the other hand, though, we should dismiss the assumption, Alan Golding notes, that this process of canonization was a simple extension of Eliotic principles through a New Critical monolith into the postwar university (see *Outlaw* 105–10). Brooks and Warren's influential textbook *Understanding Poetry* uses, across its successive editions, more works from Robert Frost than from any other twentieth-century poet, including T. S. Eliot, while poets like Ezra Pound were represented no more fully than the now obscure Mark Van Doren. *Understanding Poetry* also discusses themes and poetic content in ways that seem antithetical to the New Critical program, and its shifting inclusions and exclusions indicate that the canon was both open around the edges and in need of reinforcement at its core.

As we will see in this chapter, even when the New Critical school began to wane in the late 1950s, its influence (along with that of F. R. Leavis and I. A. Richards) continued to shape generations of scholars, teachers, and students who even now employ its techniques of close reading and aesthetic valuation. In fact, many of those postwar figures who diverged from, or even attacked, New Critical approaches still managed to shore up the rough outlines of a canon that is still defined by figures like Joyce, Eliot, Pound, and Yeats. But the dominance of academic high modernism at midcentury was ultimately built on things like studies of authors' lives, historical contexts, and extra-literary influences that were hardly New Critical concerns. These studies, along with speculations on the meaning of "modernism" in aesthetic history, were produced amid the growing institutionalization of literary study between the 1950s and early 1970s, when modernism helped define a literary, intellectual, and historical quantum of study—a bounded area of expertise, teaching, and professional practice that fit easily within the academy's structure. Indeed, the death of the movement's primary figures meant that modernism had become a historically limited era with a demarcated aesthetic canon that could be dissected with the same rigor as that of the Renaissance or the Victorian age.

This chapter examines, through groupings of representative works by figures ranging from Richard Ellmann and Hugh Kenner to Frank Kermode and Fredric Jameson, a broad-based project that despite many disagreements managed to produce cables of aesthetic tradition and professional practice capable of binding modernism into a distinct field. Certain authors and texts became cornerstones, the First World War became the central historical event, 1922 became the annus mirabilis, and a wide swath of cultural objects from the early twentieth century was silently cordoned off. This consolidation nevertheless offered some opportunities for expansion since it established a relatively clear set of standards of literary innovation for what might properly count as "modernism"— which, itself, had become an increasingly literary configuration. Nagging questions about biography, ideology, history, and politics, however, kept plucking at the "strandentwining cable" that drew together this first modernist canon. Thus, we have a curious and rather unlikely process: first, postwar critics attempted to codify and energize "modernism"—the same brand name that their creative predecessors fashioned—as a field of study by abutting their close readings of modernist texts with book-length studies of canonical authors, exhaustive biographies, analyses of unpublished drafts and revised texts, and sketches of the historical contexts of the modernist world. "Modernism" still signified diverse things, from mid-century architecture to Latin American literature, but the grounds on which it was debated and the purposes for which it was used had shifted. In contrast to what we saw in Chapter 1, the figures in this chapter are taking a sense of "modernism" that has been relatively stabilized and attempting to give it *depth*, often in the form of moorings that fit the paradigms of university study. And while modernism still had its detractors, such figures were now critiquing a poetic and critical institution far more established than when John Crowe Ransom pondered its legacy in 1924.

This work, in turn, had at least two divergent effects: one was that the very figures who helped move modernism into classrooms asked what the movement could possibly mean in such contexts. As some of the figures we discuss in this chapter noted, the unwitting result of the New Critical configuration of modernism and its academic legacy was what Cary Nelson calls "a remarkable reversal of the revolutionary strain in modernism, a reversal that is still empowered today, [in which] literary theory . . . covertly fused the disjunctive modernist poem with the idealized view of poetry in the genteel tradition [against which modernists rebelled]" (241). The other was that all of this new research opened doors to new definitions of modernism, throwing into question the canon formation itself, with its exclusions and privileges, and beginning what became the drift of modernism from the anchorage established in the New Criticism. In essence, the figures we address in this chapter—even the Marxists like Raymond Williams and Terry Eagleton who critiqued the concept of "modernism" itself—helped create modernism as an aesthetic tradition, an ideological formation, and a narrow field of professional practice, often by reaffirming the canon and its character, though for different ends or purposes. As we'll see, however, this remarkably successful process of concentration begins to turn on itself in the 1980s, prompting a move away from such grand narratives to alternative modernisms and theories of postmodernism that might be drawn from the diverse media and texts of the twentieth century.

# Forging traditions

As the term "modernism" coalesced, the kinds of art, literature, and cultural production that often began as oppositional practices within little magazines, bohemian salons, and radical sociopolitical movements found a ready home within the university—and especially in literary studies. This emerging field of modernist studies, however, needed a core group of Great Works and Great Figures. Crucial to the constitution of the modernist canon, then, was the arrival of full-length studies and biographies of key figures that helped make the authors themselves into embodiments of genius, innovation, and free thought. This process was aided by the fact that, by the late 1940s, Yeats, Bergson, Mann, Gide, Eliot, and Faulkner had all won Nobel prizes. Prior to 1960, Herbert Gorman and Harry Levin both produced biographical studies of Joyce, as did A. Norman Jeffares of Yeats; Malcolm Cowley, Robert Graves, and

Robert McAlmon published memoirs that mythologized the sites and figures of modernism; and modernists themselves—Wyndham Lewis, Gertrude Stein, and William Carlos Williams—wrote forms of autobiographies.[1] All of these works lent a mystique to certain figures and places, and indeed helped make some modernists into celebrities. This process was facilitated, in turn, by lengthy profiles in magazines like *Time* and *Vanity Fair* and by texts such as Viking's *Portable Hemingway* (1944) and *Portable Faulkner* (1944), which brought modernist texts to broader publics.[2] Writer-critics and younger associates of the high modernists, like Stephen Spender, Cyril Connolly, and Anthony Burgess, navigated between academic and lay audiences to further this work, and in important journals with similar crossover circulation, such as the *Sewanee Review*, *Kenyon Review*, *Hudson Review* (1947–), and *Encounter* (1953–91), "modernism" was promulgated as a rubric for categorizing and judging new writing according to its formal qualities. No text, though, matched the ambitious scope and thoroughness of Richard Ellmann's groundbreaking *James Joyce* (1959)—a colossal biography that effectively put Joyce on a par with Shakespeare or Dante and still powerfully shapes our understanding of one of modernism's most important figures. In its wake appeared a flurry of other academic studies that eventually reached to most every figure of the new canon, including Proust, Hemingway, Pound, Eliot, Lawrence, Woolf, Stein, Strachey, and others.[3] Hemingway's *A Moveable Feast* also appeared posthumously in 1964, and this autobiographical work definitively placed the romantic heart of literary modernism in Paris in the 1920s.

Furthermore, as the authors of the modernist era died, their letters, drafts, unpublished writings, and other archival materials became available as objects of academy study for a new generation of scholars and critics. Joyce's *Stephen Hero* (1944), an abandoned draft of *Portrait of the Artist as a Young Man*, was published, and in 1971, a facsimile version of Eliot's *The Waste Land* typescript offered scholars a fascinating document that records Pound's heavy editorial transformation of the poem. Founded in 1957, the Harry Ransom Center at the University of Texas at Austin began an aggressive campaign to collect the archives of modernist writers. It was joined by Norman Holmes Pearson and Donald Gallup of the Yale Collection of American Literature (later housed at the Beinecke Library) as well as by the Rare Books and Manuscripts

Library at the University of Buffalo and McFarlin Library at the University of Tulsa. These archival and biographical projects were supported by the creation of professional societies devoted to single authors and by cognate journals such as the *James Joyce Quarterly* in 1963, *Conradiana* in 1968, *Paideuma* (which studies Pound) in 1972, *Virginia Woolf Miscellany* in 1973, *Yeats Eliot Review* in 1974, and *The Wallace Stevens Journal* in 1977.[4]

These journals, archives, and societies all established a set of professional standards and practices around which the study of high modernism might be coordinated and made visible within the academy. Although this meant that modernism was treated as a now closed historical period, many of these critics insisted that the works themselves remained essential to the understanding of contemporary life and culture. The signature works and careers of two prominent mid-century scholars of modernism are exemplary here. Ellmann famously begins his biography of Joyce by writing that "we are still learning to be James Joyce's contemporaries, to understand our interpreter" (3). This suggests that Joyce is somehow more "modern" than the world he depicted and that his writing still directly engages, even anticipates, readers now removed by decades from early twentieth-century Dublin. Ellmann's Joyce is a universal humanist, one who, "in spite of [his] reputation of having skirted his age, . . . is unexpectedly at its center" because of his ability to turn the "ordinary" into the "extraordinary" by way of a literary style that is as "difficult" as it is "rewarding" (4, 5, 7). In his equally influential *The Pound Era* (1971), Kenner too helped craft the narrow canon of high modernism as the twentieth century's central aesthetic movement. This work—part biography, part conceptualization, and part close reading—culminated a revival of the reputation of Pound, who had been vilified for his pro-Mussolini radio addresses and his anti-Semitism, and put him squarely at the center of modernism. Across 600-plus pages, Kenner, a former student of Cleanth Brooks, covers Pound's life and major works in various contexts, from his thoughts on Henry James to his ideas of Chinese culture, in order to demonstrate how Pound created through his poetics a system for "the invention of language" and thereby set the course for twentieth-century literature (94). For Kenner, the "province" of Pound's *Cantos*, Eliot's *The Waste Land*, and Joyce's *Ulysses* and *Finnegans Wake* is, "as never before in history, . . . the entire human race speaking"; their method is so modern that it "has been possible for only a few decades, and is still not accessible to all readers" (95). Although Ellmann and Kenner often differed starkly with one another, they both nevertheless built the core of a high modernist canon around linguistic innovation, difficulty, and autonomy—elements embodied in the works of the "Men of 1914" (Joyce, Pound, Eliot, Lewis). For both critics, these writers' works represent a synthesis of language, medium, and form that demanded close examination and could still yield surprising discoveries about what it meant to be modern.

The successes within the university for grounding the new field of modernist studies, and especially the value placed on single-author studies, were borne out when Ellmann, also a biographer of Yeats and Wilde, was named Goldsmiths' Professor of English at Oxford University in 1970, while Hugh Kenner moved to Johns Hopkins University in 1973 just after the publication of *The Pound Era*. Indeed, many universities began to hire a specialist in figures like Joyce or Pound, typically mirroring the larger emphasis on major figures like Shakespeare, Dante, and Wordsworth.[5] "Modernism" was now a respected academic subject; its main figures were elevated to the pantheon of literary titans, and survey courses in English or American literature now ended with their works.

Furthermore, between 1965 and 1974, three major anthologies appeared, and all of them became very popular in classrooms, where they served as the introductions to modernism for generations of students.[6] Their work was simultaneously historical and conceptual, and oftentimes they built directly on the projects of the edited anthologies that helped launch and spread modernism: Pound's *Des Imagistes* (1914) and *Catholic Anthology* (1915), Parker Tyler's *Modern Things* (1934), Michael Roberts's *New Signatures* (1932) and *Faber Book of Modern Verse* (1936), and Yeats's *Oxford Book of Modern Verse* (1936), to name a few. Richard Ellmann and Charles Feidelson edited the first major anthology of high modernism in 1965. Their book, *The Modern Tradition*, acknowledged that critics had not yet defined "the modern," but rather, had merely used it in a chronological sense. Setting out deliberately to establish a canon rather than just a collection of historical works, however, they propose that "the modern" is a "distinctive kind of imagination," one whose characteristic works "positively insist on a general frame of reference within and beyond themselves. They claim modernity; they profess modernism" (v). In "a large spiritual exercise" ranging across disciplines and genres, modern writers created a paradoxically antitraditional tradition rooted in the new urban environments and the internationalism of the era. Ellmann and Feidelson sketch out modernism's primary traits as a series of elevations of the individual over the social, the unconscious over the conscious, passion over morals, and dynamism over stasis, all coupled with a sense of a historic mission among the writers who feel, ironically, that they have no connection to the past. The influential modernism they define through commentary on selective texts absorbs the past, but knows it cannot contain it, and thus, "in this sense, modernism is synthetic in its very indeterminacy" (vii).

The anthology identifies the nine historical and social influences that contributed to modernism's formation: Symbolism, Realism, Nature, Cultural History, The Unconscious, Myth, Self-Consciousness, Existence, and Faith. These sections weave a cable of tradition together that threads artists and writers as diverse as Paul Klee, Samuel Coleridge, and Alain Robbe-Grillet through thematic ideas like the purification of fiction, historical determinism, social realism, and deified man. The core thread running through this cable is the idea that modernism appears as the culmination of the steadily developing doctrine of aesthetic autonomy. It's there, for example, in the Symbolist premise that "human imagination actively constructs the world we perceive or at least meets it more than halfway, and does not merely reflect the given forms of external objects." The Symbolist, Ellmann and Feidelson note, relies not on reason or perception, but on the "artistic image or symbol—and especially the verbal symbol, the language of a poem—[as] the key to the relation of mind and nature" (7). As Ellmann suggested in his biography of Joyce, this implied that modernism, although historically bracketed, was not yet entirely spent—that its works remained connected to the lives of teachers, students, and readers willing to puzzle their way through its difficulties.

Just two years later, in the introduction to his anthology *Literary Modernism* (1967), Irving Howe took a different approach by arguing that "modernist literature seems now to be coming to an end," though he admitted that the movement itself remains "elusive and protean, and its definition hopelessly complicated" (12, 13).[7] This "end," or a vision of the end, is a defining trait for modernism, for it is a "sign of modernity" to always struggle but never triumph: in "modernist culture," Howe claims, "the object perceived seems always on the verge of being swallowed up by the perceiving agent, and the act of perception in danger of being exalted to the substance of reality" (14). Despite arguing that modernism might have ended, however, Howe also stresses that the "central diction in modernist literature is toward the self-sufficiency of the work" (27). Aesthetic order is "abandoned or radically modified," and instead, *"modernist literature replaces the traditional criteria of aesthetic unity with the new criterion of aesthetic expressiveness, or perhaps more accurately, it downgrades the value of aesthetic unity in behalf of even a jagged and fragmented expressiveness"* (29; italics in the original). Modernists also replace nature with psychology and rely on "shock, surprises, excitement" as dominant motifs, a description that productively links difficulty to a larger critique of Victorian Realism (30). Howe outlines, too, a modernist investment in primitivism, a new antihero, and nihilism before concluding that this aesthetic movement "will not come to an end; its war chants will be repeated through the decades." It will instead succumb, he insists in a reading of what later critics will call postmodernism, to "publicity and sensation, the kind of savage parody which may indeed be the only fate worse than death" (40).

The Idea of the Modern presents essays by Spender, Lionel Trilling, José Ortega y Gasset, William Phillips, David Jones (who earns a good deal of attention as a poet too), Harold Rosenberg, Randall Jarrell, and several others. It provides overviews of movements, figures, and trends rather than polemics on what modernism is or was. It is in Howe's attempt to sum up the movement for students and in his ambivalence on the question of whether modernism was over that we see some of the implicit contradictions that will ultimately undo the consensus surrounding the high modernist canon in the 1980s (a process we'll explore at length in the next chapter). As a politically committed leftist associated with the New York Intellectuals, Howe sought to find a way to link political readings with the focus on aesthetic order derived from the New Criticism. His work notes, with some discomfort, the diverse, often troubling, political beliefs of the writers themselves: Yeats, Lewis, and Pound went far to the right; Brecht, Malraux, and Gide to the left; only Joyce remained "pure," he believes. The anthology ultimately manages to sidestep its own contradictions, essentially ignoring the question of whether a single movement or concept called "modernism" can adequately encompass such deep political divides. This problem never quite goes away, however, and will contribute significantly to the fracturing of modernism in the ensuing decades.

Several years later came the most influential and certainly the most enduring anthology of high modernism, Malcolm Bradbury and James McFarlane's *Modernism: A Guide to European Literature, 1890-1930* (1974). It became the standard text for at least two decades of courses on modernism in universities and remains in print. Bradbury had begun elaborating their underlying theory in 1971 by focusing on difficulty as modernism's defining element, arguing that its opposition to realistic representation arose through an "international revolutionary fervor in all the arts" in the new century ("Modernity" 71). Codifying what is now a familiar account of experimentations with representations of reality and consciousness among Joyce, Eliot, and other metropolitan expatriates, he suggests that the movement is over, having exhausted itself by 1930. In *Modernism*, the editors therefore explicitly use "modernism" as a historical rather than temporal term, transforming it effectively into a professional concept used narrowly "to locate a distinct stylistic phase which is ceasing or has ceased (hence the current circulation of counters like Proto-Modernism, Palæo-Modernism, Neo-Modernism and Post-Modernism)" ("Name" 22). It captures the feeling of living in "totally novel" and "chao[tic]" times and builds on the experiences of the First World War, modern industrial technologies, and the decline of community, and it employs the theories of Werner Heisenberg, Marx, Freud, and Darwin. Thus, Bradbury and McFarlane claim that "Modernism is . . . the art of modernization," no matter how the artist reads it or tries to avoid it. It is "not art's freedom, but art's necessity" (27). And "Modernism, while not our total style, becomes the movement which has expressed our modern consciousness; . . . it may not be the only stream, but it is in the *main* stream" (28, 29; italics in the original). This focus on style played an important role not just in consolidating the modernist canon that developed after the Second World War, but also in emphasizing the genius of creators like Joyce, Eliot, and Picasso as they became both the subject of major specialized research and cultural icons in their own right.

Their anthology dates modernism from 1890, but they admit that that the movement's origin is difficult to isolate, with its progenitors scattered across Europe. They note that one could look back to bohemian Paris of the 1830s, to Émile Zola, to Walter Pater, to

Charles Baudelaire, and even to John Donne or Laurence Sterne. This kind of rhetorical move is common in many attempts to fashion the canon of high modernism: the movement's origins remain fuzzy, but always end with certainty in a European context that preserves a clear distinction between the imperial center and colonial periphery, between innovation and derivation. Bradbury and McFarlane argue that modernism is the culmination of a developing sense of historical crisis in the West, but that such a definition only holds true for the New York-London-Paris nexus. Modernism, that is, looks different from Berlin, Prague, or St. Petersburg—an apparent contradiction that again points to the debates that will begin to remake the field in the 1980s. Whatever its origins or its differential locations, however, they contend that the movement came to an end in 1930 because, after the onset of the Great Depression, "it seems that certain elements of Modernism seem to be reallocated, as history increasingly came back in for intellectuals" and writers who had subjugated politics to art (51). Bradbury and McFarlane's introduction thus helps preserve the idea of aesthetic autonomy as an essential part of a modernist tradition, and does so by declaring it a generally exhausted practice that nevertheless speaks to the contemporary moment. The collection itself concentrates on topics like "The Cultural and Intellectual Climate of Modernism," "A Geography of Modernism," and "Literary Movements," then explores three primary genres—lyric poetry, the novel, and drama. Movements from Imagism to Expressionism, authors from Robert Musil to August Strindberg, and topics from metaphor/metonymy to radical politics are all addressed. It finally features a now somewhat infamous "Chronology of Events" that overlooks or mischaracterizes (and often misspells) many non-Anglo-European or peripheral European writers and works.

In all three of these foundational anthologies, the boundaries of the movement remain loose around the edges, but restricted primarily to white, male, European (and to a lesser extent American) figures. Across all of them, for example, the Harlem Renaissance does not appear; women like Djuna Barnes, Mina Loy, and Elizabeth Bowen are absent; the colonial and postcolonial world barely exists; homosexuality, as a theme or in the lives of writers like Proust, Stein, Forster, or Woolf, is barely present (aside from some discussion of Wilde); and American figures likes F. Scott Fitzgerald, Amy Lowell, Marianne Moore, and many others receive only scant notes. Despite what later critics will come to see as these enormous gaps, these anthologies—especially Bradbury and McFarlane's—established a pervasive and still resonant definition of modernism focused around difficulty, autonomy, novelty, and a historical imbrication from the late nineteenth century to roughly the Great Depression.[8] Their avoidance of political stances, too, helped them effectively push aside competing collections of the moment, such as LeRoi Jones's *The Moderns* (1963) and Donald Allen's *New American Poetry 1945-1960* (1960), which took radically different approaches to the question of canonicity, but whose affinities with the political left made them suspect in Cold War–era classrooms.

# Taking stock of "Modernism"

Such biographies, anthologies, and single-author studies helped bind together a canonical high modernism that was both rooted in tradition and exceptional within twentieth-century culture. Helping further professionalize and institutionalize this handful of works, another set of influential scholars set out simultaneously to *conceptualize* modernism itself. What exactly did it mean, they asked, to think of modernism as a "movement," an "era," or a "tradition"? And how were the revolutionary elements of that movement being reinterpreted and revaluated in new contexts, far removed from modernism's own volatile world? As Harold Rosenberg summarized in his *The Tradition of the New* (1959), "the famous 'modern break with tradition' [that Baudelaire initiated] has lasted long enough to have produced its own tradition," but "the new cannot become a tradition without giving rise to unique contradictions, myths, absurdities—often, creative absurdities" (9). Four key documents published in 1960–61 all share a certain illustrative ambivalence about, and even hostility to, a term so fraught with ambiguity—especially as it had been absorbed into the postwar universities in which some of them worked. First, Harry Levin, an early champion in the United States of college-level courses on modernist writers, posed the simple yet provocative question: "What Was Modernism?" (1960).[9] In the article of that name, Levin pointed out that a new apartment building in New York City was named "The Picasso." Half a century ago, Picasso launched a revolt against everything this building was and represented, both aesthetically and functionally. Now, his name not only headlines MoMA, but also has had commercial appeal conferred upon it. This shows, Levin writes, the ways in which "the development of the arts is registered through a series of shocks to the public . . . with a dialectical pattern of revolution and alternating reaction" aimed at "cultural emancipation" that eventually becomes absorbed by the larger consumer-driven culture (611, 612). The late prominence, even stardom, of figures like Eliot, Picasso, Joyce, and Schoenberg clearly marks out this strange path, as they move from avant-garde provocateurs to the "living embodiment of tradition" (611). "Joyce's books," he writes, "which were burned and censored during his lifetime, have become a happy hunting ground for doctoral candidates"; Beckett, who once staged an elaborate prank on the Modern Language Association, was now carefully studied in its official journal, *PMLA*; experimental poets had left bohemia to take up university appointments; and the pages of little magazines had become academic texts (614).

Levin, like the anthologists we have discussed, concludes that the modernist revolution has passed into history, becoming part of a now defined and thus contained—one distinct, he believes, from the reactionary realism of the era (embodied by the novelist G. K. Chesterton) and large swaths of mass and popular culture. Here, he turns again to authorial style and language as means of interpreting revolutions in the social and political spheres: the modernists were commenting on and revising the theories of liberalism and individuality of the late nineteenth-century world in which they were born. They read Bergson, Proust, and Freud, and they made themselves paradoxically both belated and up to date. They thrived on exile, international style, and cosmopolitanism, so that "if the object is unity, that must bear an organic connection to the multiplicity; its collective pattern must be revealed and confirmed through individual lives; its outward view of social interaction must be combined with an inner focus on psychological motivation" (624). This yielded new modes of writing and new characters, and Levin claims that *Finnegans Wake* was the endpoint of a project of recreating fallen cities, grasping an apocalypse, and discounting science, rationalism, and positivism. Modernists, he concludes, instead "create[d] a conscience for a scientific age," a modernity whose dawn was located in Rabelais (630). In short, modernism has a strong tradition behind it for Levin—a tradition of skepticism in which the individual depicts the social whole through aesthetic innovation.

By contrast, Lionel Trilling, a cultural critic from the overlapping *Partisan Review* and New York Intellectual groups, focused less on a concise definition of modernism than on its political contexts. In "On the Modern Element in Modern Literature" (1961) (which was later republished as "On the Teaching of Modern Literature," 1965), he agrees with Levin that the cables now protectively drawing together modernism as an aesthetic canon and professional discipline also threaten to squeeze the life from it by consigning it to the dustiness of literary history. Drawing on his experiences of teaching modern literature at Columbia, he detects a "disenchantment of our culture with culture itself" and argues that "the characteristic element of modern literature, or at least of the most highly developed modern literature, is the bitter line of hostility to civilization that runs through it" (3). Trilling laments the "susceptibility of modern literature to being made into an academic subject" and worries about students who respond to what had only a few decades earlier been revolutionary work "with a happy vagueness" (4). He is surprised at "how little resistance language offers to their intentions"; despite the fact that, for him, modern literature "shows its difficulties at first blush" and that "no literature has ever been so shockingly personal as that of our time—it asks every question that is forbidden in polite society" (7).

Why have the revolutionary and controversial texts of modernism become less challenging in academic settings? Trilling asks. He rejects the idea that the university is solely at fault—it can open up works that time has domesticated, he argues—and he similarly rejects the proposition that literature is only an ahistorical structure of words. For him, the early anthropologist Sir James Frazer[10] is the key to understanding modernism, and he focuses this point through his notes on the "terrible message of ambivalence toward the life of civilization" in Conrad's *Heart of Darkness* (1899) (17). The novella is, in fact, a portrait of modern artists, he claims, much like Thomas Mann's *Death in Venice* (1912). The "darkness" is revealed in Kurtz, the painter who descends to "hell" and prefers "the reality of this hell to the bland lies of the civilization that has overlaid it" (18). Trilling marvels that his students were ready "to engage in the process that we might call the socialization of the anti-social, or the acculturation of the anti-cultural, or the legitimization of the subversive" (23). But they were not shocked by the outright attacks on civilization implicit in Conrad; indeed, they appreciated the critique of middle-class life and even shared the desire to escape from its "civilization." Modernist literature, he concludes, has been successfully domesticated, its self-proclaimed energies transformed into a historical, even traditional mode of aesthetic experience that can no longer reach beyond the text or even the classroom.

The poet-critic Karl Shapiro's *In Defense of Ignorance* (1960) similarly recognizes this apparent strangling of modernism's energies. Shapiro, on the heels of having edited the famous modernist journal *Poetry* from 1950 to 1955, vehemently proclaimed that

> the dictatorship of intellectual "modernism," the sanctimonious ministry of "the Tradition," the ugly programmatic quality of twentieth-century criticism have maimed our poetry and turned it into a monstrosity of literature. . . . In the religion of modern poetry the Trinity is composed of Pound, Eliot, and Yeats. All three men are provincials, the two Americans being Europeans by adoption. (ix, 24)

For him, modernism, now embedded within and constitutive of the long Western tradition, blunts subsequent literary production by rhetorically cutting it off from some larger modernity. As a result, judgment in criticism has been neutralized, public opinion has given way to the expertise of critics, and popular works have been debased by being removed from modernism. The same modernist figures who railed against the poetic establishment in their day were now instrumental to an oppressive establishment themselves. Incensed by the awarding of the inaugural Bollingen Prize in poetry in 1949 to Pound, Shapiro furthermore believed that critics have neatly separated poets and politics completely, leaving some canonical figures untouchable. This blinds critics to the fact that Eliot and Pound actually fail in their form because they desire religion, but cannot find it; they disavow mysticism too, so instead they "gravitate toward orthodoxy" in monarchism and fascism (84). Like Trilling, Shapiro sees modernism as a potentially dangerous force that the conventions of teaching and scholarship have managed to defuse through an excessive attention to form and tradition. They were not alone: modernism had become a constrictive rather than inspiring legacy for a variety of postwar groups who decisively rejected its aesthetics—the Beat Generation, the burgeoning Black Arts movement, Pop Artists, the Movement, and the Angry Young Men, to name only a few—and suggested that perhaps modernism was dead and was best left that way.[11] (And yet, these figures, we must note, still needed "modernism" to signify something definitive.)

Likewise, in his *Reflections on a Literary Revolution* (1960), Graham Hough shares this frustration with the rapid professionalization of modernist studies and claims that the literary "revolution of 1914 was quite as momentous as the Romantic one of over a century before, but it was different" because it did not last (6). For Hough, modernism was mostly successful in creating a mode of reading now mastered by undergraduates—the New Criticism— while its "direct effect on literary practice has been strangely small." Eliot and Pound, he asserts, "have had no successors whatever," and Joyce and Lewis have no heirs in prose (7). Understood this way, modernism has successfully accommodated itself to the literary tradition, but it has paradoxically brought that very understanding of a tradition to an end, leaving no "workable tradition" (7). Dismissing "modernism" as a now routinized practice, Hough instead tries to break its connection to a still unfolding modernity by restricting the era's key innovations to Imagism alone, which he then contends was little more than a "by-blow from Symbolism" (10). "Imagist poetic theory was inconsistent with itself," he holds, "and large parts of it were contradicted by the contemporary poetic practice" (44). In a series of attacks on Hulme and Eliot, Hough lays out what he sees as a pattern of great talent, great bombast and self-promotion, "but no sense of direction; none of that sense of a deeply felt, all-organising human purpose that we cannot fail to notice in the work of the Romantic critics . . . [and in] Dryden, Pope, and Johnson" (44–5). Hough insists, then, that what is called "modernism" managed only temporarily to disturb the greater development of English writing in the twentieth century.

In these four critics—Levin, Trilling, Shapiro, and Hough—we see, captured in the space of just over a year, a conviction that modernism was an ingrained concept, even if misnamed and exaggerated in its reach; that it rapidly fit itself to the demands of academic practice; and that its attempts to deny its own history and historicity could not hold. Even Spender, who had been a vital commentator on the high modernists, now attempted in a series of lectures between 1959 and 1961 to differentiate between "modernist" and "contemporary" writers by their respective attitudes toward the notions of progress and modernity (see *Struggle*). He distanced himself from modernism, especially as Eliot became more politically conservative, while Robert Graves—one of the first explicators and defenders of "modernist" poetry— by the 1960s had dismissed the movement. Rosenberg further lamented that not only had modernism become an ossified term, but also, during the Cold War, "the very internationalism that created modernism [in Paris] was under attack by critics who saw nationality as the highest level of aesthetic communication" (211). Modernism, in short, for these figures had been powerfully refined into a specific set of aesthetic practices, exemplified by a group of canonical artists and texts that were then segregated further for analysis within the same staid national traditions that modernists famously attacked and sought to rewrite. They were interpreted primarily through formalist critical techniques or traditional modes of scholarly practice (like biography) that defanged and relegated them to a foreclosed historical period only faintly resonant with the ongoing challenges of the contemporary world.

# Modernisms

As modernism began to harden around its still most influential definition at midcentury, contradictions continued to trouble the growing critical consensus. Even when viewed through the narrow prism of a canon, the authors and texts were simply too diverse to sustain a consistent sense of order or aesthetics. This led the influential British critic Frank Kermode to introduce, for the first time, the idea of "modernisms," suggesting that the concept itself contains a number of divergent strands woven loosely around a single core. Like Hough, Wilson, and others, he links modernism to both Romanticism and Symbolism, arguing in *Romantic Image* (1957) that all these movements share a belief in the image as a source of "radiant truth out of space and time," the perception of which requires the estrangement or isolation of the author who perceives it (4). A decade later, in *The Sense of an Ending* (1967), however, he abandons this image of a grand historical synthesis as he inquires into the critical and artistic attempt to order and design the past, present, and future. Seen from this vantage, his modernism becomes less about a coherent aesthetic program than about various attempts to induce crises and thus to force endings or declare new beginnings (such as the onset of "the modern" era).

Kermode uses this rubric to analyze two different "modernisms," one "traditionalist" and the other "schismatic": "Traditionalist modernism has its roots in the period before the Great War, but its flowering came later than that of anti-traditionalist modernism, which was planted by [French poet Guillaume] Apollinaire and reaped by Dada. This anti-traditionalist modernism is the parent of our own schismatic modernism; but at both periods the two varieties have co-existed" (103). Each of these seeks to declare different kinds of endings: one marked by the general sense of continuity shared by the "traditionalists" and the other looking to break entirely from the past into a radical, even apocalyptic newness shared by the "schismatics." Writers like Pound, Yeats, Lewis, and Eliot were profoundly skeptical about the present, but they "hated decadence, venerated tradition, wanted renovation, and had an eschatological mood," which Kermode believed led them all to purist doctrines typically associated with the political right (104). Pound's anti-Semitism, for instance, was part of his belief in destroying the "demonic host" before "positive eschatological change" could take place (109). For Lewis, Lawrence, and Eliot, fascism provided varying levels of structure and tradition—what we've called a cable that binds their work to the past—and Kermode saw here both the roots of their authoritarianism and their efforts to reconstruct a "living relation to the past" (114). Thus, for Eliot, "newness is a phenomenon that affects the whole of the past; nothing on its own can be new. That alone distinguishes his modernism from avant-gardism," and from French New Novelists, Sartre, Beckett, and other "schismatics," who seek to cut entirely the entwining cables of the past (120).

The following year, in *Continuities* (1968), Kermode takes up this notion of a splintered collection of modernisms even more directly by exploring how the word "modern" was used to encompass things as diverse as John Lane's *Yellow Book* (1894–97), Aubrey Beardsley's controversial art, Wilde's excesses, and French obsessions with novelty. He sees the roots of the "modern" as a "Flaubertian alliance of formal experiment and realism" that shunned politics only to have politics return later, then disappear again; and he sees the apocalyptic tone present since the 1890s, before the aesthetic innovations associated with the canonical version of modernism emerged from 1907 to 1925 (2). Building on his earlier work, Kermode proposes the terms "palæo-" and "neo-modernism" as elaborations of his earlier opposition between the "traditionalists" and "schismatics," and they proved influential for theorists of postmodernism (a thread we will pick up in Chapter 3). Modernism, he insists, is not over—though modernism's leading figures abandoned the movement when they abandoned humanism for fascism or religion—nor do we have the new art of a revolution. Rather, we have a "palæo-modernist conspiracy which made a cult of occult forms [and] is not unrelated to the extremist denial that there are any. These are the self-reconciling opposites of modernism" (13). Palæo-modernism is, for Kermode, the modernism of Eliot, Pound, and the pre-1945 generation that had been centralized, canonized, and declared over by midcentury. Neomodernism, on the other hand, includes still living artists like Beckett and the composer John Cage, who sought to dismantle tradition along with many of the very institutions of art and its reception. As a movement, Kermode writes, it "prefers and professes to do without the tradition and the illusion" because it believes that its predecessors did not go far enough in overthrowing the past, and it substitutes the randomness of aleatory pleasure for the order of an exquisite formalism (12). The two are inextricably linked, though: "There is, in short, a family resemblance between the modernisms. 'Indifference' and the abrogation of 'responsibility' are the wilder cousins of the more literary 'impersonality' and 'objectivity'" (13). Neomodernism chooses anarchy in place of modernism's authoritarianism, rebelling against the modernists' claims—by now institutionally cemented by critics—to have been "original" and "modern" for all time.

Among this first generation of scholars in the 1950s and 1960s to work in the wake of the modernist movement—to work with a full sense that "modernism" might be over—Kermode stands out for having offered new genealogies, divisions, and schematic vocabularies for studying the movement. As an academic and a public intellectual, he also illuminates a good deal about his own cultural context. Working with a now increasingly unified canon, he finds within it a set of contradictions and a diversity of practices that point inevitably beyond the cables from which it was woven. In the curious, even paradoxical concept of riven "modernisms," he attempts to preserve a coherent set of texts and critical concepts—a compromise that keeps the focus on a set of agreed-upon major works and figures, even as it broaches the potentially irreconcilable differences between them. This compromise becomes essential to the next wave of critics, who sought to manage its contradictions while the very idea of a modernist canon itself came under enormous pressure. Other critics like Charles Altieri distinguished between different modes of modernism; in 1976 he was the first to use the term "high modernism" to describe the canon fashioned by the New Critics. To differentiate high modernism from contemporary poetry, Altieri posits "an opposition between the earlier, essentially Symbolist poetics concerned primarily with the powers of the imagination to create values and structures for interpreting experience and the more recent concern for discovering the energies and possible moral forces inherent in acts of perception and in our immediate prereflective experiences of nature and society" ("Objective" 101; see also *Enlarging*; Breslin). Altieri's language here is abstruse, but he makes the influential argument that "high modernism" should be redefined around experimental attempts to represent formally the complex processes of observation and experience by which we might come to know the world.

This bifurcation of the modernist project is the subject of his *Painterly Abstraction in Modernist American Poetry* (1989). Like many critics of modernism, Altieri attempts to link painting and the fine arts to poetry and literature. "Modernist art," Altieri argues, "demonstrated the capacity of formal energies to reject mimetic structures and still retain extraordinary semantic force by relying directly on the production of exemplary attitudes that an audience might project into extraartistic contexts" (7). This process of abstraction, whether in poetry or in painting, required creators to define their ethical positions toward others—especially communities—in ways that made modernism at once an epistemological and an ethical project. Altieri continues this argument in his *Art of Twentieth-century Poetry* (2006) by claiming that modernism came from a refusal of sensitivity and symbolism in representation toward a "new realism" in science and "presentational realism" for poetry (4, 12). Thus, he moves here not to displace or discount modernism, but to reweave the cables that bind it together from a number of increasingly distinct strands. Modernism was both a living and a dead tradition of which we still had a loose grasp, and these critics' works testified to the ways in which "form" had been narrowed. For Altieri, modernism is still a tradition and still has a core of canonical writers, only they needed to be understood on different terms that bring with them different sociopolitical stakes.

Another key theorist of the relationship between modernism and emergent postmodernism, Marjorie Perloff, invited in the 1980s a reconsideration of what "form" had, in fact, excluded by functioning as a certain type of gatekeeper for definitions of modernism. Perloff forcefully argued against the version of modernism that Kenner had proposed in *The Pound Era*, which she saw as depoliticized, and asked provocatively in the title of an article, "Pound/Stevens: Whose Era?" (1982). Perloff's *Poetics of Indeterminacy* (1981) proposes an alternative and argues that rather than deriving from Symbolism, modernism inherited from French writers Arthur Rimbaud and Guillaume Apollinaire a poetics that passed through the avant-gardes (Cubism, Dada, Surrealism) to Stein, Williams, and Pound, and then to a still vaguely defined postmodernism exemplified by Beckett, Ashbery, David Antin, and John Cage. She holds that Yeats, Eliot, and Stevens were less modernists than Symbolists, a tradition that came from English Romanticism. She then traces a different kind of modernism to the work of Rimbaud, who embraced an anti-Symbolist and literalist indeterminacy that favored contradiction, metonymy, and synecdoche. The carefully chiseled formal structures of Symbolism, which had become the cornerstone of New Criticism, Perloff argues, gave way to an "open field of narrative possibilities" (11).[12] She then builds on Roland Barthes's and Tzvetan Todorov's readings of Rimbaud, both of which praised his antiexpressionism, "undecidability," and destruction of linguistic relationships. She writes that Stein's "Melanctha" (1909) and *The Making of Americans*, for instance, are "examples of verbal compositions in which indeterminacy is created by repetition and variation, sameness and difference, a rhetorical pattern of great intricacy, which is set up so as to create semantic gaps" (98). Williams's antisymbolism in *Kora in Hell: Improvisations* (1920) performs a similar function by preferring process and improvisation over a constellation of signs and meaning, indicating a move away from the word as symbol to the word as reality. And in his *Cantos*, Pound breaks signs, asking the reader to fill them in; the text's signs misquote, point to nothing beyond themselves, and glorify distortion over quotation and allusive discovery. All of these examples, Perloff believes, explain why the New Critics ignored these works and championed the Symbolist-modernists, thereby rendering their canon fragmented and incomplete. Like Kermode, she too constructs a canon of modernisms, now woven from multiple strands but nevertheless set in place to bind together and thereby isolate a group of elite works.

In her complementary study *The Futurist Moment* (1986), Perloff advances this argument about the multiplicity of modernism even further by focusing powerfully on the immense range of cultural production that flourished around the First World War. She notes that until 1915, many poets and artists celebrated the war; their revolutionary fervor, reactionary bombast, belligerent nationalism, and aesthetic internationalism produced a particular "avant guerre" moment. Perloff here yokes together aesthetics, culture, and politics to argue that the avant-garde practices associated with Italian Futurism did not constitute a movement, but a *moment* whose movements did not live up to it. It was a "prophetic and utopian phase, the arena and agitation and preparation for the announced revolution, if not the revolution itself" (xxxv). The upshot, for Perloff, is the same for modernism, the avant-garde, and Futurism: "actual historical realities continue to elude their totalizing power" (35). That is, these concepts each represent only pieces of a larger historical moment that cannot be reduced to a single canon or concept. Her study contrasts Robert Wohl's *The Generation of 1914* (1979), which shored up an approach to a transnational "lost generation" of writers and thinkers for whom 1914 was the touchstone of disillusioning experience. Similarly, she rebuts Paul Fussell, whose widely influential study, *The Great War and Modern Memory* (1975), linked modernism directly to the alienating experience of mechanized trench warfare. Perloff's late work thus puts further pressure on the idea of modernism as a canon of works that might be derived from a central set of aesthetic structures or experiences. By starting to look at cultural production more generally within this historically charged moment, she begins to develop a new definition of modernism that will eventually challenge the centrality of the very works that remain the focus of her own work. In short, Perloff's, Altieri's, and Kermode's essential compromise—encapsulated in the plural term "modernisms" and in the segregation of a "high" modernism—strained the cables of tradition to a breaking point and soon gave way to the more uncertain, even pragmatic, attempts to define modernism, which we will explore in the next two chapters. To get there, however, we first need to look briefly at how Marxist critics, themselves deeply committed to historical critique and wary of New Critical formalism, found themselves productively entangled in the cables of the same modernist canon.

# The Marxist canon

Marxist criticism, as we have seen, objected from the start to the New Critical effort to separate form from its immediate historical and political conditions. Many mid-century and contemporary Marxists who treated early twentieth-century literature thus sought to redefine the ways in which form had operated, but in the cases of figures like Lukács and Adorno, they nevertheless shared the same basic canon of authors, artists, and texts. The arguments about modernism therefore took place in a relatively constricted space where a common set of works generated often radically different meanings. Among the most important mid-century critical works that contributed to Marxism's attempt to explore and define a high modernist canon is Erich Auerbach's magisterial *Mimesis* (1946). Auerbach links modernism closely to a realist tradition that reaches back to Homer and runs through the whole of the European canon, before concluding with a chapter on Virginia Woolf's *To the Lighthouse* (1927). For Auerbach, modernism is less a radical break from the past than part of an endless attempt to grasp and represent different aspects of a complex historical reality. He points out that Woolf, for example, doesn't use a narrator to introduce "facts," but rather lets the characters introduce them from within the unfolding story itself. Focusing on one otherwise obscure scene in which Mrs. Ramsay measures her son for a stocking, he explores the ways in which Woolf elaborates the entire referential world of the text without ever resorting to a position of omniscience or certainty. As the scene continues, we do not know who speaks, who describes Mrs. Ramsay's look or follows her mind and then cuts back to her interaction with James. "The writer as narrator of objective facts has almost completely vanished," he writes, "almost everything stated appears by way of reflection in the consciousness of the dramatis personae" (534).

This mode of writing and world creation, Auerbach concludes, defines a new kind of realism that attempts to "render the flow and the play of consciousness adrift in the current of changing impressions," and in it, "the exterior events have actually lost their hegemony, they serve to release and interpret inner events" (538). This then crystallizes his definition of modernism as a mode of art and vision that suddenly widens "man's horizon" through multiple consciousnesses—a project that coincides with a wider sense of globalization. Drawing implicitly on the utopian element of Marxist thinking, Auerbach says that this radical expansion so essential to his conception of modernism offers a glimpse of the coming "common life of mankind on earth" and is visible in the "unprejudiced, precise, interior and exterior representation of the random moment in the lives of different people. So the complicated process of dissolution which led to fragmentation of the exterior action, to reflection of consciousness, and to stratification of time seems to be tending toward a very simple solution" (552–3). In attempting to redefine modernism in a more historical, and even political, way, however, Auerbach nevertheless relies upon the close connection between difficulty and close reading that was so essential to the otherwise largely ahistorical New Criticism. "The interpretation of a few passages," he maintains, "can be made to yield more, and more decisive, information . . . than would a systematic and chronological treatment. Indeed, the present book may be cited as an illustration" (548). The global vision he articulates, therefore, still emerges from the detailed, expert study of challenging works that only reveal their politics and histories in the fine grain of aesthetic form.

Auerbach's student Fredric Jameson built on this early work in order to articulate what would become perhaps the dominant understanding of modernism from within the Marxist tradition. In *Fables of Aggression* (1979), he asks why Wyndham Lewis—one of the original "men of 1914"—had fallen out of the modernist canon over time. Jameson writes that "Anglo-American modernism has indeed traditionally been dominated by an impressionistic aesthetic, rather than that—externalizing and mechanical—of Lewis's expressionism" (2). The problem, he claims, is that modernism has been defined within political and cultural institutions that have cut it off from its historical contexts and traditions—largely in an effort to accommodate it to Western liberalism. To define modernism more accurately in its moment, not in its institutionalized version, Jameson asserts, we should look anew to Lewis. He uses Lewis to explore the "affinities between protofascism and Western modernism" beyond individual authors, and he wants to explore what he calls the "political unconscious" of Lewis's works—a phrase that will become increasingly important in his understanding of modernism as well as in the critical procedures he uses to interpret it (5).

We'll look more closely at this idea in a moment, but first we need to better understand why Jameson focused on Lewis. Modernism, he claims, can best be understood as an aesthetic response to a larger process called "reification"—a term derived from Marxist theory and used to describe the fragmentation and alienation of the human sensorium. Capitalism, in this view, breaks apart the unity of the human body and its relations to the world as part of an ever-advancing pursuit of profits. This results in a deep fracturing of experience as the world is pulled into disparate, irreconcilable parts—all of which can then be sold back to us as new and distinctive pleasures. This process is alienating, but it also produces entirely novel experiences as the senses become increasingly autonomous, each open to unique kinds of pleasure and perception. In the early twentieth century, this process becomes acute as an intensifying reification renders empty and unsatisfying a realism that could no longer produce a shared sense of reality. Into this gap emerged the kind of modernist practice Auerbach describes—one in which there is no perceptual center but instead only a multiplicity of consciousness. Rejecting Auerbach's utopianism, however, Jameson instead looks to Lewis and treats modernism as a protest "against the reified experience of an alienated social life, in which, against its own will, it remains formally and ideologically locked" (14).

In his landmark study *The Political Unconscious* (1981), he develops these claims further by arguing that modernism breaks with a realism that had lost its power to represent the world accurately and had instead become deeply entangled with mass culture. This older mode of representation thus contributes to the ongoing process of reification, as art's critical edge is co-opted, its autonomy undercut, and its sites of production and reception become fully integrated into capitalism's industrial processes. This argument shares a good deal with claims made by Eliot and many of the New Critics, and Jameson's own work treats the same set of canonical texts that formed part of high modernism. Unlike his formalist counterparts, however, Jameson insists that modernism was not an escape from history and politics into pure form, but was, instead, a way of negotiating modern, fragmented life symbolically, with "substitute gratifications" (266).

To elaborate his theories of modernism, Jameson turns to Joseph Conrad's novel *Lord Jim* (1900), which he treats as a giant historical and aesthetic hinge opening onto his vision of modernism as a response to global reification. This novel often strikes readers as two distinct works that have been strangely fused together: one about romantic adventure on the high seas and the other about the recondite structures of knowledge, memory, and representation. In this jarring split, Jameson suggests, "we can sense the emergence not merely of what will be contemporary modernism, . . . but also, still tangibly juxtaposed with it, . . . popular culture or mass culture, the commercialized cultural discourse of what, in late capitalism, is often described as a media society" (206). It is not simply a shift in narrative paradigms or style, but a shift "between two distinct cultural spaces" (high and mass) that *Lord Jim* betrays—between sea tale and Impressionism. In this conjunction of forms and genres, Conrad supersedes realism at the level of form. Seen this way, the break in *Lord Jim* reveals the operations of capitalism's radical processes of reification in a "utopian" style that still allows mass culture and high modernism to magically coexist.

In Jameson's reading, Conrad's narrative logic shares with modernism more generally an aleatory quality in which perception becomes ideology, sight becomes autonomous, and there is a "new ideology of the image" based on "the objective fragmentation of the outside world, or of the objects of perception" (232). Reification, in other words, continues to shatter the lifeworld into ever smaller and more marketable fragments, but offers as recompense new modes of pleasure, perception, and representation. The arc from *Lord Jim* to *Nostromo* (published in 1904 and still engaged in the same utopian project) reflects a dialectical intensification staged not by Conrad but by the literary and cultural conditions in which he wrote. And in the end, *Nostromo* becomes a novel about novelistic self-reflection, having abandoned both history and politics. Thus, if "modernism is itself an ideological expression of capitalism, and in particular, of the latter's reification of daily life," then it "can be seen as a late stage in the bourgeois cultural revolution . . . [in which inhabitants] of older social formations are culturally and psychologically retrained for life in the market system" (236). Jameson believes that "the modernist project . . . is the intent . . . to 'manage' historical and social, deeply political impulses, . . . to defuse them, to prepare substitute gratifications for them" (266). This leads him to his now famous conclusion that

> after the peculiar heterogeneity of the moment of Conrad, a high modernism is set in place. . . . The perfected poetic apparatus of high modernism represses History just as successfully as the perfected narrative apparatus of high realism did the random heterogeneity of the as yet uncentered subject. At that point, however, the political, no longer visible in the high modernist texts, any more than in the everyday world of appearance of bourgeois life, and relentlessly driven underground by accumulated reification, has at last become a genuine Unconscious. (280)

For Jameson then, modernism pivots around Conrad—the same novelist whom Leavis had placed in his "Great Tradition," but for very different reasons. He thus offers a fundamentally new way of reading modernism, even while the constituent elements of that modernism remain essentially identical to the works woven together by Leavis, Eliot, and the New Critics.

Working in Britain, the great Marxist critic Raymond Williams turned to the question of modernism as well, taking up some of the same concerns that were shaping Jameson's work. In the essays collected in his posthumous *The Politics of Modernism* (1989), Williams contends that the canonization of high modernism condensed a complex cultural movement and defused its antibourgeois impulses. Like Jameson, Williams explored modernists' views of art through their understandings of a bourgeois-dominated marketplace, emphasizing the ways in which it seemed to be pulling art itself into increasingly isolated spheres. At one end of the spectrum, he notes, figures like Pound and Eliot pined for the antiquated system of artistic patronage. At the other end were figures like Kermode's "schismatics," who saw the revolutionary potential in art and sided with international communist movements. Where Jameson understood this as part of the process of reification, Williams analyzed what he believed were the material conditions that produced these divergent views of the place of the art-object in the commercial sphere. Like Perloff and Altieri, Williams sets the stage for the critical revaluation of modernism that we will explore in the next chapter by arguing that the formation of a narrow canon in the mid-twentieth century was itself a problem—though for different reasons than the critics we address above offered. Asking in the title of a lecture, "When Was Modernism?" (1987), he chides critics from the 1950s for their selective consecration of certain movements that are taken to represent "the whole of modernity"—for overlooking the innovations of Realism and Naturalism that made modernism possible, and for bracketing Impressionism in order to declare only Post-Impression, Cubism, and their heirs "modernist" (33). Once this winnowed concept of modernism, which ignored social forms and new media in favor of aesthetic self-reflexivity, was canonized, it was then closed off for participation; everything that came after it was not part of modernism, but was somehow belated, "counted out of development." Modernism furthermore "achieved comfortable integration into the new international capitalism" and thereby lost its oppositional character (35). Aesthetic history, in this sense, had been brought to a forced and artificial close, choked off by the very cables of tradition that had been used to weave it.

Despite this robust critique of modernism as a cultural and historical formation, Williams nevertheless trained his critical focus on some of its key figures and practices in order to understand how and why they operated. In his essay "Metropolitan Perceptions and the Emergence of Modernism" (1985), for example, he seeks to trace the history of modernism's development beyond any one language or nation in order to better understand it as an international, even global, experiment with style and language. Europe, he argues, saw massive migrations before, during, and after the First World War, and cosmopolitan cities like London, Paris, and Berlin became the meeting grounds of writers and artists of all nationalities (or no nationality, as the case might have been). The metropolis introduced new "universals" of aesthetics, intellectualism, and psychology, he argues, that replaced those of previous cultures. These thriving cities, in turn, become significant ideological and experiential structures that condition the practices and consolidation of modernism. Here, exiles developed a common second language derived from, and continually mediated by, newspapers and advertising. Modernism lost its antibourgeois character and settled for a condition of permanent exile that proved comfortable within international capitalism's increasingly homogenized global markets—the same "modernism" that critics codified. By celebrating the "elements of strangeness and distance, indeed of alienation" highlighted in the metropolis, modernists broke from their native, familiar, and provincial cultures; they saw language as a *medium* more than a "social custom"—indeed, they saw "the medium as that which, in an unprecedented way, defined art" (45, 46). Turning back to his thesis about the conformity of modernism, Williams concludes: "So nearly complete was this vast cultural reformation [in linguistics, architecture, painting, and more, that] . . . what had once been defiantly marginal and oppositional became, in its turn, orthodox, although the distance of both from other cultures and peoples remained wide. The key to this persistence is again the social form of the metropolis," which relativized "native" languages and accents (46).

In "The Bloomsbury Fraction" (1980), Williams examines specifically the well-known circle of liberal modernists that gathered in this now iconic London neighborhood—a group that included Leonard and Virginia Woolf, E. M. Forster, Vanessa Bell, John Maynard Keynes, and Lytton Strachey, among others. He wants to understand, in his own terminology, the "structure of feeling" of this privileged, artistic minority who were not simply withdrawn elitists (155). Indeed, many of the group's members were politically engaged with a number of groups on the British and international left. Williams thus sees them as something relatively new, a "fraction" of the upper-class elite who sympathized with the lower classes out of principle, as a *"matter of conscience"* rather than political solidarity (155; italics in the original). Williams saw that Bloomsbury represented a "new *style*," a new "critical frankness," but that they were an "oppositional fraction" who only wanted individual freedoms, not an entirely new society—they fought for style and not for social revolution (154; italics in the original). They were, in short, a disaffected, inconsequential bourgeois minority.

Claims such as those made by Jameson and Williams were tied even more specifically to English history by other Marxists who, in the 1970s and early 1980s, voiced concerns about the meaning and implications of an essentially formalist and canonical modernism. Perry Anderson asked what it meant that England, "the pioneer of capitalist industrialization and master of the world market for a century," was home to modernist exiles such as Eliot, Pound, and Conrad, but that it produced no "native" modernist movement of the type that its European peers did. Noting that England did not have the kind of sweeping political revolutions like those in Russia, France, and Germany, he argues that its modernism emerged from the "imaginative proximity of social revolution" (32, 36). Rebutting Marshall Berman's emphasis in *All That Is Solid Melts into Air* (1982) on the exhilarating "experience of modernity" and his adumbration of modernism into phases that coincided with the major revolutions in Europe since 1790, Anderson holds, instead, that this proximity combines with a reaction against official academicism and the mass consumption of media enabled by technology to produce modernism: the three "triangulate" to create modernism as a "cultural field." All of this occurred, he writes, "at the intersection between a semi-aristocratic ruling order, a semi-industrialized capitalist economy, and a semi-emergent, or -insurgent, labour movement" (36). In contrast to, say, Karl Shapiro, Anderson finds the concept of "modernism" hollow, noting that what we call "modernism" was actually the disparate and incompatible practices of "symbolism, constructivism, expressionism, and surrealism," which have only been joined together by the "blank" passage of time. The "ideology and cult" of modernism was not born until the 1950s, he writes, when it gained widespread currency as a postwar token of a break with an imagined unruptured classical world of art (39). Modernism used to be able to resist capitalism partially, but is now fully incorporated, he asserts in accord with Williams.

Terry Eagleton, a thinker who shared much of his intellectual spirit at this time with Anderson, tackled the similar question in his *Exiles and Émigrés* (1970) of why "the seven most significant writers of twentieth-century English literature have been a Pole, three Americans, two Irishmen and an Englishman" (9). This, he argues, "points to certain central flaws and impoverishments in conventional English culture itself," for unlike the Romantic or realist eras, in the modernist moment, English culture was "unable, of its own impetus, to produce great literary art," left with an "absent centre," as Anderson called it (9–10). He relates great English literature to social commitment and says that the entry of émigrés started to remove that (11). Furthermore, the great writers of the late nineteenth century (Gissing, Shaw, Bennett, Wells) were all "lower middle-class," while the modernists are "upper class" (Forster, Woolf, Myers), thus we find gaps between Bloomsbury and the Fabians. The upper-class novel, he believes, was trapped "within a world so partial, rarefied and fragmentary that it could express little more than the relatively untypical living of a rootless, dispossessed sector of the dominant social class" (14). First, Thomas Hardy and D. H. Lawrence began to challenge this cultural hegemony as they brought working-class experience to bear on metropolitan high modernism. This foreign and "alien experience is allowed radically to question civilized structures which in turn gain fresh validation from the encounter" (31). In this exchange, Eagleton argues, the idea of modernism begins to fragment into different sites and practices—a process hastened by the enormous dislocations produced by the First World War. We thus see again a tension or even a paradox within Marxist thought on modernism, especially in the 1970s and 1980s. On the one hand, the canon and its underlying conceptual structures had become splintered and appeared now as a false creation designed to routinize art with revolutionary potential. On the other, this ideological critique continued to rest on close readings of the very same texts and figures, influenced by the same historical events (imperialist capitalism, the First World War, modern urbanization and metropolitan immigration) that constituted that canon.

# Modernism's discontents

Despite Marxist and historicist critiques, modernism in the early 1980s was still largely confined to a canon and deeply embedded in a shared set of professional practices, anthologies, museums, journals, and other institutions. The term itself remained subject to debate, but even critics suspicious of it often ended up reaffirming its stability by developing arguments around a shared set of texts and ideas. Maurice Beebe's 1974 essay "What Modernism Was" captured this sense of uneasy consensus clearly. He reiterates, with some reluctance, his own earlier claims that the four characteristics of modernism were formal autonomy, detachment or irony, myth as an ordering structure, and a self-reflexive turn toward its own composition. These characteristics, he believes, are, for better or worse, fixed and that the term "modernism" is so institutionally entrenched that it is "too late to rechristen the era with a less confusing name." Even critics like Peter Faulkner, who believed that "modernism" was still open for definition, found it increasingly difficult to escape this agreement. Modernism, he argues, hinges on an "awareness of the problems of art, an unremitting self-consciousness" that he locates most fully in Woolf, Pound, and Joyce—the same figures (with the exception of Woolf) whom many others had already concurred lay at the center of the movement (19). His anthology, *A Modernist Reader* (1986), reinforced the canon of its day by presenting readings from the Men of 1914 at the center, surrounded by James and Hulme on one side, Lowell and Woolf on the other, all bounded between 1910 and 1930.[13]

Perhaps there exists no better indicator of this dilemma in this moment of conceptualization and definition—along with questions about the stakes and goals of those very processes—than Michael Levenson's *Genealogy of Modernism* (1984). This influential study argues that "modernism," despite its widespread usage and apparent familiarity, is an undefined term. He notes, though, that "vague terms still signify. Such is the case with 'modernism': it is at once vague and unavoidable" (vii). His concerns are not authors and definitions, but "the structure of English modernism, as it slowly assumed coherence, as aesthetic concepts received new formulation, as those concepts were worked into doctrine. Among the concepts were image, symbol, tradition, expression, and objectivity. The doctrines were successively called Impressionism, Imagism, Vorticism and Classicism" (vii). His account pinpoints 1908, 1914, and 1922 as the key dates in a general movement toward hardness and geometry in literature as well as in the visual arts. Reaching back to early debates among Hulme (who had been largely ignored by mid-century scholars), Pound, and Ford, Levenson writes that "early modernist criticism, in the period stretching from roughly 1908 to 1913, was largely apologetic in character. Its urgent aim was to defend the right of innovation against the hasty dismissal of both the literary establishment and the general public" (153). Pound remains vital for Levenson, because with Imagism, "the avant-garde achieved the status of a recognized *movement*" of oppositional character, while Eliot stands as the crucial transitional figure who, with *The Waste Land* and his "London Letters" columns for the *Dial*, inherited the mantle of the avant-garde and became English modernism's emblem (138; italics in the original). In essence, across the combined careers of Pound and Eliot, modernism was transformed from a provocation to a structured, symptomatic movement. Its consolidation, therefore, took place even earlier than a critic like Beebe allowed; it was, in fact, built into the very logic and practices of the movement itself.

The term "modernism" had ushered into the professional world of teaching and critical study an entirely new set of texts and ideas about how to read them. These processes, as we have seen, depended on the ability to construct, preserve, and carefully elucidate a select canon of works. They connected formal difficulty and aesthetic autonomy to the larger cables of Western art and culture—cables that now seemed increasingly constrictive. Beneath the surface of these many solidifications of modernism, however, powerful questions still rumbled: Why had form—and particularly difficulty—become so foundational an element of modernism that Levenson could simply assume that it was the through-line of his genealogy? What happened not only to the idea of content, but also to the rest of the enormous cultural output of the early twentieth century? Why had high modernism been defined in a way that excluded women writers, racial minorities, political activists, popular artists, and so much work from new media like film, radio, and phonography? Had modernism as a term and concept brought the very idea of cultural innovation to an end by wrapping novel or disruptive works in the enervating cables of tradition and institutionalization? As the late work of Williams suggested, however, there was a growing sense that modernism might be expanded or transformed by looking to new sorts of spaces, texts, producers, and institutions. In the next chapter, we will explore how another set of critics began to offer new definitions of the term "modernism" by unraveling familiar artists from the cable of tradition, thereby freeing them up to enter into new contexts and constellations. Like Pound's idealized poet, whose imagination could draw patterns from the "iron filings" of a disparate and disordered past, they looked beyond a now claustrophobic canon to a whole new range of artists, media, movements, and cultures.

# Notes

1   See Gorman, *James Joyce: His First Forty Years* (1924); Graves, *Good-bye to All that* (1929); Cowley, *Exile's Return: A Literary Odyssey of the 1920s* (1933); Stein, *The Autobiography of Alice B. Toklas* (1933); Lewis, *Blasting and Bombardiering* (1937);

McAlmon, *Being Geniuses Together* (1938); Levin, *James Joyce* (1941); Spender, *World within World* (1951); Williams, *Autobiography* (1951); and Roger Shattuck, *The Banquet Years* (1961). Cyril Connolly's annotated list *The Modern Movement: 100 Key Books from England, France, and America, 1880-1950* (1965) also helped name and delimit "the modern." This is only a partial list, of course, and does not include titles such as Zora Neale Hurston's *Dust Tracks on a Road* (1942) and Langston Hughes's *I Wonder as I Wander* (1956), nor anthologies such as Alain Locke's *New Negro* (1925) and Nancy Cunard's *Negro: An Anthology* (1934), which were only treated by modernist scholars much later, for reasons we discuss in Chapter 3.

2   Woolf appeared on the cover of *Time* magazine (in April 1937), for example, and Joyce appeared twice (in January 1924 and again in May 1939).

3   A partial list includes George D. Painter's *Marcel Proust* (first volume in 1959), Michael Holroyd's *Lytton Strachey* (first volume in 1967), Carlos Baker's *Hemingway: A Life Story* (1969), Hugh Kenner's *The Pound Era* (1971), Quentin Bell's two-volume *Virginia Woolf* (1972), S. P. Rosenbaum's *The Bloomsbury Group: A Collection of Memoirs, Commentary, and Criticism* (1975), Janet Hobson's *Everybody Who Was Anybody: A Biography of Gertrude Stein* (1975), Lyndall Gordon's *Eliot's Early Years* (1977; *Eliot's New Life* followed in 1988), and Keith M. Sagar's *The Life of D. H. Lawrence* (1980). Here again, Robert E. Hemenway's *Zora Neale Hurston: A Literary Biography* (1977) was contemporaneous but was not figured as canonical.

4   The *James Joyce Quarterly* was not the first journal dedicated solely to Joyce's work (it had been preceded by brief runs of the *James Joyce Miscellany* and *James Joyce Review* in the late 1950s), but it quickly became the most widely circulated journal dedicated to a single modern author. Titles such as the *Partisan Review*, *Southern Review*, *Sewanee Review*, *Commentary*, and *Journal of Modern Literature* were key sources for these commentaries, too, while Hilton Kramer sought to revive Eliot's editorial project with his journal *The New Criterion* in 1982. See also the emphasis on form in influential studies such as Frederick J. Hoffman's *The Twenties* (1949) and Monroe K. Spears's *Dionysus and the City* (1970).

5   In 1974, the University of Tulsa, under the leadership of Thomas F. Staley, launched the first graduate program focused exclusively on the study of modernism called the Program in Modern Letters. Almost all of its faculty were specialists in single authors, and over half focused

on Joyce. Staley later became the director of the Harry Ransom Center at the University of Texas at Austin, where he led the assembly of what has become one of the world's finest archives of modernist literature, film, and art.

6   Such anthologies continue to play a powerful material role in maintaining modernism as a pedagogical and professional field. Their reach, furthermore, was extended by the fact that they also appeared inexpensively in paperback, thus making them readily accessible to the burgeoning number of students who began to attend colleges and universities in the second half of the twentieth century.

7   Howe's book was printed identically in the same year as *The Idea of the Modern in Literature and the Arts* (New York: Horizon), and his introductory essay appeared that year as "The Culture of Modernism" in *Commentary*.

8   The first volume of David Perkins's contemporaneous *History of Modern Poetry: From the 1890s to the High Modernist Mode* (1976) aimed to provide a more US-centric account. Perkins writes that he is working "against the long hegemony of high Modernist poetry and criticism," but he effectively enshrines the heroic, triumphal story of high modernism itself, and while he treats women and minority writers, he does so in distinct chapters not tied to his discussions of modernism (viii).

9   Levin's title was recycled self-consciously in an essay some two decades later, Robert Martin Adams's "What Was Modernism?" *Hudson Review* 31, no. 1 (Spring 1978): 19–33. Adams mostly surveys the achievements of the familiar Men of 1914 and their European peers, but argues, contra Levin, that "the 'modernist' period has never ended and will never end, though as a perceptible piece of time it has ceased to exist, . . . [and] will just attenuate and diffuse itself more and more" (32). Thus, he concludes that "modernism was an inaccurate and misleading term" for an authentic cultural movement between 1905 and 1925 (33).

10  Frazer studied world religions and argued that human culture evolves through three major stages from primitivism to science. His work, though largely now outdated, was of enormous interest to Eliot and other modernist writers looking for inspiration beyond the West.

11  In an important essay from 1950, the poet-critic Louise Bogan assessed contemporary American poetry specifically through its debts to modernism (for which she had little sympathy); see "Modernism in American Literature." The critic William Van O'Connor's volume *The New University Wits and the End of Modernism* (1963) meanwhile

declared that its subjects—Philip Larkin, John Wain, Irish Murdoch, Kingsley Amis—had indeed killed off their literary forebears.

12  Perloff is quoting John Ashbery's description of Stein's discourse.

13  Indeed, in the early to mid-1980s, a host of monographs appeared—and many made a significant scholarly impact—that gave nuance and complexity to modernism while stabilizing the canon. Studies by Art Berman, Frederick Karl, Ricardo J. Quinones, C. K. Stead, and Sanford Schwartz, alongside the more culturally focused explorations of modernism by Marshall Berman and Stephen Kern, simultaneously aimed to fend off the growing chorus of critiques of modernism by postmodernist, feminist, ethnic, and Marxist scholars, which we will consider in the next chapter.

# 3

# Iron Filings

## Overview

We have been tracing thus far the development of modernism as an Eliotic "cable" that both binds together a collection of privileged works into a canon and ties them to an established cultural and aesthetic history. This process itself was embedded within a network of professional, critical, and pedagogical practices that emphasized the importance of close reading, the value of difficulty, and the removal of art to an autonomous sphere. The result was a remarkably stable definition of modernism, one so powerful that many critics and creators alike tried to declare it dead or exhausted in order to open the way for other forms of aesthetic innovation. Even now, the most common use of the word "modernism" generally refers to this foundational set of ideas and the core texts around which they were articulated. Marxist critics who sought to contest this idea of modernism, like Fredric Jameson and Raymond Williams, still did so within the confines of the canon and its formal terms themselves, while early attempts at expanding the canon (by scholars interested in race and gender, for example) typically proceeded by adding new works to an otherwise fixed firmament.

The aesthetic practices of the early twentieth century, however, extended far beyond the imaginative reach of the New Critics and the mid-century figures who sought to discipline it, to weave it into a single, coherent idea or era. This period, after all, witnessed the rise to prominence of not only Joyce, Picasso, and Schoenberg, but also detective and science fiction genres, commercial graphic design and advertising, and jazz, the blues, and Western swing. Entirely new forms of media, including film, radio, and phonography, became ubiquitous, while older forms underwent massive changes. Books were suddenly inexpensive, light, and easy to carry in a pocket or handbag, while cheap magazines and newspapers filled newsstands. Political movements like suffragism, prohibition, anticolonialism, socialism, and fascism ushered in innovative modes of rhetorical expression, often by making prodigious use of these new media. The evidence of these cultural and media revolutions, in fact, is everywhere evident in even the texts and figures most closely identified with the reigning canon of modernism. Leopold Bloom is an advertising agent, and Joyce himself founded Dublin's first cinema; Picasso pasted newspaper headlines directly onto his canvases; the avant-garde magazine the *Little Review* organized an exhibition of machine-made items including ball bearings and an airplane propeller; and Djuna Barnes first made a name for herself as a kind of shock journalist who attended prize fights and submitted to the force feedings being administered to suffragists on hunger strike. Surely, all of this is modernism too—but not of a sort that could be easily accommodated within a narrowly conceived canon.

The question of what to do with all these other modern aesthetic and cultural practices—all these things that cannot be easily or only assimilated to the elevated tradition—gave way to alternative definitions of modernism. Furthermore, the work of articulating these definitions showed how robustly the process of canonization had been contested from the start, with critics and writers alike straining against the cables of tradition, whose formation we have detailed. Interwar Marxist critics like Walter Benjamin and Siegfried Kracauer looked to both elite art and mass culture for their own definitions of modernism, writing powerfully about everything from chorus lines to slow-motion photography to horror films. They worked alongside critic-practitioners like Woolf, who wondered how culture would change if women could write freely in rooms of their own, and W. E. B. Du Bois, whose editorship of *The Crisis* (1910–) linked black political liberty to distinct new kinds of cultural expression. Such revisionary definitions of modernism were recovered and reframed, largely in the academy in the 1970s and 1980s, as an increasingly vocal collection of critics asked whether modernism was an elitist, hegemonic movement to be discarded (as some postmodernists would claim); a broad-based movement whose minority contributors had been overlooked and must be recuperated (as some scholars would claim); or a combination of the two. These questions meant carving modernism up along new, often explicitly political and identitarian lines that responded to the institutionalization of the field around matters of form. New writers, new experiences, and new kinds of politics all increasingly fell within the horizon of the modern, offering new visions of a culture that was too diverse and too widely distributed through time and space to be enveloped by a singular modernist tradition. These alternative modernisms, which first drew on prominent figures from women's, African American, and political histories, began to draw even the high modernist canon itself into new patterns and alignments with the iron filings of a vastly expanded archive. In the last chapter, we saw how these pressures began to register in the work of critics like Frank Kermode, Marjorie Perloff, and Charles Altieri. In this chapter, to understand how modernism was freed from the constrictive cable of one tradition, we have to look at the many ways in which critics began to arrange twentieth-century literature and art around new kinds of political, aesthetic, and social magnets.

From roughly the mid-1970s through the early 1990s, the idea of modernism developed along intertwining, divergent, parallel, and sometimes contradictory paths. Less and less a knowable canon, it became chaotic and complex, in part because it had not concluded in 1939 or 1945 or 1950, but remained instead a central part of contemporary debates about who gets to speak and about what art actually is, where it can happen, and how it is consecrated. Modernism served as both an object of critique and a source of inspiration; critics demonstrated, for example, the ways in which experimental formalism was also a means of articulating new identities in the early twentieth century. Much of this coincided with the revolutions in the professional study of literature that spawned departments and programs in women's and gender studies, ethnic studies, cultural studies, and other such configurations. As the literary text lost its sacred power over critics, the claim that a text was "modernist" or "postmodernist" or "feminist" now became an invention that redounded upon the critic rather than a dispassionate description of essential formal features. To borrow Pound's metaphor again, attention shifted to the different kinds of historical, intellectual, and political magnets that might be used to organize the filings of a twentieth-century culture that seemed to be growing through addition, recovery, and massive revision.

Loosening the consolidating cables of "modernism" that we traced in the previous chapter was an immense project, a paradigm-shifting transitional phase in the history of the idea of modernism. At times, this project was cooperative: the claims for feminist or black modernisms, for instance, are inseparable from the claims made by French poststructuralists about the nature of language and texts. French Theory, in turn, was itself inseparable from the battles for civil and geopolitical rights through which it was articulated (see Friedman, "Theory"). By the same token, many of the figures we discuss here saw themselves as continuing the work of the alternative modernisms and modernists that they were uncovering and analyzing. Rather than asking whether Yeats could interpret the Atomic Age, they asked whether Woolf laid the groundwork for a contemporary feminist movement fighting everyday battles. This work was mostly academic, though important voices came from outside the university precisely because institutions themselves became suspect. The culmination of the work that this chapter traces, arguably, was the multipronged critique of modernism that took shape around the idea of a "postmodernism." We'll build up to that by studying the ways in which these revisions of modernism found their critical purchase. Some of this work continues into the present, some of it has passed, and some of it has taken on new forms. In each of the sections below, we'll thus draw an admittedly arbitrary line between phases of certain projects—feminist, avant-garde, Marxist—within modernist criticism, and Chapter 4 will pick up after these nonetheless crucial junctures. In sum, by rethinking literature and art of the early twentieth century from the ground up, the groupings of scholars addressed in this chapter turned the pressing question of modernism's essence into debates about its construction, production, and consumption as a concept still in transformation and undergoing a series of fragmentations that threatened to leave it in ruins.

# Marxism and mass culture

As the earliest definitions of modernism began to take hold in the 1930s, the prominent Marxist critic Walter Benjamin resisted the consensus by ambivalently embracing mass cultural products for their ability to demystify the "aura" of the work of art. Benjamin, who is best known as an essayist and a thinker who resisted the totalizing elements of Marxist thought, saw art not as the symptom of some underlying ideological structure, but as a fascinating, uncountable plentitude of cultural forms. He devoted much of his life to a critical and historical study of nineteenth-century Parisian arcades that he called the *Passagenwerk*; it was left unfinished after his suicide in 1940 and was published decades after his death.[1] This archaeological excavation of modern culture was a bulky, piecemeal manuscript and an enormous collection of notes that he was assembling not into an overarching narrative, but into a kind of modernist experimental collage. In these notes, elite and mass culture mix haphazardly along with observations about personalities, architecture, and nearly every facet of art, culture, and history. Like Pound—and unlike many of his contemporary Marxist critics—Benjamin treated the past as a heterogeneous mass of data, a pile of iron filings that could be pushed and pulled into different, often incommensurate, shapes. Drawing on his interests in Jewish messianic thought, in fact, he believed that the job of the critic or the artist was to create patterns that would shock viewers into revolutionary consciousness. In this way, we can see that while the Marxist critics whom we have treated thus far effectively helped build the modernist canon and affirmed its terms, Benjamin—whose works also became better known in English translation beginning in the late 1960s—offered a set of tools and perspectives for undoing that work.

In his most widely cited essay, "The Work of Art in the Age of Its Technological Reproducibility" (1936),[2] Benjamin questions how the art-object has, over time, developed in capitalist society an "aura" associated with the mystification of its mode of creation. This aura relied on the artwork's existing uniquely in a certain time and space tied to its origins, which were also "embedded in the fabric of tradition" of masterworks and great creators (223). The possibilities of mechanical reproduction in contemporary technology like photography and mass printing, however, now threaten this aura: the *Mona Lisa* can be a million *Mona Lisa*s, as Andy Warhol's work would later illustrate. The result is emancipatory, but could also destroy aesthetic traditions. Worse, fascism exploits this phenomenon, Benjamin argues, and aestheticizes politics, while

Marxist criticism seeks to politicize aesthetics. Therefore, against the Aestheticist movement and its claims of autonomy, he preferred those who charged Symbolism with politics, and he praised the flâneur Baudelaire as the first poet of modernity. He also elevated the works of the Surrealists, who used fragments, as Dadaists and Cubists had done, to destroy the illusion of autonomy in art and to break down the spheres of public and private existence that the bourgeois world had created. Benjamin saw that their antichronological discontinuities, their use of commodities, their refusal to see art as a closed world created a liberating aesthetics that was, for him, akin to Brecht's theater and to Proust's ability to *produce* memory in involuntary, collage-like time-spaces.

Benjamin's ideal modernist work creates a new tradition for itself by ceaselessly churning mass and elite cultural objects into radically new formations. He thus looks to figures like Alfred Döblin, whose *Berlin Alexanderplatz* (1929) he treats in "Crisis of the Novel" (1930). Döblin, he writes, employs the "stylistic principle" of "montage. Petty-bourgeois printed matter, scandalmongering, stories of accidents, the sensational incidents of 1928, folk songs, and advertisements rain down in this text. The montage explodes the framework of the novel, bursts its limits both stylistically and structurally, and clears the way for new, epic possibilities. Formally, above all" (301). Benjamin therefore outlines two paths along which the modern novel might proceed: the tendency toward pure formalism (inner life) or toward montage and heterogeneity (everyday life) *as* form. This ceaseless mixture and juxtaposition of elements in the latter offers an alternative to the idea of a cable-entwined "high modernism" we saw evolve in the last chapter. Form is not a retreat from mass culture, but a way of interpreting it toward potentially revolutionary ends. Benjamin expounded upon this in "The Storyteller" (1936), which argues that the novel ruined the role of storytelling in traditional villages. In order to revive and maintain the form's potential for individual as well as social integration, Proust turned inward to focus on the power of memory to sustain a fractured identity, while Kafka drew on Jewish mysticism and folk traditions to preserve their power within a homogenizing modernity. For Benjamin, however, these writers nevertheless fail to capture the fundamental connection to social life that has been lost, and thus their modernism lies at a crossroads between nostalgia for tradition and anxiety about a bleak future.

This fascination with mass culture and with the idea of fragmentation was integral as well to the early work of Siegfried Kracauer, another German critic who, along with Adorno, Benjamin, Max Horkheimer, and Herbert Marcuse, was part of a loosely affiliated group called the Frankfurt School. These critics generally sought to resist the growing doctrinal rigidity of Marxism by reworking its economic and historical claims with insights from new disciplines like psychology and sociology. The group was particularly interested in the role of ideology and its power to deform, or even entirely fashion, our perception of the world. For critics like Adorno and Horkheimer, art offered the tenuous possibility of enlightenment—a potential means of escape from capitalism's deformation of human consciousness. But where they saw modernism as a real (if threatened) site of resistance to the disaster of the "culture industry"—the facile popular cultures produced by modern capitalism in order to deceptively lull the masses into a passive acceptance of their own exploitation—Kracauer, like Benjamin, saw mass culture as a vital part of modernism. In his work as a journalist for the newspaper *Frankfurter Zeitung* (1856– 1943), Kracauer wrote about topics like photography, tourism, and detective novels. Much of this work was gathered as a collection of essays in 1927 book titled *The Mass Ornament*, which sought to understand both the significance and the politics of these new middle-class forms. In this book, he argued that the Tiller Girls, a popular traveling dance troupe from the United States, exemplified life and culture under contemporary capitalism. They were "products of American distraction factories," deprived of their organic beings and routinized into a consumable spectacle—and yet the aesthetic pleasure they produced was undeniably "real" (75, 79). A Jewish thinker who eventually settled in the United States, Kracauer was deeply suspicious of much of this art, seeing in it—as Benjamin did—the seeds of Nazism. However, he insisted on its importance as an aspect of modern culture and on its disparate phenomena and practices that could never really cohere into a single tradition or even object of analysis.

Following the end of the Second World War, this early strain of Marxist thinking about modernism and the various movements associated with it moved to the margins of university and professional practice in the West. At the same time, the Cold War made any affiliation with Marxism suspect in the United States, which contributed to the consolidation of New Criticism and its understanding of modernism as a largely autonomous, formalist, and apolitical aesthetic practice. In Britain, however, key modes of leftist thinking remained vibrant, and their growing concern with the narrowness of a canonical high modernism contributed to a burgeoning interest in modernism as an object of sociological rather than purely aesthetic analysis. That is, critics asked—as we saw in the case of Raymond Williams and Perry Anderson in the last chapter—not only what modernism was, but also what kind of work the idea itself enabled or concealed. Such questions were salient in and around the Birmingham Centre for Contemporary Cultural Studies, an influential institute founded in 1964 that drew on Marxist thought in order to analyze all forms of cultural expression in explicitly political ways. Here again, modernism was seen to be fully enmeshed in the popular culture from which it tried to separate itself. Thus, CCCS did not seek to teach readers how to segregate, identify, or appreciate genuine "modernist" works. Rather, it looked more at how "modernism" was received than at how it was produced—and by implication, how it might be challenged or undone.

Meanwhile in France, the sociologist Pierre Bourdieu began to publish an influential series of books that took the iron filings model of modernism to its extreme. Looking closely at how taste forms and why different kinds of social groups are attracted to or bored by various cultural objects, he argued that modernism can best be understood as a socioeconomic rather than artistic formation. That is, instead of having any intrinsic value, it concentrates what he calls "cultural capital" in a relatively autonomous field of operation (43). For Bourdieu, modernism is essentially "the economic world reversed," in which difficulty, critical attacks, scandal, and neglect all become markers of a special kind of value (29). Commercial failure, in other words, becomes equated with artistic success, a process that divides the world of art and literature into two groups: one we now call "modernism" that is distinguished by starving artists creating difficult art and the other containing mass culture whose very popularity signifies its aesthetic bankruptcy. Expanding on this argument throughout his work, Bourdieu argues that all cultural production—from *Superman* comics and pulp novels to *Ulysses* and *The Rite of Spring*—takes place within separate fields, each with its own way of measuring and rewarding value. The radical conclusion of such an argument is that modernism is just one such field among many others, itself no more valuable, no more critical, and no more special than any other. The sociological critic thus confronts not only the idea that culture is a wildly profuse collection of iron filings, but also the realization that these objects can be arrayed into dramatically different patterns depending on the fields in which they emerge and through which they circulate or recirculate. There is no unifying field in the end, no vantage from which absolute value can be measured. The kind of wide-ranging cultural critique practiced by Kracauer and Benjamin, by British cultural studies, and by sociologically informed critics like Bourdieu thus helped elaborate the idea taken up everywhere toward the end of the twentieth century that all aesthetic value is relative, and therefore modernism can be found everywhere or nowhere depending on the fields of intellectual, political, or social force used to align its fragments.

# Feminism and revision

Where Marxists used social class and analyses of the economics of cultural production as ways of stripping away the cables of modernism, feminist critics looked instead to gender and sexuality. As we have seen, by the 1980s, anthologies and essays on modernism had created an almost exclusively male, and indeed masculinist, canon. Lisa Rado notes, however, that this was an almost entirely retroactive process set in motion by male critics—particularly those working in English departments—who occluded topics like lesbianism, suffragist protests, and critiques of patriarchy, along with the wealth of aesthetics they all promulgated. Generations of mostly male critics had essentially followed a lead established by Pound when he took over a radical feminist little magazine, Dora Marsden's *The New Freewoman* (1913). He quickly purged its "feminine" content, replaced it with his own stable of preferred writers, and then retitled it the *Egoist* (1914–19). Pound disparaged "Amygism" as Amy Lowell's inferior, feminine version of his own Imagism, and thereby helped set a course for treating "true" modernist writing as "hard" and "virile," against the "imitative" poetry of female sentimentality, in Hulme's terms. This erasure of women was striking because women writers and editors were vital parts of most every movement of the era, thanks in part to rising literacy rates, expanding educational opportunities, and the slow opening of the professions. Indeed, in the early decades of the twentieth century, innovative aesthetic practice was often linked directly to feminist politics and to a growing sense of sexual liberation more generally. Remaking the world through art meant opportunities for imagining a "New Woman"—the term often used to describe this significant rethinking of sex and gender identity.

As we saw in Chapter 2, biographies and the publication of letters, memoirs, and drafts played an important role in creating the masculinist canon. Feminist critics thereby set about recovering the lives, letters, and works of women. This included biographies of Woolf and Stein, essays such as Alice Walker's article "In Search of Zora Neale Hurston" (1975) and Susan Stanford Friedman's "Who Buried H. D.? A Poet, Her Critics, and Her Place in 'The Literary Tradition'" (1975), and even late-career autobiographical publications by H. D. and Anaïs Nin. Initially, the process of recovery sought primarily to expand the idea of a modernist canon, and thus writers of particularly difficult or challenging works like Rhys and Barnes were "rediscovered" in the 1970s. Now, writers such as Dorothy Richardson, Katherine Mansfield, Marianne Moore, Rebecca West, Mina Loy, Djuna Barnes, Jean Rhys, Amy Lowell, and Kate Chopin, and editors and publishers such as Sylvia Beach, Harriet Monroe, Jane Heap, Adrienne Monnier, and Margaret Anderson, are all seen as essential to the development of modernism. But the initial attempts to bind a selection of women writers to the modernist canon led ultimately to new conceptions of modernism that again saw cultural production as a diverse and ultimately irreconcilable set of practices. It would not do, as groundbreaking works such as Kate Millett's *Sexual Politics* (1969) suggested, simply to unearth the work of women writers who somehow belonged in the masculine Pound Era. Instead, feminist critics set out to rethink the very idea of modernism by using gender and sexuality as magnets capable of creating entirely new patterns in the art and culture of the period.

Woolf, who hovered around the margins of the canon that mid-century scholars had consolidated, was and remains the central woman in the feminist revision of modernism. Her essays, which had been overlooked for decades, gained greater attention in the work of scholars such as Jane Marcus and Carolyn Heilbrun and became the cornerstones of a politicized and specifically feminist-modernist movement. In *A Room of One's Own* (1929), an essay based on two lectures she delivered at the relatively new (and woefully underfunded) women's colleges at Cambridge, Woolf argues that women writers need both money and physical space in order to carry out their profession, and that, historically, both have been severely lacking. In other words, the material conditions necessary for anyone to create aesthetic innovations had been gendered for centuries—and when we look at the careers of Pound, Joyce, and Eliot, we find a history of female patrons such as Harriet Shaw Weaver, Ottoline Morrell, and Harriet Monroe who supported them. Economic and artistic freedom were entwined. Woolf, who came from a socially privileged family herself, asks what would have happened to a fictional figure named Judith Shakespeare, the sister of the famous playwright. Judith is denied the opportunity to attend school, has her aspirations to become a writer blunted by the men in her family, is beaten and forced into marriage by her father, and eventually commits suicide, her genius lost to history. Woolf proposes a countertradition and, building on her earlier essays such as "Modern Fiction," a new way of gathering together the fragmented shards of women's writing in English history. Aphra Behn, Jane Austen, the Brontës, and George Eliot—all of them attacked and disavowed by Woolf's male peers and ignored by most modernist critics—are made into a line of literary "monuments" that offer an alternative to Eliot's male-only "tradition." Woolf eventually extends her argument beyond gender to encompass sexuality, developing across *Orlando* (1928) and *Three Guineas* (1938) a theory of "androgynous" creativity that incorporates both the stereotypically masculine and feminine traits of psychology and writing.

Woolf's writings and the feminist return to them in the 1970s and 1980s offered a new approach to thinking about women and modernity through literature that, once recovered in the Anglo-American academy, shifted the landscape of the field.[3] Two central figures in Anglophone feminist scholarship, Sandra Gilbert and Susan Gubar, synthesized and consolidated much of this work. Their three-volume *No Man's Land* (1988–94) carried the arguments of their landmark study of Victorian women's writing, *Madwoman in the Attic* (1979), forward to twentieth-century literature. They summarize two different models of feminist thinking about modernism, one loosely aligned with the cables of canonicity and the other with the potentially bewildering abundance of history's iron filings:

> On the one hand, thinkers from Julia Kristeva and Hélène Cixous to Rachel Blau DuPlessis, Alice Jardine, and Marianne DeKoven have celebrated the subversive linguistic *jouissance* that they see as having been facilitated by the "revolution in poetic language," the fragmentation of traditional forms, and the decentering of the "subject" which they associate with modernist experimentations [and the avant-garde]. . . . On the other hand, such thinkers as Susan Suleiman, Cheryl Walker, Suzanne Clark, and Shari Benstock have implicitly endorsed our own view that, first, there is a distinction between the projects of male and female modernists and, second, the feminine should not necessarily be conflated with the so-called avant-garde since the rhetoric of innovation—for instance, Ezra Pound's "Make it new"—may, as we have shown, camouflage regressive or nostalgic sexual ideologies even while it inscribes a rebellion against what Walter Jackson Bate has called the "burden of the past." (xiv)

In elaborating this position, they redefine modernism as a product of the "battle of the sexes" that was brought about by the feminist movement of the late nineteenth century; "modernism" was said, in newspapers in the 1910s, to be caused by women, they note, and Dorothy Richardson understood aesthetic innovation in the period to be inseparable from the feminist movement (xii). Yet, subsequent attempts to confine modernism exclusively to experimental art retroactively concealed the way that the sudden expansion of women's rights and women's writing was transforming Western cultures. They point out the hostility to women—sometimes a violent misogyny—voiced by many canonical artists and writers, from F. T. Marinetti to Ernest Hemingway, and discovered in their ideals of "cold," "masculine" lines and style many problematic assumptions about gender. Pound, Lawrence, and Eliot were attacked not just for their anti-Semitism or their fascist affinities, but also for their misogyny and homophobia.

When taking up male writers, Gilbert and Gubar indict even Joyce (who often escaped the "canon wars") by pointing to his highbrow "disgust with the lowbrow scribbler [epitomized by his] parody of Maria Cummins" in the "Nausicaa" episode of *Ulysses* (146). Male modernists, they write, both hated and feared women in the marketplace—a problem compounded by the fact that so many women were editors, patrons, and mentors. Similarly, male writers regularly disparaged the fiction of the New Woman movement, which had the effect of limiting innovation solely to form and thereby excising new voices, new experiences, and new kinds of imagined communities. Gilbert and Gubar trace these responses through key pieces of modernist criticism, including "Tradition and the Individual Talent," *ABC of Reading*, *Seven Types of Ambiguity*, and *The Well-Wrought Urn*; all of these texts, they claim, write women out of the very possibility of literary history. This trend continued, they assert, in the writings of Norman Mailer, Amiri Baraka, and Robert Lowell, until feminists began to recover and continue exploring Woolf's suggestion that, in fact, the truly new art of the twentieth century was women's literature.

This resifting of the filings of a now much broader and more varied culture took place in a number of capacious and important recovery projects. Shari Benstock's influential *Women of the Left Bank* (1986), for instance, focuses on Paris—long seen as the capital of canonical modernism—but explores the networks of women writers, editors, and publishers who worked in the city. In the process, Benstock posits a new vision of modernism that includes figures like Stein, Sylvia Beach, Kay Boyle, Colette, Nancy Cunard, H. D., Maria Jolas, Mina Loy, Adrienne Monnier, Anaïs Nin, Alice B. Toklas, and Edith Wharton. (The story she tells was compelling enough to be made into a film, *Paris Was a Woman* [1996], that documents the creative, sexual, and political ferment of the city.) Benstock argues, furthermore, that "the roots of the misogyny, homophobia, and anti-Semitism that indelibly mark Modernism are to be found in the subterrain of changing sexual and political mores that constituted *belle époque* Faubourg society, and it is here that the story of these women begins—in Edith Wharton's drawing room" (x). Deliberately disconnecting the restrictive nodes of the institutionalized concept of modernism, Benstock asserts that the movement was chaotic and individualistic—far different than the epoch guided or created by Pound that Hugh Kenner outlined—and that lesbianism was a powerful yet overlooked component of it.[4]

Building on and revising such work, Bonnie Kime Scott's *The Gender of Modernism: A Critical Anthology* (1990) collects writings, letters, documents, and more from the period, including contributions from male modernists who either praised or disparaged their female peers (Eliot's introduction to Barnes's *Nightwood* [1936], for instance). Scott redresses a version of modernism that had been "unconsciously gendered masculine" by mid-century critics and dedicates her text to the "forgotten and silenced makers of modernism" (2). She operates not by offering a timeline nor a theory of modernism but by pulling together the actual filings of the culture she seeks to reexamine and by publishing original texts from many of the figures Benstock treated, then adding others like Willa Cather, Cunard, Jessie Fauset, Joyce, Lawrence, Jean Rhys, Hugh MacDiarmid, Charlotte Mew, May Sinclair, Sylvia Townsend Warner, and Woolf. In contrast to Ellmann and Feidelson's anthology, which (she notes) devotes only nine of 948 pages to women's writing, Scott's text offers what she calls a dense "mesh" of modernist connections, which she strikingly illustrates in a famous image showing the fantastically interwoven connections between writers, editors, and publishers in the period (Tangled Mesh of Modernists). She aims, in short, to show that modernism "as caught in the mesh of gender is polyphonic, mobile, interactive, sexually charged; it has wide appeal, constituting a historic shift in parameters" (4). In a two-volume monograph that carried this work further, *Refiguring Modernism* (1995), Scott then shifts modernism's locus classicus from the "Men of 1914" to the "Women of 1928," a year she chooses because her three subjects—Woolf, Barnes, and West—had at that point "found strategies to succeed as professional writers and a degree of formal license" (xxxvii). They made domestic and political connections alike, and Scott recommends here the "web" as a metaphor for understanding their version of modernism that springs from the suffragist movement and the trial of Radclyffe Hall's lesbian novel *The Well of Loneliness* (1928) rather than the outbreak of the First World War.

This work of feminist recovery and its evolving tension between adding to the canon and ultimately unmaking it depended on new kinds of theoretical models in which philosophies of art and language intersected with new ideas about political and social power. These ideas were often derived from psychoanalytic models and from Frankfurt School criticism. Consonant with Gilbert and Gubar's project, Susan Stanford Friedman's *Psyche Reborn: The Emergence of H. D.* (1981), Alice Jardine's *Gynesis: Configurations*

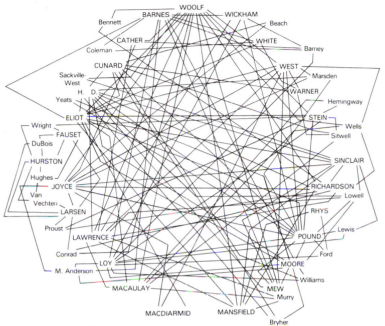

A Tangled Mesh of Modernists

*of Woman and Modernity* (1985), and Rachel Blau DuPlessis's *Writing Beyond the Ending: Narrative Strategies of Twentieth-Century Women Writers* (1985) all looked to figures such as French theorists Hélène Cixous and Luce Irigaray in their efforts to rewrite modernist literary history. Lynette Felber drew on the work of French psychoanalytic theory to argue that modernist stylistics were a form of *écriture féminine* (a French term describing a distinctive kind of women's writing), and Christine Froula approached Joyce through Freud, Jacques Lacan, Jacques Derrida, and others, all with an eye to issues of gender. Seen this way, women's writing offered revolutionary creative resources that could undermine what these critics saw as the dangerous hierarchical binaries (male-female, active-passive, conscious-unconscious) inherent in language itself. Topics such as lesbianism began to receive more attention too, with readings of "Sapphic modernism" through Woolf, Stein, and Amy Lowell, and even with claims that Pound, for instance, identified with women in his early poetry. (Male homosexual modernism, and queer modernisms in general, however, were not treated at great length until later, as we will explore in Chapter 4.) Bringing together sexuality, psychoanalysis, and politics in her *Rich and Strange: Gender, History, Modernism* (1991), Marianne DeKoven charged that New Criticism had "valorized, at the expense of the progressive implications of its forms, modernism's reactionary features" in order to produce an aestheticist portrait of the movement (11). This obscured several possibilities that feminist critics have since recovered, she contends: that some innovations, regardless of the gender of the author, had progressive implications for women; that the syntax, pre-Oedipal or aural language, and antilinearity of *écriture féminine* could offer models for reconceiving linguistic difficulty in terms other than those proposed by male writers; and that the subversive critique of culture presents a moral and ethical position that is consonant with women's writing. Here again, we see an attempt to produce a new understanding of modernism that appears less as a totalizing tradition than as a disparate collection of practices and politicized movements widely scattered in time and space. Thus, for DeKoven, modernism reveals itself not only in art, but also in its alignment with feminism and social life that offered a revolutionary alternative to a patriarchal world just beginning to decay in 1900 (21).

# Black modernism

Like feminist critics, those attentive to race—and particularly to African American arts and letters—indicted the canon of high modernism and the terms used to constitute it. Initially, they set out to revise it by adding forgotten artists and writers, but this project too eventually yielded new definitions of modernism that cast twentieth-century culture in revealing new lights. The first critical opening for this work came in the revaluations of the Harlem Renaissance in the wake of the Black Arts movement and during the rise of academic African American Studies. Before the 1980s, critics typically treated the Harlem Renaissance—itself part of the New Negro movement—as almost entirely separate from modernism, much as the history of women's literature had been seen. Now,

Langston Hughes, W. E. B. Du Bois, Claude McKay, Zora Neale
Hurston, Nella Larsen, Richard Wright, Ralph Ellison, and others
are essential to nearly every definition of modernism. Du Bois, for
example, was not only a thinker about race and consciousness in
the United States, but also a novelist and theorist of a leftist, activist
modernism who argued in 1926 that "all Art is propaganda and
ever must be, despite the wailing of the purists" (161–2). Similarly,
Hughes issued a call for racial independence and artistic autonomy
in "The Negro Artist and the Racial Mountain" (1926), writing that
"I am ashamed for the black poet who says, 'I want to be a poet, not
a Negro poet,' as though his own racial world were not as interesting
as any other world. . . . An artist must be free to choose what he does"
without fear (213). Journals like Du Bois's *Crisis* and the short-lived
*Fire!!* (1926) published black modernists ranging from Gwendolyn
Bennett to Countee Cullen, and anthologies such as Alain Locke's
*New Negro* (1925) and Nancy Cunard's *Negro* (1934) presented
global portraits of literary production across the African diaspora
in which modernism was articulated. But where women's texts and
feminist movements were overlooked for reasons ranging from
misogyny to a bias against popular culture, black modernism was
often overlooked because of critics' racialized assumptions about
literariness. These assumptions were bound up with beliefs in black
art's alleged provinciality (it was made by black writers for black
audiences only), its "low" cultural status (the denigration of jazz,
for instance), and its often leftist politics that, as we have discussed,
found little place in institutionalized studies.

The elision of these authors and texts from discussions of
modernism furthermore obscured the role, as critics have since
shown, that black figures played in developing the term itself. In
*The New Negro*, Locke, for example, praises James Weldon Johnson's
musical "transfusion of racial idioms with the modernistic styles
of expression" and Jean Toomer's ability to give "a musical folk-
lilt and a glamorous sensuous ecstasy to the style of the American
prose modernists" (51). In his 1963 edited collection *The Moderns*,
Amiri Baraka (writing as LeRoi Jones) gathered the work of what
he called "populist modernism" from marginal groups: racial and
ethnic minorities, homosexual writers, the poor, outcasts, writers
from Jack Kerouac to Robert Creeley, Charles Olson, William S.
Burroughs, and himself. He claimed that they draw on Joyce for
aesthetic reasons, but are more urgently continuing a "tradition that

has characterized the best of twentieth-century American writing"
(xvi). Several years later, he opened his poem "Return of the Native"
(1967)—itself a play on Hardy's title—with the declaration that
"Harlem is vicious/modernism." Baraka thus developed in his
poetry and criticism an expansive vision of black modernism that
connected to the largely white canon yet looked well beyond it.
This same impulse is evident as well in some of the first mid-century
collections of black writing, such as Hughes's *Anthology of Negro
Poets* (1955) and Addison Gaylem, Jr.'s *The Black Aesthetic* (1971),
with this latter text placing Baraka himself alongside Du Bois,
Hughes, Locke, and Wright.

Nathan Irvin Huggins's important and influential study *The
Harlem Renaissance* (1971) was one of the first works to move
these questions about black writing into the academy, but there still
remained few connections to a portrait of a modernism that was
almost exclusively white. In the 1980s, however, a new generation of
scholars grew frustrated with previous treatments of this literature
and attempted to define the distinguishing, if not autochthonous,
features of black expression across time, and thus to place black
literature within, alongside, or in dynamic tension with what was a
de facto white modernism. Drawing on the exciting and engaging
work by figures like Robert Stepto and scholar-activists like Cornel
West, both Houston Baker and Henry Louis Gates, Jr. questioned,
in two monumental studies, the previous dismissals of the Harlem
Renaissance as a failure, either because it was too provincial (as
Huggins claimed) or because it was too assimilationist (as David
Levering Lewis claimed). Baker's *Modernism and the Harlem
Renaissance* (1987) thus begins with the premise that the Harlem
Renaissance—a "movement" only in retrospect, he notes—produced
a "mastery of form" and "deformation of mastery," both of which
are concepts necessary for comprehending its "sound" and realizing
more fully its successes (50). Building on his own theories of the
"vernacular"—which refers both to a local mode of speech and,
etymologically, to a "home-born slave" (from the Latin *verna*, a
slave born in the master's house)—Baker looks for a Jamesonian
"ideology of form" in black expression, whether in the blues or in
sonnets (2). Baker does not argue that Harlem Renaissance writers
were *like* Eliot, Pound, and others in their formalism. Rather, they
developed a "*modern Afro-American sound* as a function of a
specifically Afro-American discursive practice" (xiv; italics in the

original). The myth of the Harlem Renaissance's failure, he later argued, was a legacy of the Black Arts movement's larger rejection of modernist forms. "Further," he notes, "the very *histories* that are assumed in the chronologies of British, Anglo-American, and Irish modernisms are radically opposed to any adequate and accurate account of the history of Afro-American modernism" (xvi; italics in the original). This argument, in effect, balances a formalist definition of modernism that might include innovative black arts and a more expansive rethinking of modernism that encompasses the enormous contrasts of twentieth-century cultural production, and, in fact, had been practiced for perhaps centuries by black subjects.

Baker challenged the very idea of modernist formalism by seeking to provincialize white modernism instead—to undermine its claims to universality by pointing to the ways in which it is "exclusively Western, preeminently bourgeois, and optically white" (6). In a sometimes personal study, he winds together a new cable of black modernism around figures like Du Bois, Locke, Paul Lawrence Dunbar, and Charles Chesnutt; in an allusion to Woolf, he traces its origin to "on or about September 18, 1895" (8). This date was the "commencement of Afro-American modernism" in Booker T. Washington's famous Atlanta Compromise speech (15). Washington masters form, Baker argues, not for individual aesthetic purposes, but for the survival of a nation. Baker focuses on articulations of a black nation, and Locke's *New Negro* "is the first fully modern figuration of a nation predicated upon mass energies [that] returns us to the present discussion's exploration of definitions of Afro-American 'modernism'" (91). The blend of "class and mass" in 1930s literature, in which formal mastery and folk elements came together, was epitomized for Baker by Sterling Brown, who was for him "the essence of black discursive modernism" (93).

Like Baker, Gates aimed to trace an essential tradition of black modernism—one separate from the New Critical canon but nevertheless engaged with some of its key concerns with aesthetic forms. His book, *The Signifying Monkey* (1988), fused race studies with poststructuralism (a topic we discuss in more detail below) in order to bridge studies of "high" literature and vernacular art. This broadly influential study treats Wright, Ellison, Hurston, and Ishmael Reed within what Gates calls a "black tradition [that] has inscribed its own theories of its nature and function within elaborate hermeneutical and rhetorical systems" (xiv). He traces through this

tradition a longstanding practice of "signifyin(g)," a term he takes
from black culture to describe the double-voiced wordplay and
exploitation of the inherent gaps between denotative and figurative
meanings of words. For Gates, Ellison and Reed are constantly
"signifying upon" a white literary heritage that they blend with
their own black vernacular creations (221). Likewise, Hurston's
employment of multiple voices at play with one another in *Their
Eyes Were Watching God* (1937) is a rhetorical strategy, he asserts,
that depends vitally on both the development of black vernaculars
outside of the white gaze and the superficial intelligibility, among
white audiences, of her depictions of it. Black writers also signify
upon one another, as Ellison does by parodying "Wright's distinctive
version of naturalism with a complex rendering of modernism"
(106). Gates, in effect, posits an alternative modernism in which
Wright represents a persisting Realism and Naturalism in the
modernist era, and Ellison represents the subtle revolt against it.
In doing so, however, he also challenges the very idea of a singular
tradition and the many institutional and pedagogical structures that
subtend it by excluding vernacular form. By Gates's account, Reed's
*Mumbo Jumbo* (1972), rather than *Finnegans Wake* or the Second
World War, marks an endpoint of modernism since it recasts the
"implicit relation among modernism, realism, and postmodernism"
(xxvi).

     Baker's and Gates's work, which focused on delineating and
archiving black modernism both parallel to and in tension with
high modernism, extended along different lines, both domestic
and international. In 1990, for example, James de Jongh's *Vicious
Modernism* further developed a conception of African American
modernism located in Harlem, reaching from the neighborhood's
origins as a center of 1920s' black culture to the Black Arts movement's
readings of the neighborhood's riots of the 1960s. Bringing these
interventions to a treatment of canonical high modernism, Michael
North's *The Dialect of Modernism* (1994) argued that vernacular
African American English crucially informed the creation of
modernist idioms. North contends that white writers used black
dialect to operate against the impulse to "standardize" English
that was growing in this era (the *Oxford English Dictionary* was
completed in the 1920s after forty years of work). Three modernist
classics thereby depend on racial ventriloquism—Conrad's *The
Nigger of the 'Narcissus'* (1897), Stein's "Melanctha" (1909), and

Eliot's *The Waste Land*—and for Pound, "black dialect is a prototype of the literature that would break the hold of the iambic pentameter" (78). Reading these texts alongside McKay's novels and the film *The Jazz Singer* (1927), North holds that linguistic mimicry was not a fad, but an array of "strategies without which modernism could not have arisen" (Preface). Like Gates and Baker, then, North finds that the attempt to sustain a notion of modernist canonicity inevitably leads to a substantial revision of what can now count as art. Thus, as we see the shift between our two metaphors, blackness again becomes less an alternative cable running independently alongside high modernism than a critical magnet that both recasts the look of the canon and exposes new fields of cultural production.

North's book, along with ones by Ann Douglas, Kenneth Warren, Laura Doyle, and Barbara Foley, marked in the mid-1990s a new "integrationist" direction in studies of modernism that, at the same time, put new pressures on many of the ideas that had contributed to the term's mid-century consolidation. The same is true of George Hutchinson's *The Harlem Renaissance in Black and White* (1995), which criticized previous accounts of black writing for focusing too narrowly on language and semiotics. Hutchinson instead investigates institutions and "fields," as theorized by Bourdieu, in order to fashion what he calls an "interracial perspective" on the era (31). Seeing structural links among "modernist American cultural nationalism, cultural pluralism, and the Harlem Renaissance," Hutchison argues that the black "brand of modernism is actually closer to Latin American *modernismo* than to high modernism" in its "realist localism" and its attention to "low" or vernacular cultural forms (119). The integrationist search for formal properties by which the two might be wedded, therefore, was in vain. Instead, he argues that we should consider their shared participation in a rapidly changing literary marketplace in which black figures had white patrons, but also in which white writers courted black audiences.

# The arrival of "Theory"

Deeply entwined with studies of gender, race, and ethnicity came an approach to art and literature known simply (and often bafflingly) as "Theory" (with a capital T).[5] This unwieldy term generally serves as shorthand for structuralism, poststructuralism, and post-Freudian psychoanalysis, though it also encompasses aspects of Marxism and sociology that together offer ways of thinking about the grounds (or groundlessness) of meaning. These overlapping schools developed in the 1960s in the works of Philippe Sollers, Maurice Blanchot, Tzvetan Todorov, Michel Foucault, Jacques Derrida, Roland Barthes, Julia Kristeva, Louis Althusser, Gilles Deleuze, and others—a group mostly centered on the journal *Tel Quel* (1958–82) and with politics that crystallized in and after the May 1968 student revolts in Paris. Like the New Critics, they were particularly interested in language and aesthetic form, but had starkly different intellectual backgrounds and investments, including Marxism, feminism, and gay rights. Generally speaking, they believed that language offered our only access to the world and that even visual signs and signifiers had an inherently linguistic logic (an assumption that led to our current critical tendency to refer to any object of interpretation as a "text"). Such claims led many critics to argue that Theory itself might be part and parcel of modernism, a continuation of it or at the least a revisionary interpretation of it.

Indeed, many of the early French-language theorists saw themselves as a continuing part of the Parisian avant-garde of the twenties and thirties. But unlike scholars of gender or race studies, they had little interest in discovering alternative traditions. Developing some of the radical elements of Friedrich Nietzsche's writings, Theory began to dismantle the very idea of the aesthetic itself, and of the linear senses of history and tradition. Instead, these thinkers proclaimed the inherent instability of language and thus the world that it helped us constitute and understand. As a result, its main figures emphasized multi-perspectivalism, multiplicity, difference, a lack of unity, and antitotality. Borrowing ideas from Freud and from the French psychoanalyst Jacques Lacan, they even extended these insights into the very idea of human identity itself, which became increasingly riven, alienated, and incommensurable with the material world. Aesthetic objects and aesthetic experience alike became fragmented as the entire world suddenly began to look like an ever-shifting pile of shards, constantly being rearranged and pulled apart or "deconstructed" into their irreconcilable contradictions.

These insights came, in part, in and around the debates about modernism's restrictive canon and its formal features that we've already examined. Roland Barthes, for example, drew a distinction

between "readerly" and "writerly" texts, associating the former
with Realism, in which the world of the text requires little
effort from a reader called upon to assemble it imaginatively or
linguistically. Chronology and character development are mostly
stable and noncontradictory while the contradictions of language
are suppressed. Readerly texts thus create the illusion of an
objective reality, an illusion that Barthes then links with bourgeois
complacency and the acceptance of certain regimes of power.
Writerly texts, on the other hand, require that the reader construct
the textual world and discern its relation (or lack of relation) to
his or her own socio-historical contexts. This transfer of power
from the autonomous modernist text to the playful contemporary
reader is liberating for Barthes, since it potentially frees language,
and thus the perception of reality itself, from political and social
constraint, allowing semiotic play to carry readers in directions
that a single historical subject could not conceive (see *S/Z*). Unlike
the New Critics, who sought to control this kind of threatening
play by placing worthy works in a vital tradition, Barthes claimed
that *all* texts could become writerly through what Kristeva called
the reader's "aggressive participation" (181). Thus, in addition to
important studies on canonical authors like Balzac and Proust,
Barthes also wrote about wrestling and advertising, photography
and striptease.[6] Initially, he hoped to unlock a notion of the core
structure of meaning, but his work quickly tilted, instead, toward
the process that allowed the writerly imagination to drag all kinds
of artifacts into new interpretive schemas, linking modernism to
the radical avant-garde and to the cultural detritus of industrial
capitalism alike.

In the history of modernist studies that we have been tracing,
however, it took one more layer of mediation for Theory's impact to
be felt in US and British academies—a layer that unfolded around
canonical modernist works. Both Francophone and Anglophone
structuralist and poststructuralist theorists began to articulate
their ideas through treatments of interwar writers, with Joyce, in
particular, playing a pivotal role for them. In his theories about
the role of language in psychoanalysis, Lacan argued that the
epiphanies—moments of profound realization or insight recorded
in literary fragments—in Joyce's early works were instances of
the real foreclosing meaning. Lacan also saw in Joyce's mature
works a successful penetration of the Symbolic order by the private

*jouissance* of the subject (see *Le séminaire*). In an illustrative moment in 1978, Colin MacCabe took up various threads of Theory's work and published *James Joyce and the Revolution of the Word*, which claimed that Joyce's writing "produces a change in the relations between reader and text, a change which has profound revolutionary implications" (1). MacCabe argues that it is "only by the acceptance of the most reductive account of the relation between politics and literature that Joyce's texts can be dismissed as non-political," even though they are ultimately politically ineffective (152). By way of such contentions, MacCabe was attacking the Leavisian and practical modes of reading that still reigned in British universities, and that figures like Williams had also attempted to revise. MacCabe's book thus caused a scandal at Cambridge, where he was denied tenure, presumably on the grounds that his use of French Theory to read Anglophone literature was, in essence, spurious.[7]

Throughout the 1970s and 1980s, there was often a gulf between French-inspired Theory and Anglophone academic approaches, though at least initially both shared a common set of canonical texts. As we have seen, however, Theory offered a way for critics of many stripes to expand what got to count as a "text." This, in turn, put great pressure on the very idea of modernism as an entangled collection of experimental work embedded in a Western tradition. Derrida's ideas about deconstruction—in which language seems constantly to undermine itself—offered new ways of thinking about the difficulty many critics still believed essential to any definition of modernism. In "Literary History and Literary Modernity" (1971), Paul de Man further argues that "modernism" could never be truly "new"; it is only a series of metaphors through which we imagine having now become more modern. For him, every era calls itself "modern" but lives off the capital of predecessors; modernity and history are thus locked in a union that constantly kills both. There is no concept of "modernism" for de Man, only a *desire* to wipe out the past. The concept is thus contradictory and vacuous, a self-deceiving category. Similarly, Harold Bloom, who first made his name as a scholar by defending the Romantics against Eliot-derived attacks, also claimed that "modernism in literature has not passed; rather, it has been exposed as never having been there" (28). Instead, he charged, it was a series of gossips among certain writers turned into myth by the New Critics and into dogma by Hugh Kenner, while all along Stevens and Yeats were actually Romantics. Bloom believed that the allegedly distinct movements called the "later Enlightenment, Romanticism, Modernism, Post-Modernism" are all part of one still unfolding phenomenon (33).

In short, modernist experimentalism, which first drew critical attention for its elevation—if not sacralization—of form, was now read as a failed effort to ward off the conditions of formalism itself. The modernist investment in what makes language and what language makes, in the hands of Theory, was a thread to be pulled until its tightly knit tapestry unraveled into new potentialities—or until it was revealed to be nothing at all. And as critics tugged ever more insistently, the cables that once held together a narrow canon snapped. The great modernist heresy of antitraditionalism came to look like nothing more than a vain retrenchment in a lost tradition. Theory, therefore, both enlivened questions about what "modernism" was as a literary-historical project and what its political potentialities were for women and black writers, and at the same time cast doubt upon whether the sharp-eyed critic with a magnet of any sort could arrange the iron filings of the past into a coherent narrative.

# The avant-garde

A new focus on questions about race and gender and the general turn toward Theory all meant the concept of modernism became increasingly unstable, its canon twisted into new, often irreconcilable patterns. As we have seen, this process led to a new awareness of the intersections among social conditions, politics, and literary form evident in formations ranging from the New Woman to Du Bois's program of propagandistic art. For the New Critics and others who sought to define modernism as an autonomous aesthetic practice, however, politics had often been set aside or waved away by the intentional fallacy. Concomitant with the rise of academic Marxism, feminism, race studies, and Theory, however, was a reconsideration of what politics itself meant—how politics were expressed, embodied, and enacted. With a common investment in addressing works that were *oppositional* in various ways, critics thus began to look more closely at a new collection of more explicitly political works across the arts that are still loosely described as the "avant-garde"—a term used to separate them from high modernism. The phrase "avant-garde" itself originated in the French military ("advanced guard"), migrated to leftist politics from the 1840s to 1870s, then made its way into the aesthetic realm in the late nineteenth century, all the while denoting a belief in the idea that art could transform society. The question arose, then: Were modernists truly the self-appointed prophets and leading voices of the "modern," or were they in fact fighting very different and sometimes misunderstood battles? And what was their relationship to the art-worlds and economies that supported them?

This idea of the avant-garde posed a series of challenges to the idea of high modernism as a largely autonomous and strictly formalist movement. A first chord was struck in the Italian critic Renato Poggioli's *Theory of the Avant-garde* (1962; English, 1968). Like Bourdieu, Poggioli was a sociologist, curious less about the content of any given work of art than about the social and institutional practices enabling its creation. Across a variety of European contexts, the avant-garde, he believes, historically thrived on a dialectic of activism and antagonism: "Linguistic hermeticism, which is one of the avant-garde's most important characteristics of form and style, would be conceived of as both the cause and the effect of the antagonism between public and artist" (37).[8] In other words, while Eliot proclaimed that formal autonomy, difficulty, and the discovery of tradition were an escape from the conditions of everyday life, critics, in fact, needed to engage fully these very conditions in order to make them cohere meaningfully. Furthermore, while evading a linear model of history and emphasizing instead the iron filings of diverse yet interlocking social and aesthetic practices, Poggioli constellates the avant-garde around concepts rather than historical events. Activism, for instance, is action for action's sake; antagonism is "acting by negative reaction"; nihilism is "attaining nonaction by acting . . . in destructive, not constructive labor; and agonism is the point at which the avant-garde accepts its own ruin and can move no further" (61–2). By configuring the avant-garde this way, Poggioli opens a path for understanding a more politically engaging, socially potent force whose energies had been concealed by an excessive focus on a high modernist canon premised on the ideal of autonomy. Avant-garde art, for Poggioli, is intensely attentive to its historical specificity and does not aspire to the condition of universality or Eliotic immortality.

Writing in the wake of the failures of the global revolts of 1968, the German critic Peter Bürger offered a somewhat different account of the avant-garde that still provokes extensive debate. In his *Theory of the Avant-garde* (1974; English, 1984), Bürger agrees with the Mexican poet and Nobel prize winner Octavio Paz, who believed that avant-garde art in 1967 was repeating the avant-gardism of 1917, thus bringing about the end of an *idea* of "modern" or new art (see Paz, *Children*). Bürger looks back to the German-language avant-gardes of the 1910s in order to understand these aesthetic-political failures by sharply distinguishing a conservative "modernism" attentive to its own place in an unfolding tradition from a far more radical, yet perpetually fleeting, avant-garde. He thus defines "modernism" as an attempt to evolve literary and aesthetic style—to disrupt old categories and genres and to invent new ones. The avant-gardist, however, had no faith in tradition or progress and instead launched an assault on the institution of "art" as such. Thus, for Bürger, Joyce and Picasso were modernists, while the Russian Constructivists and the Surrealists were avant-gardists. Most of all, he points to Dada as an exemplary avant-garde "movement," since it was an anti-movement of anti-art, intent on gleefully destroying the very idea and ideal of art itself. Against Poggioli and Clement Greenberg, Bürger saw the avant-garde as "historical," making it a bounded period or set of movements, not a transhistorical concept.

The underlying arguments for Bürger's account are sociological as well and involve the development of aesthetic institutions and the commodification of art in the modern (i.e., post-medieval capitalist) era. Like Bourdieu, he argues that modern art has declared its own realm of autonomy in the capitalist sphere because it can no longer rely on the church or on the court to ensure its social integration. But this was a dangerous development because it has removed art from its integration in what he calls the "praxis of life" (51)—the idea that theory and practice should be inextricable from one another. Aesthetic autonomy is a bourgeois fiction for him, and one that hides the labor of art's origins and separates it from life. Drawing on the Frankfurt School theorist Herbert Marcuse, he holds that art can no longer be politically engaged *as art* under these conditions; it becomes complicit with the institutions (museums, collectors, taste-makers) and thus the capitalist regimes that sustain it. He calls this the "neutralization of critique" and writes that "this neutralization of impulses to change society is thus closely related to the role art plays in the development of bourgeois subjectivity" (13).

Thus, in an ironic reversal, the success of the avant-garde in the institutional art-world of its moment guaranteed its failure, which is why its legacy is unsustainable. Dadaists were anti-original, anticreative, antirational, ahistorical, but they too were quickly institutionalized—put in museums and elevated as paradoxical anti-artistic artists—in a process that emptied out the fundamental core of their work. Bürger's account thereby turns away from analyses of the *content* of avant-garde or modernist works: we cannot discern the differences between modernism and the avant-garde, or indeed between the "social function" of any movements, through questions of language or style alone, he believes (44). That is to say, even Theory's claims about the instability of language and its political potential fail to apprehend the truly radical nature of the avant-garde. In an extended analysis of the concept of autonomy in bourgeois society, building on Adorno's insight that the "autonomous" work attempts to mask the social conditions of its production, he argues that the "avant-garde not only negates the category of individual production but also that of individual *reception*" (53; italics in the original). The endpoint of the emphasis on autonomy, he holds, is that we accept the modernist separation of art and life, which signals the end of art (see *Decline* 44–5).

Bürger's theories have been a powerful magnet for rearranging cultural production in the early twentieth century along new lines—institutional, aesthetic, and political—and they have provoked some hostile responses, especially from Anglo-American scholars, as we'll discuss more fully in the following chapter. Some scholars, ranging from Ann Ardis to Raymond Williams, criticized Bürger's stark distinctions and have proposed more fluid, overlapping conceptions of modernist and avant-garde arts, or even a "modernist avant-garde" (Ardis 175). Others have noted that he universalizes several debates in German Marxism and the aesthetic history of the German left, for the most part. His work remains important, however, precisely because it attempts to untangle the idea of modernism from the cables of tradition, education, and institutionalization that had cut it off from its social life and context. For him, the avant-garde is a way of thinking about the costs inherent in creating modernism as an aesthetic and historical category, and thus it continues to invite us to think about the powers of institutions—from the high school classroom to the fine arts museum—to align even the most radical works with a potentially deadening tradition.

# Postmodernism

Across the 1970s and 1980s, the growing ferment and debate around the definition of modernism that we have been tracing had developed into a kind of crisis. As we have seen, concepts like "modernisms" and a special category like "high modernism" sought to retain a core rubric, but the old canon itself still weighed heavily on a number of theorists and producers who felt increasingly constrained by it. Amid these debates, "postmodernism" took shape. Postmodernism launched a highly effective set of aesthetic and intellectual attacks on modernism as a whole, far different from the critique of its exclusivity or complaints about difficulty and amorality that we've already seen. High modernism, in particular, came to be seen as stodgy, antihistorical, apolitical, and elitist; as Lillian S. Robinson and Lise Vogel charged, "Modernism . . . seeks to intensify isolation. It forces the work of art, the artist, the critic, and the audience outside of history. Modernism denies us the possibility of understanding ourselves as *agents* in the material world, for all has been removed to an abstract world of ideas" (198; italics in the original). The problem wasn't simply modernist authors who disempowered readers, either: Susan Sontag's landmark book *Against Interpretation and Other Essays* (1966) charged that New Criticism and a variety of other myopic academic strategies had sapped the inherent energy, erotics, and playfulness of art by focusing too heavily on form and thereby ignoring other, often more embodied, approaches to literature and visual art. Seen from this vantage, modernism had exhausted itself and become thereby not an exceptional gathering of still urgent ideas and aesthetics, but a quiescent and institutionalized historical period that fell roughly between 1890 and 1940. No longer connected to modern life, it was entombed alongside Romanticism and the Renaissance as just another literary-historical period to be dispassionately dissected.

Postmodernism, in turn, positioned itself rhetorically as a new, vital, and immediate configuration of aesthetic, political, and even social practices. But what was postmodernism itself, and what were the implications for declaring an end of modernism, whether in *Finnegans Wake*, the Second World War, or the premier of *Waiting for Godot* in 1953? And, as in the case of "modernism," was (is) it a set of literary traits, a movement, an era, a mode of criticism, or a "condition" under capitalism? The concept itself is diffuse and still widely contested, in part because it rejects outright canon and tradition while embracing the idea that the world is an unstable field of textual play. In this sense, it radicalizes Pound's metaphor of the cultural past a pile of iron filings, concluding that we are caught in the perpetual attraction of different magnets constantly tugging language, identity, and politics into ever-changing designs that cannot be rooted in a shared reality or aligned with some vision of totality. "Postmodernism," in fact, ran into many of the same conceptual problems as the "modernism" it hoped first to constrain, then to escape or surpass—problems compounded by the fact that it too drew on ideas from several different intersecting fields ranging from art and architecture to literature and performance.

Once the term caught hold, definitions proliferated, all of them charging or, at least, implying that modernism had collapsed into an institutionalized canon. We can say, then, that "postmodernism" gathered the various energies of revision, rejection, criticism, and recontextualization that we have seen developing in thought on modernism at least since the early 1960s. In what was perhaps the first and most influential exposition of postmodern literature by a writer who would become identified with it, John Barth's "The Literature of Exhaustion" (1967; later revised in "The Literature of Replenishment" [1980]) looks back to a certain grouping of canonical modernists as avatars, if not initiators, of postmodernism. Celebrating Joyce, Kafka, Jorge Luis Borges, and Samuel Beckett, along with Pop Art and intermedia art, Barth sees new possibilities in the ways that—as he writes of Borges—one "confronts an intellectual dead end and employs it against itself to accomplish new human work" (69–70). He calls for "novels which imitate the form of a Novel, by an author who imitates the role of Author" (72). This mode of writing, he claims, has its own tradition running back through Vladimir Nabokov, Miguel de Cervantes, Henry Fielding, the *1001 Nights*, and more; it aims not for novelty, but for the farce of novelty. Silence, miscommunication, metafiction, and parody, from Beckett's empty stages to John Cage's *4'33"* (1952), become

the hallmarks of "new" arts—though seen here as writing with a
tradition of its own. Barth, in other words, parses "modernism" by
way of the possibilities it opens and forecloses for contemporary
writers.[9] For him, Borges and Joyce were both modernists *and*
postmodernists; he did not see such potentiality beyond the novel
as it existed in their moment in Forster or Woolf, for instance, and
so he relegated them to a fixed historical period.

As postmodernism began to develop its own canon of authors,
these lines of influence and revisionary readings of modernism
became more variegated. The shift toward "modernisms" and the
splintering of tradition into mobile iron filings thus quickly overtook
postmodernism as well. In fact, as early as 1964, Leslie Fiedler
had declared "The Death of Avant-Garde Literature," in which he
claims that major American novelists now positioned themselves
against the European avant-garde, itself in its final throes. He calls
Beckett and Alain Robbe-Grillet the "European gravediggers of
the avant-garde," but argues that commercial media are the true
killers of this spirit: "with the aid of the mass media, antifashion
becomes fashion among us at a rate that bewilders critics and
writers alike" (454, 455). Avant-garde literature is now banal, he
says; offensive literature is impossible, and though "highbrow or
truly experimental art aims at *insult*; and the intent of its typical
language is therefore exclusion," its attacks on the bourgeoisie
have been foreclosed now that the bourgeoisie adore it (456; italics
in the original).[10] Lenny Bruce, the edgy and obscene comedian, is
the last true avant-gardist in the United States for Fiedler. In "The
New Mutants" (1965), Fiedler named as his "mutants" Burroughs,
Barth, William Golding, Anthony Burgess, and Kurt Vonnegut: all
writers, he believes, who wrote in a style that would have been
considered science fiction in the past, but is now accepted as a
"literary" genre. "These mutants who are likely to sit before us in
class . . . beatniks or hipsters, layabouts or drop-outs we are likely
to call them with corresponding hostility," he writes, are attempting
to create a "revolutionary or prophetic or futurist function" for
the novel (381, 383). They are "dropouts from history," have
withdrawn from school, and "strive to disengage . . . the tradition
of the human, as the West . . . has defined it, Humanism itself, both
in its bourgeois and Marxist forms" (383). Fiedler does not praise
or condone the "mutants," but rather offers a descriptive account
of how the "young lose us in literature as well as life, since here

they pass over into real revolt, i.e., what we really cannot abide, hard as we try" (398).

Soon after, in a series of studies gathered in *The Dismemberment of Orpheus* (1971; revised 1982), Ihab Hassan offered a rough but useful schema for demarcating the differences between modernism and postmodernism. Like the early attempts to define modernism we discussed in Chapter 2, his work attempts to define postmodernism through a series of oppositions while embedding it in a distinct aesthetic tradition. Hassan draws out dichotomies between modernism and postmodernism such as form/antiform, purpose/play, design/chance, hierarchy/anarchy, synthesis/antithesis, metaphor/metonymy, paranoia/schizophrenia, signified/signifier, metaphysics/irony, and transcendence/immanence (267–8). While scholars have found a host of counterexamples in the years since he published this list (and the author himself conceded at the time that plenty of "inversions and exceptions" could be adduced), Hassan crucially defines postmodernism as a "revision of Modernism" rather than an absolute break with it ("POSTmodernISM" 15). As with Barth's conceptualization, this allowed certain key figures like Joyce and Stein to move between categories, a process that both helps locate postmodernism within an aesthetic tradition and allows it to draw upon the very processes of institutionalization and professionalization that many critics believed had brought modernism itself to a close.

Drawing new lines in his essay "Modernism and Postmodernism: Approaching the Present in American Poetry" (1972), the poet-critic David Antin questioned the enshrined "tradition" of English-language American verse that critics had pointed to Eliot as originating, and he separated Eliot's legacy from Pound's. Eliot's reading of the metaphysical poets became the basis for Brooks's and Richards's distinctions between "Modern" and "Romantic" poetry, or the poetry of "inclusion" or "exclusion." Antin looks for a nuanced approach that will not "reduce the complex 'hyperspace' of modernist collage (Pound, Williams, Olson, Zukofsky) to the nearly trivial, single-dimensional ironic and moral space of Eliot, Tate, Lowell, and so on" (183). He credits Charles Olson and the Black Mountain poets for initiating

the beginning of the end for the Metaphysical Modernist tradition, which was by no means a "modernist" tradition but an anomaly peculiar to American and English poetry. It was the result of a collision of strongly anti-Modernist and provincial sensibilities with the hybrid modernism of Pound and the purer Modernism of Gertrude Stein and William Carlos Williams. (183)

Antin here uses aspects of postmodernism to posit an alternative and a more lively line of development for American modernism, one that celebrated figures like Olson, Creeley, John Ashbery, and many of those collected in Donald Allen's *New American Poetry* (1960). Marjorie Perloff agreed, adding that "New Critical" poets such as Karl Shapiro, Delmore Schwartz, Richard Wilbur, and Hayden Carruth represent the end of modernism, which became rigidified in the ten years after the Second World War (see *21st-Century*). For her, the experimental Language Poetry is indebted to Eliot's early work: attempting to weave together a new cable, she argues that Eliot, Stein, Duchamp, and Khlebnikov were the neo-Romantic avant-gardes of early modernism—especially the Eliot of 1910–11, before he changed his modes of experimentation. Both Antin's and Perloff's works were supported by new journals such as *boundary 2*, founded in 1970 on the premise that an older version of modernism was dying, postmodernism was emerging, and Western metaphysics was in its final stage. For its editor William V. Spanos, modernism withdrew from existential time into simultaneity in art; postmodernism, on the other hand, aims for contingency in temporality. In all of this work, we see theorists of postmodernism who were creating genealogies that enlivened the present in ways that made modernism variously, yet simultaneously, a burden and a source of aesthetic liberation.

Furthermore, less dichotomous in their approach were studies like Tyrus Miller's *Late Modernism* (1999), which draws on Fredric Jameson's work to find a space between, or straddling, modernism and postmodernism—or what he calls, following the architectural historian Charles Jencks, "late modernism." (We'll talk more about architectural postmodernism in Chapter 4.) Others, too, explored this transitional phase, including Art Berman and Brian McHale; Miller asserts that

at first glance, late modernist writing appears a distinctly self-conscious manifestation of the aging and decline of modernism, in both its institutional and ideological dimensions. More surprising, however, such writing also strongly anticipates future developments, so that without forcing, it might easily fit into a narrative of emergent postmodernism. (7)

Miller's methodology is to begin between modernism and postmodernism, then to look back before he looks forward in hopes of reshaping narratives of both. He ultimately dates late modernism's origins to around 1926, and he points to Beckett's readings of Joyce and Proust, which, contra Eliot, claimed that both had become slaves to their commitments to form. Beckett wanted not a "'unification' of the historical chaos," but the "straws" and "flotsam" of the modern world (qtd. 17, 18). Late modernism appears in works by writers like Nabokov and Zukofsky and is identifiable by a self-aware yet "disruptive, deforming spell of laughter" as modernism steps knowingly into its own formalist grave (19).

As postmodernism opened up new vantages on its own inheritance from and resistance to the immediate past, it helped forge new and increasingly dissonant definitions of modernism. As a result, the attempt by postmodern theorists to fashion a tradition for themselves that ran outside, in parallel, or beyond the New Critical and mid-century canon ended up shifting modernism itself into ever more protean shapes. Indeed, the term postmodernism itself often referred vaguely to a general sense that the very idea of tradition had come undone and that the fragmentation of twentieth-century culture into a collection of mobile iron fragments was, in fact, now general across the arts and humanities. The past, indeed all of culture itself, could be clustered by powerful interpretive magnets into confusing, often dissonant patterns.[11] For Perloff, as we've seen, the early Eliot is postmodern, the later Eliot is modern. Other authors too were bifurcated in equally strange ways. Joyce's *Portrait of the Artist as a Young Man* might be modernist, for example, and *Finnegans Wake* postmodernist, but even a single book like *Ulysses* was reduced to a mass of iron filings so that the first few chapters could be aligned with modernism, the later more experimental ones with postmodernism. Professional and institutional prestige was at stake in these debates as widely studied figures like Eliot and Joyce retained significant cultural capital and thus could be profitably aligned with innovative modes of reading and critique. But this had the effect of further fragmenting both modernism and postmodernism, undermining the early attempts of critics like Hassan to distinguish between the two.

Calling postmodernism a product of "late capitalism," Jameson argues that it is less a distinctive aesthetic movement than an ideological structure. For Jameson, postmodernism emerges from a rupture with modernism that breaks down high and mass culture into a depthless field, one of pastiche and not parody, with no history, no critical distance, no symbolic correspondence or resonance, only unassembled fragments. He believes that there will be as many postmodernisms as there were high modernisms because the former are a reaction, characterized by schizophrenic metafictions, to the reification of modernisms. Seen this way, modernism did not have a stranglehold on fragmentation: rather, it must now be delineated by a certain *type* of fragmented aesthetics that were entangled with mass culture. Modernism resisted commodification; postmodernism embraces it. Thus, for him, "camp, better than anything else, underscores one of the most fateful differences between high modernism and postmodernism" since it announces "the disappearance of *affect*, the utter extinction of that pathos or even tragic spirit with which the high modernists lived their torn and divided condition" ("Baudelaire" 359; italics in the original).

As Jameson's account indicates, the stakes of this debate about modernism and postmodernism were pervasive, though they arrived unevenly in different fields. Architecture, for example, was one of the first fields to take up the idea of postmodernism, while it came somewhat late to art history—in part because Greenberg's influential definition of modernism encompassed numerous postwar movements like Minimalism and Abstract Expressionism. Across all these fields, however, there coalesced a growing sense that modernism and postmodernism could now be easily separated from one another. Michael Fried, a disciple of Clement Greenberg, argued in "Art and Objecthood" (1967) that Minimalism in the 1960s had betrayed the experimental legacy of Modernist aesthetics by refusing to absorb the viewer, instead constantly pointing up its status as being-viewed and closing itself within its own "theatricality" alone (157). That is, modernism had self-consciously analyzed and explored its own materiality, whether in visual arts, language, or music. "Literalist" (or Minimalist) art had taken this premise too far, he suggests, to the point that it betrays the modernist revolution by becoming absorbed in its own "objecthood"—its physical presence—in a "theatrical" manner (148). Through her interpretations of French Theory, Rosalind Krauss turned to the legacies of modernist form

in sculpture, photography, and installation art, concluding that
art criticism had needlessly sustained the myths of originality and
aura that surrounded modernism—and thus kept modernism alive
artificially. She proposed that postmodernism, unlike modernism
and the avant-garde, celebrates inauthenticity through copies
that remove themselves from any notion of aesthetic history (see
*Originality*). Hal Foster holds that "modernism . . . was marked
by . . . 'negations' [of art or of representation as such], espoused
in the anarchic hope of an 'emancipatory effect' or in the utopian
dream of a time of pure presence, a space beyond representation,"
but that in postmodernism, we are supposedly never outside the
politics of representation (xvi). And Charles Jencks dates the death
of modernism in architecture—a field in which the postmodern
rejection of modernism was perhaps most pointed—to the exact
moment when the Pruitt-Igoe housing development in St. Louis was
dynamited, on July 15, 1972 at 3:32 p.m. (9).

Within philosophy, Jean-François Lyotard's *The Postmodern
Condition* (1979; English, 1984) had a profound effect on thinking
about modernism, both directly and indirectly, by defining
postmodernism through its lack of faith in metanarratives, and
calling it "that which, in the modern, puts forward the unpresentable
in presentation itself" (81). Modernism, on the other hand, only uses
its technical experiments to *point* to the unpresentable. Drawing on
figures such as Thomas Kuhn and Paul Feyerabend, Lyotard points
to a crisis in the legitimation of knowledge in order to claim that
the postmodern

> is undoubtedly a part of the modern. . . . A work can become
> modern only if it is first postmodern. Postmodernism thus
> understood is not modernism at its end but in the nascent state,
> and this state is constant. . . . Modern aesthetics is an aesthetic of
> the sublime, though a nostalgic one. It allows the unpresentable
> to be put forward only as the missing contents; but the form,
> because of its recognizable consistency, continues to offer to the
> reader or viewer matter for solace and pleasure. (79, 81)

Proust and Joyce allude to this condition, he argues, in writing and
in their treatment of the signifier, but they do not go far enough,
even when their "modernism" challenges what it makes "yesterday."
Postmodernism, for Lyotard, thus revolves around a paradox: it is

"future (*post*) anterior (*modo*)" (81). Most important, it moves away from a desire for totality that plagued the nineteenth and twentieth centuries: he writes, in a manifesto-like claim, "Let us wage a war on totality; let us be witnesses to the unpresentable; let us activate the differences and save the honor of the name" (82). Elaborating these claims further, the geographer David Harvey returns to the modernist recastings of time and space to claim in his *Condition of Postmodernity* (1990) that "modernity, therefore, not only entails a ruthless break with any or all preceding historical conditions, but is characterized by a never-ending process of internal ruptures and fragmentations within itself" (12). Modernism, for him, seeks to manage this crisis in language in form by attempting to "speak to the eternal only by freezing time and all its fleeting qualities" (21).

Lyotard's argument remains one of the most influential attempts to define postmodernism as a critique of knowledge, totality, and aesthetic tradition. But it was met almost immediately with significant resistance by the German philosopher and Frankfurt School associate Jürgen Habermas, who organized a conference on modernism just a year after Lyotard's book appeared. Habermas proposes that any culture that is heir to the Enlightenment must contain both modernism and the avant-garde, progressive modernity and reactionary postmodernity. He insists that the task of the present moment is to refuse the normative but beware of false negations and a potentially vitiating antimodernism. In his "Modernity Versus Postmodernity" (1981), he notes that the Enlightenment posited a belief in the infinite progress of knowledge and moral betterment, and this gave way to the modernist consciousness. The "romantic modernists sought to oppose the antique ideals of the classicists," but now, the division between the modern and the classical has "lost a fixed historical reference" (3). The result is that "modernism is dominant but dead," and conservatives—most famously Daniel Bell—now make cultural modernism responsible for the ills of capitalism (5). For Habermas, postmodernism is a consequence of the unraveling of modernist philosophy; its refusal of totality and embrace of fragmentation thus becomes a new, even hazardous kind of intellectual conservatism. His critique, like Bürger's and Bourdieu's, is institutional: he insists that the development of the bourgeois public sphere led to the historical construction of an autonomous individual who can experience art without interest—as art alone—liberated from theocracies and religion. As the arts developed according to what seemed like internal rules—a hallmark of modernism—they paradoxically confirmed the fact that society as a whole had been totally instrumentalized. Modernism, however, still holds for Habermas the potential to elucidate and critique that historical process.

# Modernism in transition

Three major studies published between 1986 and 1990, by Andreas Huyssen, Matei Călinescu, and Astradur Eysteinsson, captured in contrasting ways the many pressures that had unraveled the cables of tradition once so essential to the institutionalization of modernism. All of them became touchstones for many of the New Modernist critics we'll examine in the next chapter. As a schematic and oppositional approach that sparked transformational debates within modernist studies, Huyssen's *After the Great Divide* (1986) argues that "modernism constituted itself through a conscious strategy of exclusion, an anxiety of contamination by its other: an increasingly consuming and engulfing mass culture." He dates the modernist insistence on autonomy to the mid-nineteenth century and locates at its core an "obsessive hostility to mass culture" and a "programmatic distance from political, economic, and social concerns" (vii). This produced what he calls the "Great Divide" within modern culture that tries to make a clear division between high art and mass culture, and which postmodernism—the true heir of the avant-garde—now rejects. Huyssen sees this antagonism toward mass culture in the critical writings of Adorno and in Greenberg, in French poststructuralism and in the Frankfurt School, and in New Criticism. All of them, he claims, shared a reading of mass culture as feminine; thus, he contests readings of modernist *écriture féminine* (Kristeva, he insists, is only genial to modernism because she focuses on Mallarmé, Lautréamont, and Joyce rather than on Flaubert, Mann, and Eliot), and argues that the debates about mass culture are subtexts for modernist discussions of how to pacify women.

According to Huyssen, modernism makes itself appear autonomous and separate from everyday life by way of self-reflexivity, irony, ambiguity, and intense individuality. Its scientific style, explorations of language and medium, rejection of classical systems of representation and subjective narration, and scorn for realism lead to the conclusion that

> only by fortifying its boundaries, by maintaining its purity and autonomy, and by avoiding any contamination with mass culture and with the signifying systems of everyday life can the art work maintain its adversary distance: adversary to the bourgeois culture of everyday life as well as adversary to mass culture and entertainment which are seen as the primary forms of bourgeois articulation. (53–4)

With these claims, which he later revised in "High/Low in an Expanded Field" (2002), Huyssen, in effect, tied together numerous strands of critique from feminism and postmodernism to launch a powerful attack on modernism as an elitist formation now strangled by the very forces that had helped define and institutionalize it.

Moving away from the binary opposition between modernism and postmodernism, Călinescu's *Five Faces of Modernity: Modernism, Avant-Garde, Decadence, Kitsch, Postmodernism* (1987) offers a prismatic etiology of the term and the senses of "modern" through the terms listed in his subtitle. In these contexts, Călinescu traces the courses of *l'art pour l'art*, the Salon of 1846, and Baudelaire's Symbolism, but notes that they were each viewed as discrete movements. It was not until 1890 that an outsider, Rubén Darío, saw a throughline of "modernism" in their collective impulses. Călinescu follows the parallel between this and Catholic modernism, pointing out that the priest Loisy himself recognized the plurality rather than the doctrine of modernism: "There are as many modernisms as there are modernists" (79). The pope, however, made it into a single line of thought and said it should be rejected globally. In contrast to continental Europe, he notes while looking to New Criticism, the United States and the United Kingdom were slow to evolve a sense of the term "modernist," remaining stuck on "modern" as "contemporary." In short, Călinescu aims to replace "modernism" as a *term* back in the messy, criss-crossing milieux from which it developed.

By studying this process of the gradual accretion of meaning around modernism, Călinescu turns to the ways in which aesthetic modernity was offered as an alternative to capitalist modernity. As this occurred, the five movements he traces butted against one another. The avant-garde offered a "radicalized and utopianized version of modernity" once the Romantics turned its military connotations to culture; postmodernism offered an ironized fatalism in contrast to this utopianism; decadence "synthesize[d] and unif[ied] a great many related ideas (decline, degeneration, sickness, etc.) that had become constitutive elements of his dialectic of life against death"; and kitsch, "a specifically aesthetic form of lying," is "'efficient' art, . . . one of the most direct manifestations of the triumphant aesthetics and ethics of consumerism" (95, 187, 229, 247). Thus, for Călinescu, modernism is best understood in a historical complex from which a number of unions of politics and aesthetics came together, all moving still in different directions. Although he does not explicitly consider the role of women or people of color, his work helps build on the growing sense that modernism was not one thing, but instead a mobile arrangement of works and ideas that could be pulled into innovative, and often irreconcilable shapes. Rather than the restrictive legacy Huyssen imagined, it was instead a way to productively gather the various assaults on the effects of capitalism on art scattered across cultural productions ranging from aesthetic decadence to everyday kitsch.

    With a more specific focus, Eysteinsson's *The Concept of Modernism* (1990) aims to "disentangle modern literature from the salient forms of its 'institutionalization'" (100). He begins by working around paradoxes such as modernism-as-disruptive versus modernism-as-apolitical (or purely aesthetic). He agrees with Adorno that modernist texts grant the reader a measure of distance for social critique, but he does not aim to offer a definition of modernism. Rather, he attempts to take some measure of its conceptual resistance in order to echo Stein's remark (and indeed, the one that guides this book as well): "Is there a there there?" Eysteinsson notes the slipperiness across languages, especially between "modernism" and "avant-garde"; Lukács, he notes, used the German term "*Avantgardeismus*" to refer to what we now call "modernism," while Wilson called it "symbolist." Modernism gains its signification, he argues, by "highlighting and 'naming' the complex relation between nontraditional or postrealist literature and history in the broader sense" (3). And ultimately, for Eysteinsson, modernism does not reflect modernity, but interrupts it. He thus sees a contradiction in theories such as Lukács's: "They illustrate how the historical conception of a modernist paradigm can (and has tended to) vacillate between mimetic notions of a modern 'chaos' reflected in one way or another by modernist works and an understanding of modernism as a chaotic subversion of the communicative and semiotic norms of society" (24). "We need to ask ourselves," Eysteinsson urges, "how the concept of autonomy, so crucial to many theories of modernism, can possibly coexist with the equally prominent view of modernism as a historically explosive paradigm" (16).

Eysteinsson finds another contradiction in accounts of modernism when he discusses the notion of subjectivity. Some claim that modernism is "highly subjectivist"; others say that it was "highly antisubjectivist or impersonal," even in the same works, like Eliot's (27). But through Eliot's Joyce, modernism becomes "aesthetic heroism" in the face of a chaotic world, and from here, the deep structures of high modernism's content—negation, crisis of the subject, discontent, subversion—began to find grounds (9). This was altered by New Criticism, which made it formal and nonreferential, and Marxism, which made it a "historical counterpart of social modernity . . . a cultural subversive enterprise that revolts against dominant notions of bourgeois subjectivity or of bourgeois-capitalist historical development" (39). How then, he wonders, does modernism, which was so bent on destroying tradition, enter literary history? In part, Eysteinsson says, because—as we have seen throughout this book—it could be aligned effectively with the processes of institutionalization and professionalization. He admits that his own book is a partial account of the partiality that has been made universal—offering more questions than answers—in other attempts to make modernism as a concept cohere along any lines—economic, feminist, or otherwise.

Eysteinsson thus shares with Huyssen and Călinescu a sense that a kind of rictus had set into modernist studies—that its once foundational and still powerfully institutionalized structures could no longer adapt to the diversity of twentieth-century art, literature, and culture. Thanks to the critique of the high modernist canon, to the recovery of works that had been ignored or suppressed, and to the development of innovative interpretive practices beyond the New Criticism, the very idea of modernism seemed on the verge of a crisis. This is not to say that the canon itself disappeared, but the intellectual, critical, and aesthetic consensus supporting it had largely dissolved. Its once core texts were either seen within the broad pluralism of "modernisms" or held aside in a hazily defined space called "high modernism." As we have seen throughout this chapter, the range of texts and objects that could be counted as modern underwent enormous expansion—a process that first strained and then unwound the cables of tradition that once held together the New Critical canon. We were left with Pound's disaggregated iron filings and there ensued vibrant debates among critics whose interpretive magnets promised to arrange this material into new, ever-revealing patterns and networks. Instead, modernism—despite powerful efforts by critics such as those we saw at the end of Chapter 2 to shore up its significance—effectively came to refer to a historical period stretching from roughly 1890 to 1945, and even these temporal boundaries were relatively loose and varied across intellectual fields. It was, in effect, a container in which all manner of cultural work can be collected and critiqued, sorted and analyzed.

As we will see in the next chapter, this process of fragmentation has opened up rich new areas for exploration and set new terms for the debate about the relationships among art, culture, history, and politics. The iron filings were piling up rapidly on the critical workbench and now included not only work by women and people of color, but genre fiction, commercial illustration, popular music, and a myriad of other forms. Indeed, new fields and subfields like film studies, women's studies, and area studies, blossomed—many of them having done so precisely because of the reconsideration of what could be counted as art and literature. Indeed, the characterizations of modernism most closely identified with postmodernist critiques often had the ironic effect of prompting a revision of modernism as already containing the politics that postmodernism accused it of ignoring. Sanford Schwartz argued, for instance, that the oppositions and antitheses that postmodernism used to distinguish itself from modernism "once played a major role within modernism itself, a role obscured by the institutionalization of modernism in the postwar era and perpetuated in the successive reactions against it" (12). We remain bedeviled, however, by the conceptual contradictions inherent in modernism even as we use that term to try and create new conceptions that can now be drawn from across the globe, from sophisticated digital archives, and from the vast stores of mass and popular culture. Paradoxically, "modernism" itself has become a fully institutionalized field of study, research, teaching, preservation, and exhibition. Thus, pictures of Joyce and Woolf appear on shopping bags and coffee mugs; exhibitions of work by Matisse or Picasso draw huge crowds; Stravinsky's music has become "classical" rather than riotous; and Frank Lloyd Wright's designs appear in chain stores. Despite this institutionalization, the term itself seems as fraught and uncertain as it was when Woolf put her pen to paper, and Picasso his brush to the canvas. Pound's own ambivalence near the end of his *Cantos* bespeaks the problem: he writes in Canto CXVI, "My errors and wrecks lie about me/ . . . I cannot make it cohere," then adds somewhat reluctantly several lines later, "i.e. it coheres all right/even if my notes do not cohere" (*Cantos* 817). Amid this uncertainty, a "new modernist studies" found life and began to give a different intellectual, professional, and institutional shape to the field—an ongoing process to which we turn in our final chapter.

# Notes

1   A German edition of nearly 15,000 pages entitled *Das Passagenwerk* was published in 1982. In 2002, a team of editors and translators assembled a slightly shorter and somewhat controversial English version entitled *The Arcades Project.*

2   This essay was originally published in English in 1968 as "The Work of Art in the Age of Mechanical Reproduction" in the collection entitled *Illuminations*, which Hannah Arendt edited. This older version is still commonly used despite some concerns about the translation.

3   Woolf's work also provoked debate within the feminist movement: Alice Walker, for instance, noted that her reliance on economic support for producing brilliant writing places too much emphasis on material deprivation as an insurmountable obstacle and thus ignores a figure such as the slave Phyllis Wheatley.

4   Similarly, Virginia L. Smyers and Gillian Hanscombe's *Writing for their Lives: The Modernist Women, 1910-1940* (1987) made a notable case for adding Barnes, Richardson, Monroe, Moore, and others to the modernist canon, and for considering more robustly the women who edited and published modernist works, including Harriet Monroe, Dora Marsden, and Margaret Anderson.

5   This term came in to use primarily among Anglo-American academics, who used it primarily to distinguish literary history

and the New Criticism from a range of other approaches that had
originated primarily (though not exclusively) in France during the
1970s and 1980s.

6   His 1957 collection of essays, *Mythologies* (translated into English
in 1972), brings his interpretive practice to this widely diverse array
of texts. The book remains an important document not only for
Theory but also for cultural studies and other critical practices that
look to treat mass cultural objects as meaningful aesthetic and social
practices.

7   MacCabe himself built on other contemporaneous works by
Margot Norris, Derek Attridge, and Stephen Heath. The scandal of
his departure from Cambridge, however, helped focus widespread
attention on the growing critical divide within the Anglo-American
academy.

8   Here, Poggioli is consciously drawing on the sociological approaches
to the avant-garde taken by the Spanish philosopher José Ortega y
Gasset, who offered a theory of new aesthetics and their broader
ramifications in his *The Dehumanization of Art* and *Notes on the
Novel* (1924–25). Ortega believed that viewers' responses to anti-
mimetic works of art separates them into two camps: the elite (who
understand the art) and the masses (who do not). He cites examples
like Joyce, Proust, Pirandello, and Ramón Gómez de la Serna as well
as Expressionism and Cubism. Ortega claims that this new kind
of art is a revolutionary strike at Realism and its decaying notions
of temporality and materiality. It aims to alienate the public and
to avoid evoking easy sentiment or pathos: a deathbed scene full
of emotion in a Victorian novel, Ortega believes, would now be
rendered with shapes, forms, and self-consciousness so that the reader
would feel no sympathy with the dying character. And because of
the interconnectedness of the modern world, writers and artists, no
matter their locations, would embrace these new conditions as part of
a self-conscious vanguard politics.

9   Here, we see a connection between his work and the recovery work
done by feminist writer-scholars such as Alice Walker, who fashioned
new historical literary alliances with then mostly neglected twentieth-
century writers such as Zora Neale Hurston and Jean Toomer.

10  Furthermore, Hemingway's *The Sun Also Rises*, Fiedler disdainfully
notes, "has ceased being a dangerous book to become a required one,
a bore assigned in class," while "Kerouac provides fantasies for the
future $40,000-a-year ex-Beatniks" (458).

11  This sense of epistemic crisis reached a head in the 1996 "Sokal
Hoax," which seemed to reveal a kind of intellectual abyss at the

heart of postmodernism. Alan Sokal, a physicist at New York
University, submitted a paper about the arbitrariness of gravity to the
leading postmodern journal *Social Text* (1979–). It was accepted and
published, at which point Sokal revealed that the essay was basically
nonsense. The event led to serious debate about postmodernism as an
intellectual concept.

# 4

# Networks

## Overview

Modernist studies arrived at a complicated, even precarious juncture in the early 1990s. In a 1992 survey of the field, Marjorie Perloff wrote that modernism once denoted "the site of all that was radical, exciting, and above all *new*," but now it "found itself under attack as a retrograde, elitist movement," a belated and unimportant byproduct of Romanticism, or even an essentially fascist aesthetic ("Modernist Studies" 154; italics in the original). It had become the "roadkill of contemporary theory," George Bornstein lamented (162). The rise of gender, ethnic, and cultural studies, postmodernism, Theory, new Marxisms, media history, and New Historicism had unwound the cables that had bound together the high modernist canon. As a result, its once central works had become a mass of iron filings that could be pulled into new configurations around topics like engaged politics, subversion, semiotic play and self-reference, multiplicity and difference, and the destruction of boundaries between "aesthetic" or "literary" and other types of texts, such as newspapers or commercial music. Perloff noted, however, that despite a newly sharpened sense of crisis, the field was still growing as more and more material was opened up for serious critical and historical examination. In retrospect, we see that from this nexus in the 1990s, what we now call the New Modernist Studies began to take shape.

Rather than a singular approach or line of argument, the "New Modernist Studies" denotes the collective work of thousands of scholars who are engaging conversations that, while difficult to categorize and perhaps ultimately incommensurable, share some important traits. Most significantly, it describes an attempt to synthesize rather than to bracket or isolate forms of cultural expression across multiple media and throughout the world. Once foundational concepts like autonomy and difficulty, for instance, are now no longer essential to the branching definitions of modernism, but instead are treated as one of many complex, multifaceted responses to a bewildering variety of historical, literary, cultural, and other forces that created a global twentieth-century modernity. Thus, critics now speak increasingly of "modernisms," in the plural, forged in vastly different historical circumstances, but nevertheless held together loosely by an interrelated array of creative impulses. Digital technologies continue to open up new archives; new modes of intellectual interrogation and exploration have ruptured the stabilizing structure of canon, language, and nation; and formerly separate fields like law, economics, sociology, and design now seem integral to understanding the practice and conception of modernisms both new and old.

The current, often paradoxical challenges of treating modernism as a coherent concept are strikingly evident in the decision made by the Centre national d'art et de culture Georges Pompidou in Paris to rearrange its core exhibition in 2013. Holding one of the world's foremost collections of modernist art, the Pompidou had traditionally organized its public galleries to elaborate a canonical and almost exclusively Eurocentric understanding of modernism as a line of aesthetic practices that began with the Post-Impressionists and ended with Abstract Expressionism in the 1950s. Catherine Grenier, the curator who fashioned the new exhibit at the Pompidou, now acknowledges that this traditional notion of modernism "focused on artists whose work corresponded to established canons and who participated in collective history through their involvement in modernist movements. . . . In the name of artistic radicalism and the concept of rupture, it left aside or played down the importance of numerous individual or collective forms of expression, which were dismissed as hybrid, local, late, or anti-modern" (16). To cut the idea of modernism loose from these cables of canon and tradition, Grenier created a new exhibition entitled *Multiple Modernities, 1905-1970.* "It encompasses," she writes in the catalog, "the many forms of modernity that developed in different parts of the world . . . [and] the sheer variety and richness of modernity in the West" (17). Crucially, the museum abandons a narrative of development and opts instead simply to display as diverse an array of materials on the walls as it can. Thus, Picassos rub shoulders with architectural models from Brazil, Japanese prints, and paintings by the Moroccan artist Farid Belkahia—all placed against wallpaper made from hundreds of little magazines. Aptly summarizing the challenges surrounding the New Modernist Studies, Grenier concludes that we are in an "interrogatory" moment that invites us to ask anew about the range, constitution, and value of the modern (18).

As a result of these interrogations and revisions, "modernism" has now become an almost unintelligible concept unless it is modified by prefixes or qualifiers. Sometimes, the term is used vestigially to describe the canon consolidated at midcentury and that still endures in student anthologies and blockbuster exhibitions. More often, however, it serves simply as a kind of shorthand to mark almost any cultural or aesthetic work that appeared between roughly 1890 and 1970 (though even these dates are elastic). The traditional canon has not disappeared; indeed, in some ways it has found new life in reinterpretations of its figures and works. But a surprising paradox now exists: modernist studies has been strengthened by the lack of resolution over what exactly modernism *is*. A perpetual "definitional crisis" has been a boon, in other words, to the wide-ranging debates about the field's nature, boundaries, and contents. Caught amid this tumult ourselves, this book cannot therefore offer a comprehensive summary of the New Modernist Studies, nor will we conclude with some clear sense of what modernism—as a concept, a practice, or an aesthetic movement—now definitively means. As should be obvious by this point, the word has often been flexible, capacious, inventive, and unstable. Indeed, the adjective "new" in the New Modernist Studies invokes many of the same definitional and conceptual problems that afflicted the term "modernism" from the beginning. What was "new" in the 1990s, however, is now over a decade old, yet it still continues to charge any claim to novelty or innovation within the field. Just as modernism implicitly attempts to cut off any possibility of succession (What, after all, could be more modern than modernism?), so too the "New Modernist Studies" implicitly brings the complicated history of the idea of modernism to a premature close. We are, in some ways, at a moment similar to that of the early 1900s: "modernism" is conceptually up for grabs in ways that it was not in the mid-1900s, and it is not vilified as it often was in the 1980s.

This final chapter offers a pragmatic approach to contemporary concepts of modernism by surveying a representative variety of institutions and critical activities that call themselves "modernist." We will address here some of the topics and texts that have become available for exploration under the heading of modernism, the new methods that have been developed to examine them, and the works that have been highlighted or elided by the field's expansion. Many of these intersect. An interdisciplinary study now, for example, would likely read the robot-vamp Maria in Fritz Lang's German Expressionist film *Metropolis* (1927) through a lens equally attuned to gender, science, aesthetics, media history, and politics. Another might consider the phenomenon of the modern crowd as it interacted with new media technologies, the rise of social science, and the various instruments of government surveillance. As it has aimed for an engagement with "modernisms" from nonliterary fields, the New Modernist Studies—which nevertheless remains dominated by literary scholars—has shown little interest in identifying a single moment as "the birth of the modern" and has made almost no attempt to define modernism strictly around a set of canonical texts or conceptual magnets. Instead, it traces out an ever-expanding network of nodes, connections, and genealogies that resist taxonomy precisely because they highlight the inadequacies of traditional scholarly genealogies. Thus, as we move through this chapter, we will discuss the ways in which the sometimes parallel debates over modernism in fields like architecture, cinema, and theater cast a different light on the largely literary-critical history this book has outlined. Each section that follows aims for overviews rather than catalogs, and thus we leave aside a host of fruitful topics: modernism and psychoanalysis, modernism's legacies in contemporary literature, modernism and dance history, or modernism's relationship to any number of political structures or movements. This chapter, therefore, will point to, and rely on, the forthcoming volumes in the New Modernisms series to provide fuller accounts of the increasing complexity of the New Modernist Studies. At the end of this book, you'll also find a critical toolbox: a concise bibliography of the works we discuss as well as a handful of other major studies that will help lead you deeper into the kinds of expansive questions and experimental answers that now characterize this "interrogative" moment in modernist studies.

As we hope to show, the field continues to develop in waves that have now gathered into a protean tide, leaving us with a number of questions that frame our account: If the pushback against postmodernist attacks on modernism in the 1980s helped fuel the reinvention of the field of modernist studies, has postmodernism been effectively absorbed into modernist studies, its critiques repurposed to strengthen a reinvented and "re-branded" field? Does a pluralistic theory of modernism implicitly rely on a "prior coherence" of the concept that belies the very project of pluralization? (Gilbert 168) And what then are the boundaries of modernism as a term? Does it have a global reach? How far does it extend into the nineteenth century or into the twenty-first? What is truly "new"—and "new" to whom?—and what does modernism's expansion mean for other fields and disciplines? This chapter cannot answer these questions fully, but will instead approach them by sketching the ways in which "modernism" continues to organize itself as an assemblage of institutional practices, a capacious field of inquiry, and now a network that labors constantly to link the innovative, moving, and often unsettling cultural products of our unfolding modernity.

# The changing field and its institutions

In "The New Modernist Studies," an influential article published in *PMLA* in 2008, Douglas Mao and Rebecca L. Walkowitz attempted to take stock of the sea changes in the field since the mid-1990s. For them, and as we will see below, a radical "expansion" has taken place along multiple axes—temporal, spatial, and vertical (the last signifying high/low art)—and they focus on the effects of the "transnational turn" and of media studies as two of the many hallmarks of change (739). The former, they note, has moved away from defining modernism around a Eurocentric set of paradigms and geographies and toward examining "alternative traditions," translation and multilingual practices, anti- and postcolonial movements, and diasporic or other transnational communities (739). Meanwhile, critics now look at the new media of the early twentieth century and the ways in which it allowed the dissemination of words and images across vast spaces with previously unthinkable speed, a process that was critical to everything from the emergence of fascism to the development of Cubist collage. These two "turns,"

Mao and Walkowitz note, have intersected fruitfully in a number of ways, most visibly in studies of various elements of state-building from the turn of the twentieth century to the present.

"Expansion," as Mao and Walkowitz warn, brings with it certain dangers: If modernism, riding on multiple waves of expansion, can potentially be found everywhere, where might the New Modernist Studies end? In fact, just as the revamped field was gaining its steam, Jennifer Wicke sounded a cautious note in 2001 by describing the double-edged sword that "newness" and expansion represent for scholars. She argues that we hold onto "modernism" as a "brand" in order to confer it as a prize (even if retroactively) and to raise its value, since

> Modernism is a brand name . . . [that] lingered for decades in such a boring twilight sleep, etherized upon a dissecting table, or slumbering in a jar. . . . As with so many commercial brands, the modernist brand can only be resurrected by ironizing or implicitly denying its original cultural status . . . [by way of] rebranding. A return to modernism with a difference, and with a plural vengeance, as in "new modernisms," legitimately opens key debates, stages productive re-readings, and enacts agonistic language games of genuine import and ferocity. We cannot ignore, however, our own investments in modernism's speculative bubble. As revivers of its brand, a brand we cannot seem to do without, we re-brand ourselves as critics and theorists just as we rebrand modernist others. (395)

For Wicke, the "modernist bubble of our speculations" is part of a "retailing" effort that does not "sell out" modernism, but rather, acknowledges that "the only danger lies in failing to appreciate and give value, and thereby selling modernism short" (402). In a pointed critique of "NMS [New Modernist Studies]," Max Brzezinski goes a step further and laments what he considers the evacuation of politics from understandings of modernism in contemporary scholarship: "By considering the consolidation of the NMS brand, we can gauge the theoretical distortion and political flattening that too often accompany the transformation of a critical movement into a marketable intellectual commodity" (109).

How, when, and where did this "expansion" and "re-branding" begin? There is no single date at which the "New Modernist Studies" was founded or emerged, nor did a single publication launch or gather its force the way that Stephen Greenblatt's *The Power of Forms in the English Renaissance* (1982) did for New Historicism. But by 1999, the rejuvenated field was significant enough to be treated in a series of articles in the *Chronicle of Higher Education* that discussed the changing canon and methodologies of modernist studies. A number of scholars date the New Modernist Studies to two linked events in the 1990s, both of which opened up new institutional structures within the Anglo-American academy for broadly conceived, globally oriented scholarship that sought to work beyond the constraints of single-author scholarship and the silos of national literary traditions. First was the founding of the journal *Modernism/modernity* by Lawrence Rainey and Robert von Hallberg in 1994—tellingly, four years *after* the founding of the journal *Postmodern Culture* in 1990. By joining the terms "modernism" and "modernity," as Marxist critics had urged for decades, and by doing so with a suggestive yet ambiguous slash, the journal provided a venue for an ongoing debate about exactly what that slash signifies. The interdisciplinary journal began, Rainey and von Hallberg wrote in their editorial introduction, in the belief that

> the artistic movement known as modernism produced the most radical and comprehensive changes in western culture since romanticism. . . . We sense that the effects of modernism still reverberate through all the arts, and its products surround us in the buildings where we work, the houses and apartments where we live, and even the chairs where we sit now trying to itemize its effects. Modernism was more than a repertory of artistic styles, more too than an intellectual movement or set of ideas; it initiated an ongoing transformation in the entire set of relations governing the production, transmission, and reception of the arts. The modernists themselves seem to have understood this when they urged that changes in the arts be viewed in conjunction with changes in philosophy, historiography, and social theory, to say nothing of the scientific shifts that they claimed as part of their moment's cultural revolution. (1)

For Rainey and von Hallberg, modernism was a supremely multidimensional revolution, and it has permeated many areas of life beyond the sphere of aesthetics. Modernism is everywhere, they assert, imbricated inextricably in every facet of modernity and yet, at the same time, standing apart from it in certain ways. The journal has thus published articles and archival documents on every topic from modern medievalism to the poetics of Auschwitz. By conjoining modernism and modernity with substantive but not definitive temporal, spatial, or aesthetic boundaries, the journal opened a well-worn term to new life as a vital interpreter of the ongoing processes of modernity.

Shortly following (though initially independent of) the journal's launch, the MSA was founded in 1998 and held its first conference (called "New Modernisms") the following year at Pennsylvania State University.[1] It drew some 450 attendees—far more than expected—and in its annual meetings since then, the organization often sees attendance of more than 700 scholars from most every discipline, though literature and film remain at the core. In its founding statement, the MSA characterized itself as "devoted to the study of the arts in their social, political, cultural, and intellectual contexts from the later nineteenth- through the mid-twentieth century" (MSA). As with *Modernism/modernity*, these parameters point to a historical milieu but remain topically open-ended.[2] In 2001, the MSA allied with *Modernism/modernity*, which became the official journal of the organization.[3] As another sign of the field's revitalization, *Modernist Cultures*, the official journal of the new British Association for Modernist Studies, was launched in 2005. With similarly diverse contents, the journal also revisits the history of the field in a "Modernism Under Review" section, in which one scholar reviews a landmark work of modernist scholarship from the past—Kenner's *The Pound Era*, Williams's *The Politics of Modernism*, Wilson's *Axel's Castle*—in light of contemporary critical trends.[4]

The New Modernist Studies, in short, found its strongest support and articulations in the institutions of academia: conferences, journals, scholarly organizations, and course catalogs. Even in the troubled world of academic publishing, studies of modernism, anthologies of modernist texts, introductions to the movement, essay collections on modernism and its formation, and other such texts have flourished since the mid-1990s, far outpacing the analogous publications in the 1960s and 1970s that helped entrench the field in universities. Furthermore, several monograph book series have been founded that characterize themselves as part of this movement, including Refiguring Modernism (Pennsylvania State University Press, 2004–), Modernist Literature and Culture (Oxford University Press, 2008–), Modernist Latitudes (Columbia University Press, 2011–), Hopkins Studies in Modernism (Johns Hopkins University Press, 2011–), Historicizing Modernism (Bloomsbury, 2011–), and Critical Studies in Modernist Culture (Edinburgh University Press, 2012–). The presses of Cambridge University, the University of Texas, Duke University, Yale University, and the University of Chicago, and commercial imprints such as Palgrave Macmillan, Routledge, Wiley-Blackwell, and Ashgate, have all increased their production of titles that describe themselves as "modernist" since the early 2000s. Responding to and thereby furthering this trend, the MSA began awarding an annual book prize in 2005. Our own book and the larger series of which it is a part suggest the ongoing institutionalization of the New Modernist Studies in undergraduate classroom, syllabi, and graduate exam lists.

Since the 1990s, however, jobs in modernist studies disappeared more quickly than jobs in literary studies across the board. In part, this is an ironic result of the field's ongoing rejuvenation and expansion: since modernism now often appears to be everywhere, many universities hire specialists in twentieth-century literature who focus on postcolonial, ethnic, or world literary studies, too. Modernism is also densely connected to other fields and its institutional foundations are no longer rooted in either canonical authors or isolated aesthetic, national, or linguistic traditions. Thus, even as the field broadens critically and intellectually, the "market shelter" it once offered has become increasingly tenuous (Jaffe 19).

Perhaps no debate within the New Modernist Studies better captures both the definitional quandaries and institutional complexities that still reign in the field than the discussion of modernism's relationship to modernity. Indeed, as the concept of modernism first unwound then fragmented, it has given way to a renewed focus on the idea of modernity—some underlying historical, political, economic, or social structure that might still knit the world together into a single totality across which all forms of art and culture can be mapped. Scholars including Marshall Berman, Rita Felski, and Susan Stanford Friedman have argued that modernism is (in Friedman's words) a constitutive "expressive dimension of modernity" ("Periodizing" 432). Rather than merely

a symptom of some buried ideological structure, it is, instead, a
"domain of creative expressivity *within* modernity's dynamic of
rapid change, a domain that interacts with other arenas of rupture
such as technology, trade, migration, state formation, societal
institutions, and so forth" ("Planetarity" 475; italics in the original).
This integration of modernism with modernity—of aesthetics with
politics, economics, culture, and technology—raises new questions
of its own: *When* and *where* is "modernity"? *Whose* modernity,
and why should the practices heretofore associated with high
modernism be tied to it? Both *Modernism/modernity* and the MSA
reached back to the mid-nineteenth century as their point of origin
for studying modernism, thus equating modernity with a European
nexus of industrial development and modern metropolises, as well
as the experimental aesthetic practices that coincided with them.
Friedman points out the restrictive Eurocentrism of such conceptions
of modernity and favors instead a "polycentric" account: "Every
modernity has its distinctive modernism," she writes, and these
"alternative" modernities themselves are not confined to a specific
time and place (475, 480). In this capacious account, modernism
is everywhere and yet nowhere; indeed, it becomes difficult to find
examples of works that are *not* modernist. As a result, theorists
like David James, Urmila Seshagiri, and Eric Hayot, as well as
scholars in other fields, have critiqued this potentially imperializing
theorization.

Approaching this same set of questions from a feminist
perspective, Rita Felski's *The Gender of Modernity* (1995) argues
that canonical definitions of modernism have proven so limiting
because they have been organized around a norm that locates
modernity only in the masculine field of technological advancement.
Felski thus aimed to overcome what she saw as a division in feminist
scholarship on modernism between an attention to form and an
analysis of sociocultural conditions in order to understand how and
why women's experiences of modernity might have taken department
stores seriously, as everyday scenes of aesthetics, rather than with
ironic detachment or scorn. But her aim is not to reject modernity;
rather, she reveals that feminism both criticizes and draws upon, with
complex interweavings, the "processes of modernization" (14–15).
Thus, ranging with a comparative eye across fictional and factual
texts, high and low art, and a variety of media, Felski constructs
a broader history in which "modernism is only one aspect of the

culture of women's modernity" (25). She believes that focusing on
Woolf, West, and Stein, because their aesthetics and formalisms most
closely aligned with those of their male peers, missed an immense
amount of media—particularly mass and commercial media, which
these women did not engage as richly as did some of their peers. This
realignment of modernism and modernity around the question of
gender then requires us, Felski suggests, to rethink what the literary
and the aesthetic actually mean. Like Bourdieu, she does more than
simply create new patterns from a now significantly expanded pile
of cultural filings; she begins to inquire into the institutional and
social practices that define the very category of art itself.

The attempts by Friedman and Felski to use modernity as a
way of extending modernism into broad new domains stand
at odds with the approaches taken by T. J. Clark and Fredric
Jameson. Clark, an art historian, claims in his *Farewell to an Idea:
Episodes from a History of Modernism* (1999) that "already the
modernist past is a ruin, the logic of whose architecture we do not
remotely grasp" (2). Therefore, "modernism is unintelligible now
because it had truck with a modernity not yet fully in place," and
now that this modernity has "triumph[ed]" in our contemporary
moment, the modes of life that produced modernism—that is, the
processes of "modernization" itself—are inaccessible to us (3).
Rejecting narratives of modernism's development through aesthetic
innovations, Clark argues instead that modernism was an episodic
series of momentary reprieves from the ongoing, expanding force
of capitalism, and that "the truly new, and disorienting, character of
modernity is its seemingly being driven by merely material, statistical,
tendential, 'economic' considerations" (8). Far from a "polycentric"
experience spread across human history, modernity, for Clark, is
instead part of the globalization of Euro-American capitalism—a
phenomenon that has now successfully enfolded the entire world.
"It is the blindness of modernity that seems to me fundamental," he
concludes, "and to which modernism is a response" (8).

A consonant, but even stronger assault on the ideas of modernism's
expressive relationship to modernity and of alternative or multiple
modernities can be found in Jameson's more recent work. Returning
to and revising his thoughts on modernism from previous decades,
which some critiqued as economically deterministic, Jameson argues
in *A Singular Modernity* (2002) that there is only one pernicious
modernity: global capitalism. His conception of modernity, however,

is complex and elusive, since it is not a concept or a structure, but instead is a narrative category through which one grapples with the effects of capitalism. Echoing Paul de Man, he writes that "modernity, as a trope, is itself a sign of modernity as such. The very concept of modernity, then, is itself modern, and dramatizes its own claims" (34). At the same time, global capitalism is by nature hierarchical: there are First World and Third World nations, and they are tied together by networks of power and exchange that create irreducibly distinct conditions everywhere. First World nations then hold out the term "modernity" as an empty utopian hope for the developing world, overlooking the fact that capitalism's modernity has largely failed and often decimated those very nations. To compensate, he concludes in a sharp critique of the pluralistic approach, critics speak of "alternative modernities" in order to absolve themselves of complicity in creating the conditions outside of the First World.

While other Marxists have allowed that multiple *modernisms* have been produced by a global, totalizing modernity, Jameson aims to separate "modernism" from "modernity" in order to charge that the former is an aesthetic response to the conditions of uneven and incomplete *modernization*—to the coexistence of technologically advanced factories and traditional peasant farms in one moment. Thus, the conditions that created modernism cannot be yoked together coherently: "Any theory of modernism capacious enough to include Joyce along with Yeats or Proust, let alone alongside Vallejo, Biely, Gide or Bruno Schulz is bound to be so vague and vacuous as to be intellectually inconsequential" (104). Severing "modernism" from "modernity" in this way allows Jameson to concentrate on the "ideology of modernism" that has developed in critical history. This ideology, grounded in an essentially false notion of aesthetic autonomy, is purely "an American invention," a post–Second World War combination of New Criticism and the kind of formalism exemplified in Clement Greenberg's theories of art (165). Seen this way, aesthetic autonomy is a kind of fiction, one put in place to sustain the idea of periodization and the absolute novelty of modernism. For Jameson, however, the idea that one period has given way to another—that Realism somehow gave way to modernism—is manifestly false on its face since the former is epistemological and the latter is aesthetic. Jameson thereby offers a challenge to some of the key premises of the New Modernist Studies by rejecting efforts to attach it to the complex of modernity and to pluralize "modernism" across irreconcilably diverse historical situations. The attempt to expand modernism that Mao and Walkowitz identified thus runs afoul, for Jameson, of the very same contradictions that have always beset the term. The field, once more, finds itself caught in antinomy and contradiction: now, not only are its once canonical texts only vaguely delimited, but its conceptual links to the "modern" and even to the twentieth century are entangled in politically charged debates.

The following sections of this chapter therefore will offer an overview of the New Modernist Studies by looking at the major nodes that now make a diffuse network of ideas, objects, texts, and approaches while also framing some of the most pressing questions now being asked about modernism. Each of these sections will itself be the subject of a book scheduled to appear in the New Modernisms series, and the capsule summaries we offer here are meant only to offer a broad survey of the field's current state. These are, in other words, a way into the thicket of modernism and modernity—not a way out. Instead, the debates we survey will be taken up at length in the volumes that follow this one, each of which offers an approachable yet sophisticated guide to that still provocative question: "What is modernism?"

# Modernism, gender, and sexuality

As we saw in Chapter 2, the earliest canon of modernism excluded not only women authors and artists (with the occasional exception of Woolf and Stein), but also women's experiences of modernity. Feminism, as well as gender, queer, and sexuality studies, all contributed to a significant reformulation first of modernism and then of the way we understand the broad range of aesthetic interpretations of modernity itself. This work has altered our understanding of the era and shifted attention to landmarks such as the fight for suffrage, Oscar Wilde's trial, the development of gay and lesbian coteries, and the queer sexualities now apparent throughout even the most canonical texts. Indeed, most scholars would now agree that no facet of culture was left untouched by the transformations in thought and practices associated with gender in the early twentieth century. This fundamental shift is evident in the title of the revised and expanded edition of Bonnie Kime Scott's

*The Gender of Modernism: A Critical Anthology* (1990), which appeared in 2007 as *Gender in Modernism: New Geographies, Complex Intersections*, indicating its shifts in conception and focus. Feminist-modernist aesthetics appeared not only in Greenwich Village, Bloomsbury, and Harlem, but also in Tbilisi and Beijing, while sexuality—its reinvention, instability, and constant renegotiation—has moved to the very center of what modernism itself might mean. The New Women or the Paterson Strike Pageant organizers were not the only ones who contributed vitally to modernist revolutions; the private and domestic worlds of household objects and decorative arts were revolutionized by women as well. The picture is now becoming even more complex as digital technologies make available for teaching and study an ever-expanding archive of literature, art, and film alongside pamphlets, advertisements, and letters.

Recovery and revisionary work has remained important to gender studies in modernism, though with a shifting emphasis that coincides with what is known as "third wave feminism." As Deborah Longworth writes, previous scholars used the common experiences of women and notions of feminine writing to redraw the boundaries of modernism, whereas contemporary scholars now focus on "the *instability* of gender as the foundation of concepts of identity and difference" that are embedded in the logic of modernity itself (160; italics in the original). By a similar token, feminist critics in the 1980s relied more heavily on psychoanalysis, but its influence has waned in the New Modernist Studies, which is often concerned less with faint symptoms than with the rich cultural and aesthetic practices no longer obscured by sexism and homophobia. Thus, one sees more often intersections between feminism and cultural studies (which Lisa Rado has outlined), print and media networks (Lucy Delap), anticolonial activism (Anna Snaith), race studies (Jane Marcus), transnationalism (Susan Stanford Friedman), and an astounding variety of politics linked to what Rebecca West called the "sex war" that defined the early twentieth century (West 3). The result has been capacious attention to canonical and new figures alike. Christine Froula's *Virginia Woolf and the Bloomsbury Avant-garde* (2005), for instance, defends and renovates Woolf and Bloomsbury against their dismissals by Peter Bürger, Perry Anderson, and Raymond Williams. Likewise, Stein's work has been used to reread the relationships among modernist, postmodernist, and minority poetics, especially in more contemporary movements like Objectivism and Language Poetry. This work is juxtaposed with new studies of figures like Ling Shuhua, Mina Loy, Hope Mirrlees, Lola Ridge, Margaret Walker, and Victoria Ocampo, all of whom are now seen to bear on modernism's entanglement in a global gendered modernity. Recovery furthermore includes both archival work and reconstructions of early feminist-modernist criticism, such as May Sinclair's commentaries on Dorothy Richardson's novels or Dora Marsden's essays on how science intersects with art. Furthermore, new scholarship is exploring the ways in which gender was articulated in translation projects, including H. D.'s versions of Greek texts and Adrienne Monnier's French version of Eliot's "The Love Song of J. Alfred Prufrock."

With the increased attention to gender has come a new awareness of multiple ways in which homosexuality and queerness defined and constituted many of the works we now call "modernist." "The homosexual" was still a relatively new type in public discourse, and was studied by Freud, Havelock Ellis, and various practitioners in the new field of sexology. Oscar Wilde's testimony in his famous trial for "gross indecency" reads as a defense of Aestheticism overlaid onto a private life of then criminalized homosexual practices. This famous trial, in which Wilde defends "the love that dare not speak its name," has now become one of the historical markers critics use to denote the beginning of a modernist era. Furthermore, Stein's repetitive, incantatory style was not simply Cubist, scholars have shown, but also queer; her suppressed, posthumously published novel Q. E. D. (*Things as They Are*, 1950) and Forster's posthumous *Maurice* (1971) have received belated attention. Networks among modernism's famous editors and publishers (Jane Heap and Margaret Anderson, Sylvia Beach and Adrienne Monnier) were both material and lesbian. Scholars have looked not only to the influence of queer cultures on the making of the Harlem Renaissance, but also to the anxieties about homosexuality and the instability of masculinity in Eliot, Joyce, Faulkner, and other major canonical figures. The curious way queerness disrupts the divide between public and private life in the works of male writers ranging from Proust, Pater, and Genet to Roger Casement, W. H. Auden, and Federico García Lorca has been studied, too.

Indeed, the groundbreaking text of queer studies, Eve Kosofsky Sedgwick's *Epistemology of the Closet* (1990), treats the male-male erotics and desire in Wilde's *Picture of Dorian Gray* (1891) and Proust's *In Search of Lost Time* (1913–27) as essential elements of modernism. Sedgwick argues that the early definitions of modernism we discuss in Chapter 2 were not only sexist, but heterosexual and often homophobic as well. Their attempts to structure modernism around a split between content and form (in order to privilege the latter) is, she contends, part of a project of "universalizing, naturalizing, and thus substantively voiding— depriving of content—elements of a specifically and historically male homosexual rhetoric" (165). As queer studies developed in the 1990s, articles by Shari Benstock, Makiko Minow, and Karla Jay and books such as Joseph Boone's *Libidinal Currents* (1998) tied its insights to modernist studies. Mary E. Galvin's *Queer Poetics* (1999), for instance, traces an arc of "lesbian modernism" (a term that, like "Sapphic modernism," saw increasing use across the 1990s) from Emily Dickinson through Amy Lowell, Stein, and Loy, to Barnes (see also *Sapphic Modernities*). Others have since linked modernism's radical aesthetic experiments to everything from cross-dressing to class-distinct sexualities. Critics are also now examining the role of the "homosocial"—a term that describes patterns of same-sex but not physical relations—in influencing different conceptions of modernism. These help us better understand variegated social and aesthetic patterns that can be found everywhere from male friendship in the First World War to connections among female prostitutes and streetwalkers. Indeed, D. H. Lawrence, a once canonical figure who languished on the sidelines after being attacked as a misogynist, has been placed in new contexts informed by queer studies, thanks to his hyperbolic celebration of male-male bonds. Less-studied figures such as Lorca are also being brought to the forefront, whether for the transnational queer cosmopolitanism of his "Ode to Walt Whitman" (ca. 1930), or for the tacit identification with him seen in two of his first English-language translators, Langston Hughes and Stephen Spender.

To get a better sense of how new work around gender and sexuality contributes to a new conception of modernism, consider the case of Nancy Cunard. Although not exactly obscure, she often hovered at the margins of modernist studies as a publisher and networker in Paris. Since the 1990s, however, she has received renewed attention along multiple lines. She was an heiress to a conservative family's fortune built on international shipping lines, yet was an ardent leftist who published works such as a multilingual collaboration with Pablo Neruda in support of the Spanish Republic during Spain's Civil War. A world traveler and expatriate, she transgressed racial boundaries in her public relationship with Henry Crowder, a black American jazz musician, and she edited the cosmopolitan *Negro: An Anthology* in 1934. Cunard collected art and artifacts, was a *fashionista* known for her heavy ivory and bronze jewelry, was the subject of inventive photographs by Man Ray, and was the publisher for a number of famous modernist writers through her Hours Press. She was open about her sexuality and her body, whether during her bouts with mental illness or as she withered to a staggeringly low weight late in life.

For these and other reasons, Cunard's life, like those of many other women in this era, highlights a new interest in the materiality of the female body and its public appearance. As Liz Conor has argued, a convergence of technologies, media, and politics made "visibility" a key marker of femininity in the early twentieth century in ways that previous models of gender studies (often structured around a strict male-female binary) struggled to adequately comprehend (xiii). Essential to this "visibility" is fashion itself, which scholars now treat as a complex aesthetic, social, and even activist practice. Anne Anlin Cheng, for example, analyzes what she calls Josephine Baker's "second skin," while others have looked into the queer consumption practices of dandies and the politics of "glamour" and female celebrity (1). By a similar measure, Cunard involved herself in media networks whose vast reach has been studied by scholars such as Barbara Green and expanded by publishers such as Persephone Books, which reprints neglected books by women writers of the era. This sociological approach has also contributed to a new focus on what women were reading and thus connects to the emergent work on print culture we discuss below. Likewise, the alliances and divisions among the battles for women's rights, racial equality, and collectivist politics are made stark in Cunard's life, and scholars have treated them all as inevitably pressing on one another. In sum, gender studies is not an autonomous silo within modernist studies but is instead one node of inquiry, argument, and activism that connects to a much larger sense of modernism as a still mobile and interlinked network.

# Modernist races

Like feminism, race and ethnic studies transformed our understanding of modernism by first expanding its canon and thereby
fundamentally altering its intellectual and historical foundations.
As we saw in Chapter 3, this process began with a reconsideration
of African American writers. In the United States, in particular, the
turbulent aftermath of the Civil War and the often violent civic and
political battles that followed shaped the art and literature of the
period in profound yet troubling ways. This era saw the rise of
Jim Crow laws, legally enforced segregation, lynching, and race
riots, as well as contrasting movements like the Great Migration,
black nationalism, pan-Africanism, and the birth of jazz and
blues. America's violent racial past and its agonized struggle over
questions about race in a democratic society touched every aspect
of the nation's art and culture. These debates, however, were not
uniquely American; they radiated across the globe. One can hardly
consider "race" at the time without thinking of eugenics and its legal
and pseudoscientific regimes, caste systems, the Nuremberg Laws,
the Partition of India, the *Négritude* movement, anthropological
writing, exoticism and primitivism in numerous arts—the list goes
on. Like gender, race has thus been understood both as a constituent
element of modernity itself and as a product of modernity's forces.

Critical race theory helped reshape the idea of modernism by
attending to scenes of racially conscious cultural production, ranging
from black writers in Harlem and Paris, through the playwrights of
the Irish Renaissance, to the Jewish poets and novelists at work
in cosmopolitan cities like Vienna, Prague, and Trieste. The New
Modernist Studies increasingly examines race through global
rather than nationalist or local frameworks. This trend began
with Paul Gilroy's influential *The Black Atlantic: Modernity and
Double Consciousness* (1993), which pushed scholarship away
from questions of racial essentialism or hybridity and from the
constraints of monolingual or single-nation productions. Combining
postcolonialist approaches with cultural studies, Gilroy focuses on
diaspora in order to read the historical Middle Passage (one leg of
an international trade route that brought slaves to the Americas)
as the experiential locus for transnational cultural production; for
him, the slave thus becomes the emblem of modernity. W. E. B. Du
Bois famously described the "double-consciousness" of race in the

United States, which divides the self into "an American [and] a Negro; two souls, two thoughts, two unreconciled strivings; two warring ideals in one dark body, whose dogged strength alone keeps it from being torn asunder" (*Souls* 12). For Gilroy, this idea also describes the dialectical tension between race and modernity beyond America's borders. Rather than search for a common heritage across diasporic communities, Gilroy "take[s] the Atlantic as one, single complex unit of analysis" and sees transatlanticism as the center of the development of what had been called—too narrowly, in his view—African American literature and culture (15). Thus, his Euro-African focus claims black music, for example, as a "counterculture of modernity" (36). He sees Du Bois's studies in Europe as critical to his formation as an experimental modernist, and he treats Richard Wright's writings in Europe, previously dismissed by critics as inconsequential or even "disastrous," as fundamental to the novelist's revision of modernism because they incorporate populist, "low" genres such as detective fiction in apparently "high" modernist works (156).

One of the most important works in modernist studies to follow from Gilroy's work was Brent Hayes Edwards's *The Practice of Diaspora* (2003). Edwards situates black literary production in transnational circuits characterized by gaps inherent in the translation practices used to connect often far-flung diasporic communities. Reexamining major writers from the New Negro Renaissance such as Langston Hughes, Claude McKay, Alain Locke, and Du Bois, Edwards sees them as partners in a global network that fostered African solidarity. Many of these figures were translators and theorists of both diaspora and leftist (often communist) solidarity grounded in race—the polar opposite of the allegedly provincial Harlem Renaissance that previous scholars had seen. For them—as for the South Side Writers Group in Chicago— folk stories and vernacular forms were not the preserved essence of the premodern, but were instead politicized productions capable of resisting capitalist modernity's homogenizing effects. As a result, dialects, creoles, pidgins, and other variations on "standard" English have become newly legible as generative fonts of literary experimentation and commentaries on geopolitics—in essence the site of a heretofore entirely overlooked modernism. Capturing some of the energies emanating from the work of Gilroy and Edwards, Laura Winkiel and Laura Doyle's collection *Geomodernisms: Race,*

*Modernism, Modernity* (2005) helped excavate a global modernism that could encompass Chinese cinema, Arabic poetry, and Native American novels. Urmila Seshagiri, Samantha Pinto, and others have extended this line of inquiry further into postcolonial and diasporic contexts, especially with a focus on women writers.

Working in productive tension with this trend, we still find active debates about the intersection between race and national, regional, and even local cultures—particularly in the United States. Walter Benn Michaels's provocative *Our America: Nativism, Modernism, and Pluralism* (1995) asserts that white nativism in the United States was, in certain literary works, both a "modern and a *modernist* phenomenon" (2; italics in the original). To make this case, he links racism—in particular, a strand of racism centered on anxieties about mixing bloods—to poststructuralist ideas about the "ontology of the sign" that came from Theory. For him, "both nativism and modernism . . . [are] efforts to work out the meaning of the commitment to identity—linguistic, national, cultural, racial— that . . . [is] common to both" (2). The instability of language itself, in other words, created a corresponding instability of national and racial identities that some high modernist aesthetics tried to stabilize or resolve at the level of form. He reads Fitzgerald, Faulkner, and others as complicit in this nativist-modernist project, and the mixture of neo-pragmatism, New Historicism, and semiotic theory in his work proved so influential that it prompted *Modernism/modernity* to devote much of an issue to debating his book. Branching out from such concerns—and often revising Michaels's conclusions— minority, immigrant, "gypsy," and "melting-pot" modernisms have all received scholarly treatment; many of them have intersected, too, with studies of "deviant" Englishes, in work on Zora Neale Hurston, Henry Roth, or Carlos Bulosan.

The interdisciplinary foundation of the New Modernist Studies, furthermore, means that race can also be treated as part of a larger network of forces, practices, and identities. Scholarship on visual and material culture, for example, allows us to better understand the complex signifying practices of magazine covers featuring African Americans and the aesthetics of Parisian advertisements for Josephine Baker's performances. Likewise, a new focus on performance has led critics to examine the "black dandy" and the diverse (if often covert) sexualities of the cabaret. Such critics elaborated multifariously Henry Louis Gates, Jr.'s somewhat shocking claim in 1993 that the Harlem Renaissance was "surely as gay as it was black" ("Black Man's Burden" 233). Homosexuality had barely been mentioned in decades of scholarship on Hughes or Cullen, and the scenes of lesbian or female homosocial intimacy in Hurston or Larsen had been obscured by a singular focus on race. At the same time, scholars have revisited the patriarchies and misogynies present within twentieth-century minority communities, whether in Harlem, the Caribbean, Taos, or Warsaw. This shift in focus has enabled us both to understand an archetype like the "blues woman" as a symbol of modernist performance and to better map the interactions of gender and race in caricatures of Jewish men as effeminate or of Irish people as apes.

The attention to marketplaces, circulation, prizes, patronage, and more that George Hutchinson initiated in 1995 has also led to new questions about the ways minority modernisms have been understood as lucrative brands that both participated in and critiqued the capitalist systems of their moment. Jazz—the controversial new art form that early theorists of modernism like Theodore Adorno and Clive Bell both attacked—has been addressed from a variety of perspectives: philosophical, social, musicological, even scientific. A division remains, however, between studies of African American texts and those of racial minorities around the world: many books on the former are classified as "American studies," while the latter are "postcolonial studies." This has left a gap in the debates in the New Modernist Studies over when and where various kinds of modernism occurred, as a 2013 special issue of *Modernism/ modernity* pointed out. In fact, one of the most significant titles of recent years, James Smethurst's *The African American Roots of Modernism* (2011), declares straightforwardly that it will not address definitional questions about modernism.

Just as Nancy Cunard helped us take stock of the new kinds of questions about gender and modernism that are now being asked, so too can Jean Toomer highlight similar issues around questions of race. Toomer was an American writer from a wealthy background who was of mixed race and could pass for white. He was broadly educated and well read, but never finished a college degree. Instead, he became intensely involved in social politics and contributed to a number of leftist papers while honing experimental stories that appeared in avant-garde little magazines. His masterpiece, *Cane* (1923), is a dense collage of fictions, poems, and experimental

writing that describes aspects of black American life from rural
Georgia (with its Jim Crow laws and public lynchings) to New York
theaters and an imagined Africa. The book itself consists of many
pieces that had appeared in magazines and were then substantively
revised when removed from this print network and lodged
between covers of their own. Although a prominent figure in the
New Negro Renaissance, Toomer was reluctant to have his work
branded or marked as "Negro," a concession he eventually made
in order to boost sales. After the book's publication, he gradually
drifted away from avant-garde art; instead he studied the new
age mystic George Gurdjieff and eventually left the United States
to study with him and to promote his teachings abroad. *Cane*'s
experimental narrative form allowed scholars to treat Toomer
as a black "modernist" writer whose works could be compared
to those of Eliot and Pound. A new biography of Toomer's later
years, the publication of his correspondence, renewed attention to
his periodical writing, and finally a major new edition of *Cane*
edited by Rudolph P. Byrd and Henry Louis Gates, Jr. have all
refashioned our image of this writer.[5] No longer solely a black
writer or a member of the New Negro/Harlem Renaissance, he is
instead a diasporic figure whose work unsettles the categories of
race, nation, and modernism.

# Modernism in a global context

Along with gender and race studies, the rise of postcolonial studies
has contributed significantly to the fundamental rethinking of
modernism as a concept, a historical period, and a set of aesthetic
practices. As we've seen, work by Friedman, Jameson, Williams,
Said, and Gilroy illustrates the force of different versions of
postcolonial studies and the modes of inquiry they have launched.
These include transnational studies, global studies, and certain
approaches in comparative studies that ask profound questions
about cultural responses to modernity. The twentieth century has
been treated not just as a hothouse for aesthetic experiment, but
also as a period of massive imperial expansion and contraction
characterized by unprecedented waves of migration, widespread
revolutions, redrawn maps, and numerous colonial and civil wars,
not to mention the dynamic shifts in creole languages, cosmopolitan

thought, indigenism, and much more. Even the works at the core of the traditional canon of modernism came from "exiles and émigrés" who drew on forms, media, languages, and genres from across the globe. The generations of scholars who divided "modernism" into traditions defined by single languages and nations, that is, ignored Pound's own warning regarding the concept of "American literature": "You may as well give courses in 'American chemistry', neglecting all foreign discoveries" ("Renaissance" 218).

In addition to offering new political readings of modernism in international contexts, "transnational modernist studies," as it has been called, bears on previous understandings of modernism in three important ways. First, the question of modernity's singularity or plurality has prompted new questions of comparative modernisms. That is, the previous multiplications of "modernism" along the lines of gender or race focused largely on the West. What happens to "modernism" when non-Western modernities are analyzed? The same holds for peripheral modernisms: 1922 was an aesthetic annus mirabilis in Europe, but it was also the year in which São Paulo's Modern Art Week launched modernism in Brazil, the Peruvian poet César Vallejo published his avant-garde masterpiece *Trilce*, and the Chinese novelist Lu Xun (a penname for Zhou Shuren) serialized his vernacular landmark *Ah Q—The Real Story*. Second, the treatment of non-Western art and literature has forced a reconsideration of modernism's temporal boundaries in the first half of the twentieth century. On the one hand, the period of decolonization in Africa after the Second World War now constitutes a part of the "modernist" era, for instance, even though the movement had been declared "dead" in Euro-America. On the other hand, Hispanophone *modernismo*— the first aesthetic movement to call itself "modernist"—predates Anglophone modernism by some two decades. Furthermore, modernism was variously embraced, revised, or rejected in complex ways by non-Western figures, whether Oswald de Andrade, Chinua Achebe, Kamau Brathwaite, or Tayeb Salih, thus putting additional pressure on the concept's temporal bounds and its consequent usefulness. Indeed, postcolonialism's commitment to undoing hierarchies of (Eurocentric) originals and (peripheral) copies, not surprisingly, leads us to ask why modernism was presumed to have begun in a particular Anglo-European moment at all—and not in, say, Africa, where the masks Picasso used to revolutionize painting originated. Third, and finally, the combined importance of these trends has prompted efforts to alternately synthesize or parse the critical histories of "modernism," under many different names, from around the globe and in many different languages. This work led Mark Wollaeger to argue, in his introduction to the *Oxford Handbook of Global Modernisms* (2012), that in order to connect movements as diverse as *"modernismo, futurisme, modanizumu, moderna, vanguardismo, chủ nghĩa hiện đại,* or *avant-garde,"* we need not redefine modernism, but rather recognize in all of these a Wittgensteinian "family resemblance . . . that make[s] multiple modernisms recognizable as members of a class" (3, 11).

Postcolonial studies came to bear on modernism somewhat belatedly, relative to other fields and approaches. As a possible starting point for what has become a "transnational turn," one could look to Raymond Williams's account of the metropolis (see Chapter 3), or to his *The Country and the City* (1973), which understands the conditions of cultural relations between centers and peripheries in terms that would influence a generation of Marxists. Perhaps the most influential provocations came in a set of essays published by Jameson, Said, and Terry Eagleton, *Nationalism, Colonialism, and Literature,* in 1988. In his controversial contribution, "Modernism and Imperialism" (1988), Jameson attempts to account for modernism's formal experimentation—especially the trope of "unknowability" in works like *Heart of Darkness, Ulysses,* and Forster's *Howards End* (1910)—by reading it against the context of a newly expansive "imperial world system" that began with the Berlin Conference, which carved up Africa among the European powers (59). In this world-system, citizens at the core (in London, for instance) could not know, much less comprehend or even fully imagine, their distant colonial counterparts as subjects—indeed, as fellow citizens. Adorno accounted for modernist fragmentation through the conditions of industrial capitalism; Jameson extends this to the global plane and claims that time and space had to be represented as fragmented and incomplete because of the radical disjunctures in temporality and spatiality ushered in by this new stage of imperialism (50). Jameson asserts that modernism's mythic allusions, too, were not simply exercises in symbolic correspondence; Joyce, in fact, had "slyly turned the imperial relationship inside out, appropriating the great imperial space of the Mediterranean [by way of correspondences to the *Odyssey*] in order to organize the space of the colonial city" (68). *Ulysses,* for him, is "the epic of the metropolis under imperialism," and Joyce is not the archetypal metropolitan high modernist (*"Ulysses"* 145). Rather, he reads more like a postmodern, multicultural, even Third World modernist.

Seen this way, high modernist aesthetics are the products of geopolitical forces—a shift that has led to fundamental reconsiderations of even the most canonical works. Taking seriously the colonial condition of Ireland, for example, scholars like Enda Duffy and Emer Nolan proposed new readings of Joyce's position as a subaltern, postcolonial writer. Meanwhile, Pound's engagements with Chinese literature and culture were revisited through theories of Orientalism; Conrad's roots in revolutionary Poland were seen anew; and Woolf's protracted arguments against colonialism were recovered. In keeping with a pattern we have seen in other "expansions" of modernism, scholars next excavated the works of figures who came from non-European sites and circulated among more familiar modernist peers, as the Indian novelist Mulk Raj Anand and the Trinidadian Marxist C. L. R. James did. A step further in renovating the field was to locate modernism beyond Europe. Simon Gikandi's *Writing in Limbo* (1992) does so by tracing the "historical anxiety and ambivalence and the cultural and narrative forms Caribbean writers have developed both to represent and to resist the European narrative of history inaugurated by Columbus and the modern moment" (2). Caribbean modernism, Gikandi argues, is thus "highly revisionary," and is "opposed to, though not necessarily independent of, European notions of modernism"; it creolizes the concept through a manifestation of the "inner dichotomy" in modern experience that Marshall Berman posited, but with an attention to the issues and histories of slavery, the African diaspora, and postcolonial state-formation (4–5).

In the last two decades the kind of work Gikandi pioneered by looking at the Caribbean has now traversed the globe. Hardly a site has been untouched in the quest to rethink modernism beyond Anglo-America and the European core: former British colonies (Ireland, India, Canada, Nigeria), countries along Europe's margins (Russia, Spain, Turkey, Greece), and then an array of sites including China, Brazil, Japan, and many others have all been treated. Beyond national formations, "peripheral," "mestizo," "diasporic," "plantation," "New World," "Pacific Rim," "Mediterranean," and "cosmopolitan" modernisms have all been articulated and examined. Large essay collections such as Wollaeger's, Astradur Eysteinsson and Vivian Liska's two-volume *Modernism* (2007), and Peter Brooker, Andrzej Gasiorek, and Andrew Thacker's *Oxford Handbook of Modernisms* (2010) all devote many (if not all) of their dozens of contributions to international or comparative topics. Gikandi even turned back to English modernism and argued that it arose from a "crisis in belief in the efficacy of colonialism, its culture, and its dominant terms—a progressive temporality, a linear cartography, and a unified European subject" (*Maps* 161). Cutting across geographies, Laura Doyle's *Freedom's Empire* (2008) resituates American modernism as an end-stage in the story of the transatlantic novel since the time of slavery, while Christopher GoGwilt's *The Passage of Literature* (2011) uses a "postcolonial philology" to trace new convergences of Conrad, Rhys, and the Indonesian writer Pramoedya Ananta Toer (4). Elsewhere, Jessica Berman complicates the distinctions between "modernist" and politically "committed" writing (*littérature engagée*, as it was often called) in her *Modernist Commitments* (2012) in order to reveal an ethical vision that underscores works from Indian, Spanish, English, and working-class US cultures. Such studies, of course, represent a global expansion of the field that, as Winkiel and Doyle note, both coincides with a post–Cold War expansion of American power and influence and replicates the territorial logic of empire. Such a recognition, in turn, reignites debates over modernism's origins, which Winkiel and Doyle sought to resolve by coining the term "geomodernisms" to move away from a Western/non-Western binary of cultural production. On the whole, however, the aim of transnational modernist studies has not been to assimilate "other" modernisms to a preconceived norm, nor to provide a naive multiculturalist celebration of modernism's diversity. Instead, it has sought to disrupt the presumed center of the concept of modernism and to continually pluralize its possible interpretations.

Drawing on the methodologies of sociology and world-systems theory, Pascale Casanova's much-debated study *The World Republic of Letters* (1999; English translation, 2004) offered a much different account of modernism that placed the movement within a global battle for aesthetic autonomy centered in Paris. Like Bourdieu, Casanova argues that artists came from various peripheries to Paris with the goal of earning the "consecration" that the Parisian network of letters could offer them (20). This consecration was judged by how fully a writer had created an "international literary space" that stood as an autonomous unit unhinged from the inequalities of the geopolitical map (109). That is, Joyce was not praised for giving a realistic portrait of a poverty-stricken Dublin, nor was Faulkner valued for his portrayal of Mississippi; instead, both became canonical modernists by turning their native areas into imagined spaces full of myth, symbolism, and allusion through which they could accumulate the literary capital (by way of technical innovations) necessary to gain commendation from elite readers and critics. Casanova applies this model to a host of writers who, from peripheral or marginal locations, used a model for international success that was modernist in form, and that created a blueprint for the success of subsequent movements like Magical Realism.

Casanova's account is complicated by the career of the Bengali writer Rabindranath Tagore. Already a national icon in Bengal (British India) by the 1910s for having renovated vernacular Bengali poetry and prose, Tagore found himself catapulted quickly onto the world stage in 1912, when the British painter William Rothenstein "discovered" him and sponsored the publication of his *Gitanjali* (*Song Offerings*) in English. Yeats wrote an effusive introduction to the book and proclaimed that "I know of no man in my time who has done anything in the English language to equal these lyrics"; Pound averred that Tagore was "greater than any of us," indeed one of the greatest poets in the English language; *Poetry* published Tagore's poems with hyperbolic notes of praise from both Pound and the magazine's editor Harriet Monroe; and André Gide translated the work into French (qtd. in Longenbach, *Stone Cottage* 24, 23). Almost overnight, Tagore became an international literary celebrity whose work was translated into a half-dozen European tongues, and in 1913, he became the first non-European to win the Nobel Prize for Literature. A prolific translator himself, he often changed the genre of the original (from poetry to prose, for instance), reordered its sections, and deleted references to India that he deemed too local or obscure for English-language audiences. His star burned bright in Europe for several more years and in 1915, he was knighted by George V, but renounced the honor in 1919 in response to the Jallianwala Bagh (or Amritsar) massacre. By the 1920s, his once strong champions began to resent him and his work: Yeats trashed him, in racist tones, as a sentimental charlatan, while Pound abandoned his cause with embarrassment. He disappeared

from the map of modernism assembled by Anglophone scholars
even while his legacy in Spanish translation, to take one example,
continued to grow—so much so that sales of his works outpaced
those of Spain's leading poets in the 1920s.

Several points can be taken from Tagore's disappearance from
and recent recovery in the historiography of modernism. One is
that the arguments made by scholars of race, media, and translation
almost always bear on the international elements of modernist
texts. Stephen Yao notes that translation was a means by which
modernist writers made cultural and political statements, forged
international alliances, and undermined notions of "the foreign"
in often forgotten ways. The networks that made modernism an
international phenomenon relied heavily on a variety of translation
practices, many of them uneven and fraught with matters of
race or colonial hierarchies. Beyond the Nobel, organizations
and cultural institutions from the BBC to the Congress of Black
Writers and Artists formed important bases for such work. We
see also that modernism in England, and indeed across Europe,
exhibited its anxieties about colonialism not only in the formalist
terms that Jameson outlines, but also in the lives of most famous
figures and texts, in the networks of "consecration" and celebrity
that it fashioned, and in its reliance on multilingualism. Whether
by tracing the foundations of modern anthropology, following the
course of "stereomodernism" in Africa, or charting the development
of what Jahan Ramazani calls a "transnational poetics," the New
Modernist Studies has embedded modernism in geopolitics both
past and present.

# Modernism's print cultures

The new field of media studies, which has flourished in recent
decades, has played a central role in unraveling the idea that
modernism was an antagonist of mass culture. The critique of
high modernism's elitism was spelled out in works such as John
Carey's *The Intellectuals and the Masses* (1992), which argued that
writers ranging from Pound, Yeats, and Lawrence to Knut Hamsun,
Ortega y Gasset, and Woolf exhibited an intense Nietzschean
hostility toward mass, commercially driven reading publics. This
new public expanded rapidly in the late 1800s for a variety of

reasons, including education reform, new printing technologies, the wide distribution of artificial lighting, and the expansion of leisure time, all of which helped reading to become a popular occupation. Inexpensive paperback novels regularly appeared in shops, stands, and rail stations along with illustrated magazines, tabloid newspapers (whose vertical folds made them easier to read on a packed train), and new genres such as detective and science fiction stories. These new print media technologies fragmented the marketplace into segments and niches, making it almost impossible to assess or review the state of writing as a whole. The idea of a single national literature that Matthew Arnold once imagined might serve as a repository of thought and culture came under enormous threat, and Carey argued that many of the writers who would come to be seen as modernist reacted to this fragmentation with a jealous, often aggressive loathing. In response, he insists, most modernist writers imagined themselves and their intellectual peers as a "natural aristocracy"—elite leaders witnessing the ongoing separation of art and politics since the French Revolution—charged with preserving culture itself against the degeneracy of the rabble that modern democracy exemplified (71). Indeed, scholars and critics of modernism have noted at least since the 1930s that such a belief led many writers to gravitate toward antidemocratic, reactionary politics. John R. Harrison called it a "strange and disturbing phenomenon . . . that five of the greatest literary figures of this century, Yeats, Lewis, Pound, Eliot and Lawrence, were attracted by Italian and German fascism before the Second World War. . . . Why is it," Harrison asks, "that great creative artists can totally reject a liberal, democratic, humanitarian society, and prefer a cruel, authoritarian, bellicose society?" (15) Charles Ferrall and Tom Villis extended this critique in their associations of modernism with far-right politics, as have Paul Peppis and Jeroen Vanheste. For many of these critics, the critique of mass culture was essential to the definition of modernism, which, in turn, made its aesthetic practices hazardously antidemocratic.

Such critiques, however, cannot fully account for the way that many writers from the early twentieth century either failed to comprehend this divide or instead attempted to straddle it. Conrad and Faulkner, for example, meld adventure, sensationalist, or gothic plots with complicated, often disturbing styles. Joyce's first stories, *Dubliners* (1914), drew heavily on European Naturalism to offer his

readers a "nicely polished looking glass"; only later did his work
come to seem less direct and more experimental in form (*Letters*
2:134). And Woolf collected her essays under the title *The Common
Reader* (1925) in an attempt to fashion a hybrid public, even as she
later decried the "brain prostitution" practiced by popular writers
(*Three Guineas* 94). The New Modernist Studies reassesses the idea
of an antagonistic divide between an elite, if isolated, modernism
sheltering on the far side of a great divide from a profit-oriented
mass culture. Rather than an autonomous sphere of cultural
activity, in fact, modernism is increasingly seen as one of many
overlapping market segments, a point made clear by the cross-
section of materials studied in Michael North's *Reading 1922: A
Return to the Scene of the Modern* (1999), which weaves Joyce and
Wittgenstein together with Walter Lippmann (a pioneer of modern
theories of public opinion) and Howard Carter (who unearthed
Tutankhamen's tomb in 1922, sparking a vogue for all things
Egyptian). Jennifer Wicke's *Advertising Fictions* (1988) understands
the burgeoning world of advertising as a "radically new discursive
practice" that arose in the nineteenth century and developed a
language of its own in productive tension with the development
of the novel. High art and mass production have always been in
interplay, she posits, and in Dickens, James, and Joyce, advertising
was a "shadow partner" of literature (1). Most strikingly, she
sees in Oscar Wilde—who so brilliantly marketed himself as the
quintessential man of taste—a mirror image of P. T. Barnum, the
great entrepreneur who learned that the powerful pleasures offered
by advertising could create an aura capable of transforming the
dullest of objects into magical experiences. The jealous isolation of
modernist writers and artists, in fact, is now often treated in relation
to the brimming field of stars and celebrities in which they were
embedded. Aaron Jaffe's *Modernism and the Culture of Celebrity*
(2005) explores this dynamic interaction, arguing that "modernism
is less a periodizing term or a bundle of formal concerns than a
historically circumscribed mode of presenting value and prescribing
frameworks of expectations" (12). Faye Hammill's *Sophistication:
A Literary and Cultural History* (2010) pursues similar arguments
about the ways in which difficulty functions not only aesthetically,
but also as a kind of social and economic capital. Experimental
works, after all, advertise the intelligence of their readers, which
helps us make sense, for example, of the famous 1955 photograph

of Marilyn Monroe, in a bathing suit at a playground, reading the final pages of *Ulysses*.

Lawrence Rainey's *Institutions of Modernism: Literary Elite and Public Culture* (1998) follows this same set of concerns by exploring how movements like Futurism and books like *The Waste Land* cannily exploited the marketplace for elite goods. Noting that unstable categories of "high" and "low" art crossed daily, and that "middlebrow" only appeared in 1906 as a term, Rainey posits that "modernism's ambiguous achievement . . . was to probe the interstices dividing that variegated field and to forge within it a strange and unprecedented space for cultural production" that was both a retreat from public culture and an intersection with it. Modernism, in this telling, did not resist commodification by resorting to autonomy; it *invited* commodification through an "economic circuit of patronage, collecting, speculation, and investment" exemplified by Pound's early career in London (3). Pound learned from Marinetti's lecture tour in London how to gain both patrons and audiences; Joyce carefully crafted the first editions of *Ulysses* as high-priced collector's objects; and Eliot sold *The Waste Land* to two magazines (and considered adding *Vanity Fair* as well) in order to increase its visibility, then added his endnotes in order to meet a page-length quota necessary for its printing as a book.

For Rainey, the critiques of modernism offered by Huyssen, Bürger, and Perloff all remain trapped within the logic of the New Critical canon, "rehears[ing] a fall narrative in which an Edenic state of subversion imperceptibly yields to an appropriation, assimilation, and containment by 'late capitalism' or its cultural instrument, academic criticism" (8). Similarly, for David Chinitz, the focus on Eliot as the arch-formalist of modernist poetry, interested only in high literary allusions, overlooks the significant parts of his career that he dedicated to writing about jazz, the music halls, and detective novels. In *The Public Face of Modernism: Little Magazines, Audiences, and Reception, 1905-1920* (2000), Mark Morrisson argues that canonical modernists drew on visual techniques from the aesthetics of advertising, recast poetry around popular paradigms, and published reviews in mass media to pay the bills when their books sold only a few copies. Further entwining the fields of prestige and commerce, the "prize culture" of the twentieth century had significant roots in the establishment of awards like the Nobel and the Pulitzer during the modernist era (see English).

At the heart of work by critics like Rainey, Morrisson, Wicke, Jaffe, Morrisson, and others is a turn toward the archive. In *Material Modernism: The Politics of the Page* (2001), George Bornstein brought the tools of book history and the "sociology of texts" to modernist studies by insisting that "the literary work might be said not to exist in any one version, but in all the versions put together" (6). William Faulkner's short story about a horrific lynching, "Dry September" (1931), to take one example, seems to mean something very different when it appears in *Scribner's* magazine surrounded by articles about police brutality and an excerpt from a memoir about leaving the South than it does in Faulkner's *Collected Stories* (1950) or in the second volume of the *Heath Anthology of American Literature* (2002).[6] Much of the work on print culture associated with the New Modernist Studies, in fact, has arisen precisely from ongoing attempts to recover the many different versions of now familiar texts that circulated through complicated publishing networks of production, reception, and consumption. The early twentieth century was the golden age of magazines and nearly every significant work from the era appeared first in the pages of a periodical. "Little magazines" such as *Poetry*, *Blast*, the *Little Review*, and the *Dial*, among many others, have long been acknowledged as central media for the articulation and publication of high modernism. But before they were approached through the wide-angle lenses of media studies, they were often seen only as repositories for "first-runs" of modernist works that were later published as bound books or in anthologies—items typically of interest only to textual editors. Furthermore, when they were stored in libraries, their covers and advertisements were almost always ripped out, making it difficult to find full runs or intact issues. Scholars of periodical studies have seen these media as especially ripe for analysis since the surprising juxtapositions and collisions that take place on the pages of a magazine allow us to discover new, often unexpected meanings and contexts, and to trace the revisions that took place across multiple versions of a text. The "Hades" episode of *Ulysses*, for example, is set in a Dublin graveyard in 1904 and appears to reflect primarily on Ireland's past. It first appeared just as the First World War was drawing to a close, however, in a 1918 issue of the *Little Review* where it was surrounded by stories, poems, and letters about death, mourning, and memory. Seen from this vantage, Joyce's work becomes not just a chapter of his novel, but part of a larger set of texts reflecting on the disastrous aftermath of a global conflict. Recovering these original sites of publication, in other words, enables us to discover new meanings within even the most familiar canonical works, thereby making them more resonant and often more socially engaged than earlier generations of readers had imagined.

These new approaches to the twentieth-century archive developed out of the ongoing collection and digitization of print media from the period. Founded in 1998, the Modernist Journals Project (MJP) was the first large-scale digital repository of early twentieth-century magazines, and it continues to gather complete runs of important and overlooked modernist reviews up to 1922 (both the annus mirabilis of Anglo-American modernism and the year at which copyright law in the United States demands that the MJP's work cut off). Its searchable scans include the covers, advertisements, and even markings by previous readers in the margins. Other projects have followed, including the Blue Mountain Project, which focuses on non-Anglophone journals from Europe, especially from the late 1800s and the turn of the century. These digital collections, furthermore, have not only changed our view of modernism's traditional canon, so that writers like Beatrice Hastings and Katherine Mansfield now appear more important, but also have opened up entirely new resources. Digital editions of widely distributed magazines like *Scribner's* and *McClure's*, for example, help us better see how high modernist aesthetics permeated mass and popular culture, while activist publications like *The Masses* enable us to see how periodicals created new kinds of social networks. Finally, attention is now turning to inexpensive pulp magazines, which helped pioneer new genres such as hard-boiled detective fiction and science fiction while reaching untold audiences. Modernism, Robert Scholes argues, took place in the magazines, and a return to these media is now rapidly changing our understanding of what modernism was, where it happened, and how it circulated in spaces and temporalities beyond its traditional bounds.

And periodicals are only part of the story: books changed dramatically at the time, too. The Victorian three-decker novel began to wane and the lending library was in decline. They were replaced by newsstands and book clubs that helped create national audiences while generating new celebrity authors like Marie Corelli, Arthur Conan Doyle, Hall Caine, Zane Grey, and Anita Loos. The availability of cheap paper and halftone printing for images altered the very look and feel of books, while new printing technology allowed some authors to go around often conservative editors and publish their own works. W. B. Yeats and his sisters, for example, set up the Cuala Press in order to provide a venue for key works in the Irish Revival. Virginia Woolf and her husband Leonard Woolf founded the Hogarth Press as something of a hobby in their Bloomsbury home and quickly made it into a major venture that distributed essential works from the period—not only Woolf's novels, but also translations of Dostoevsky on which Woolf collaborated, the English editions of Freud's complete works, and C. L. R. James's landmark *The Case for West-Indian Self-Government* (1933). And Sylvia Beach, with the support of Harriet Shaw Weaver, created Shakespeare & Company in order to publish *Ulysses* after it had been rejected as obscene by mainstream publishers. Other writers, like Ernest Hemingway and F. Scott Fitzgerald, joined with major publishers such as Charles Scribner's Sons in book-of-the-month schemes in order to maximize profits. Thanks to such arrangements and marketing strategies, *For Whom the Bell Tolls* (1940) sold half a million copies in its first five months, while Stein's *Autobiography of Alice B. Toklas* (1933) helped transform the author of highly experimental prose into an international celebrity.

Paying close attention to the ways in which modernism was printed, disseminated, and supported, furthermore, illuminates the complicated ways in which print culture intersects with larger debates about gender, politics, and access to the public sphere. As Jayne Marek argued, the portraits of modernism as masculinist and opposed to a feminized public sphere fall apart when we look more fully at the little magazines that so powerfully shaped the early twentieth century. She argues in *Women Editing Modernism* (1995) that women such as Harriet Monroe, Dora Marsden, and Margaret Anderson were the intellectual (and often financial) forces behind many of the most important venues in which high modernism was launched. And they were not simply women who provided means for male authors' bidding: they pushed bold feminist agendas in the *Freewoman* (1911–12) and the *New Freewoman* (1913) and published women authors who otherwise would likely have remained anonymous. They operated through collaborations (and their inherent tensions) such as those between Anderson and Jane Heap, and they succeeded in presenting a multiplicity of perspectives on aesthetic and political issues that worked against the reigning notions of objectivity and (male) authorship in the media of the day. To overlook their contributions is to write an essentially misogynistic literary history that follows the very self-championing precepts that Pound, for one, laid out.

# Modernism and mass media

The rethinking of modernism's engagement with mass culture was not limited to the printed word, but extends to include the vast array of new media invented in Thomas Edison's Menlo Park labs. Film, radio, telephony, phonography, and later the television all created wholly new aesthetic and cultural forms, but for decades they were held at considerable distance from canonical definitions of modernism. Theodor Adorno, who used the term "culture industry" to register his deep suspicion of these new mass media, wrote in 1951 that "every visit to the cinema leaves me, against all my vigilance, stupider and worse" (*Minima* 25). This blunt assessment effectively summarizes the way many prominent theorists of modernism understood not just film but all of the twentieth century's mass cultural forms: as the dissolute other of authentic art, as the industrialization of false consciousness, as a soporific bastion of sentimentality, and as a degraded form of realism. The New Modernist Studies, however, has sought to understand these other forms as an integral part of modernist innovation with the ability to transform radically our perception and representation of the world in an age of newly mobile, electrified, and energetic things. As a result, modernist difficulty is increasingly understood as the aesthetic of the machine age, linked closely to what Mark Goble calls the "beautiful circuits" of mediated life (xv).

As we have seen, ideas about modernism have always been tied up with the mass media. For Clement Greenberg, in fact, modernism was nothing more and nothing less than the aesthetic exploration of individual media—a way of turning inward to the possibilities of paint on canvas, of words on a page, of flickering images on a cinema screen. "It quickly emerged," he wrote, "that the unique and proper area of competence of each art coincided with all that was unique in the nature of its medium" ("Modernist Painting" 86). Thus, Hollywood cinema, snapshot photos, and advertising could all be exiled to the far side of the great divide since each exploited its particular medium for other ends. At the same time, nonnarrative films (by Marcel Duchamp and Hans Richter), avant-garde photographs (by Man Ray and Alfred Stieglitz), and Dada collages (by John Heartfield and Hannah Höch) could all be preserved as authentic works of aesthetic expression dedicated primarily to the nature of the medium itself. By the 1990s, however, this emphasis on the medium's purity had dissipated. Miriam Hansen's essay "The Mass Production of the Senses: Classical Cinema as Vernacular Modernism" (1999) encapsulated this new way of thinking about media by understanding film as a popular modernist art form that enabled a wide range of engagements with conceptions of modernity among viewers. Mainstream Hollywood coincided with high modernism, she notes in an article that works back and forth across a history of modernism *in* cinema and a history of modernism *through* cinema studies. Modernist cultural practices, she asserts, both articulate and mediate the experience of modernity. Similar arguments that move between film and high modernist literature and poetry appeared in David Trotter's *Cinema and Modernism* (2007), Michael North's *Machine-Age Comedy* (2009), and Susan McCabe's *Cinematic Modernism* (2005).

In breaking with the idea that modernism was bound to media specificity, new spaces opened for the exploration of transmedia studies—ways of thinking about how media interacted with and borrowed from one another. Thus, critics began to explore in greater detail the way cinematic forms were approximated or integrated into experimental narratives like John Dos Passos's *The 42nd Parallel* (1930), which uses "Newsreel" sections to break up its chapters, and Christopher Isherwood's *Berlin Stories* (1945), in which one of the narrators declares "I am a camera" (1). And once largely ignored essays and poems about film by Woolf, Stein, and H. D. have begun to take on new prominence. Similarly, critical and historical work on the early cinema by Tom Gunning, Thomas Elsaesser, and Mary Ann Doane carry this exchange in the opposite direction in order to reveal the ways in which this medium developed its own distinctive idiom by borrowing, recycling, and reinventing conventions of print culture as well as carnivals and sideshows. Paintings like Marcel Duchamp's *Nude Descending a Staircase, No. 2* (1912) and Umberto Boccioni's *States of Mind* series (1911) explored the relation between cinematic movement and the static canvas. Although not strictly a theorist of modernism, Jay David Bolter described this process of borrowing as "remediation"—a term that captures the ways in which new media become comprehensible by first borrowing the conventions of older, more familiar forms. As Paul Young argues in *The Cinema Dreams Its Rivals: Media Fantasy Films from Radio to the Internet* (2006), this process of exchange only accelerates as even newer media like television and then the Internet arrive. Old media, Young contends, can become defensive yet aggressive, trying to contain or limit their rivals by paradoxically encompassing and rejecting them. Defined this way, modernism becomes a way of characterizing aesthetic responses to the push and pull of old and new media that at once fragment experience even while opening new possibilities for expressive connection.

Although this process of rethinking modernism as a part of media history grew initially out of film theory, it has since grown to encompass many of the twentieth century's other new Edisonian media. *Broadcasting Modernism* (2009), edited by Debra Rae Cohen, Michael Coyle, and Jane Lewty, gathers an influential group of essays on the ways in which radio became a rich site for transmedial innovation. It offers scholars a way to think about invisible connections between minds even while providing an aural correlate for specific narrative techniques like a stream of consciousness. Popular music played millions of times over on gramophones also resonates in the poetry of Langston Hughes and Gwendolyn Brooks. Taking an alternative approach, Todd Avery's *Radio Modernism: Literature, Ethics, and the BBC, 1922-1938* (2006) explores the ways in which writers like Woolf, H. G. Wells, and E. M. Forster responded to the possibilities for public engagement offered by the BBC. Such work further diminishes the idea of a great divide between modernism and mass culture by showing the ways in which writers and artists sought to exploit the new media for their own end. This rediscovery of modernist engagement is taken up in Mark Wollaeger's *Modernism, Media, and Propaganda* (2006), which helps recast experimental writers and filmmakers as information specialists who often lent their expertise to the state. This shift in focus from formal experimentation to media expansion, furthermore, has contributed to the theorization of modernism beyond the early twentieth century and into our contemporary world, where its narrative innovations especially remain salient. If modernism is redefined as a response to new media, in other words, then a movement that began with photography and the cinema has continued to unfold through television, the personal computer, and the Internet. In *Digital Modernism: Making It New in New Media* (2014), Jessica Pressman contends that the newest forms of electronic literature take up many of the same challenges and paradoxes surrounding twentieth-century literature that have made modernism so inconstant yet resonant a term. Now embedded within these wide-ranging debates about the rise of mass media technologies across the twentieth century, "modernism" has become an even more far-reaching and unstable term, one that still activates all of Walter Benjamin's famous anxieties about the way mechanical reproduction might fundamentally transform the very idea of art.

To get a sense of the way media theory might transform our understanding of modernism, consider Mark Z. Danielewski's 2006 work, *Only Revolutions*. It's difficult to call this a book, though it's printed on paper, contains lines of texts, and is bound between covers bearing the title and the author's name. Each page, however, features two loosely constructed stream-of-consciousness narratives printed at 180 degrees from the other. This means the reader (or perhaps "user") has to rotate the object constantly in order to make sense of it—a mechanical process evoked in the very title. These narratives, furthermore, begin at opposite ends of the book and run toward one another, meeting and then passing in the middle, while also moving against one another in time. Each page also has a running timeline of events from 1863 to 1963 that includes clear public markers like the end of the Spanish-American War of 1898, more mundane ones like "Tigers over Cubs," and totally obscure references like "Rocket Ranger 3" (165/196, 317/44).[7] The overall effect is of a kind of loop—like the reels of a tape machine or film projector that can tell a different story depending on which way they run. The object itself, furthermore, is filled with references to various modernist textual devices. The timeline, for example, alludes to the marginal annotations Joyce uses in one chapter of *Finnegans Wake*, while the use of different ink colors echoes Faulkner's plan to print each of the different time streams of *The Sound and the Fury* (1929) in distinctive colors. Deciphering the actual narrative of *Only Revolutions* is difficult, though it clearly contains a love story of sorts and depends heavily on the cinematic conventions of the American road film as well as on Jack Kerouac's *On the Road* (1957). Although temporally removed from the historical limits often used to periodize modernism (both "high" and otherwise), this work actually seems intensely modernist in its direct engagement with new media technologies. Not only does it clearly materialize (and defamiliarize) the book's technological affordances, but it also was created in response to the twentieth century's last new media technology: the Internet. Danielewski, for example, added events to the running timeline after urging his readers to suggest them on a webpage; many of these can only be fully unpacked through the use of massive search engines like Google. Similar to works by Dos Passos or Beckett, *Only Revolutions* self-consciously lodges itself with a larger media revolution that has been unfolding since the nineteenth century. As his constant allusions to Joyce and others suggest, furthermore, Danielewski's work seems self-consciously to redefine modernism not as a kind of formal narrative technique or historical period, but as part of an ongoing response to the proliferation of new media forms.

# Modernism and the law

The experimental art, writing, and new media of the early twentieth century often tested the limits of public taste and aesthetic tradition, thereby running afoul of government censors who sought to limit, censor, and even ban it. Indeed, the very word "modernism" still invokes a romantic, liberal narrative about banned books in which isolated, heroic authors overcome the forces of conservatism and win the right to express honestly the full range of human experience. These struggles helped define our understanding of novels like Joyce's *Ulysses* and Lawrence's *Lady Chatterley's Lover* (1928), both of which were initially banned and then later published with the legal decisions certifying their status as art bound in as introductions. The laws governing obscenity in the West were complex and varied widely across national contexts, with authority sometimes vested in official state agents (like the United States Postmaster General or the Lord Chamberlain), but often residing in nonstate offices and agents such as the New York Society for the Prevention of Vice, which initiated the prosecution of *Ulysses* when it was published in the *Little Review*. Elsewhere, churches and other nongovernmental organizations exercised similar powers, which explains why *Ulysses* was never officially banned in Ireland, but was nevertheless not available for sale. The laws governing obscenity radiated beyond these central canonical works to entangle a wide array of writing, including fiction by Flaubert, Wyndham Lewis, and Radclyffe Hall; dramatic works by Ibsen, George Bernard Shaw, and Eugene O'Neill; and nonfiction by the birth-control advocate Margaret Sanger and the pacifist editors of *The Masses*. In order to evade the censors, some authors simply withheld their works from publication (as E. M. Forster did with his queer bildungsroman, or Claude McKay with his *Color Scheme*) or circulated them privately. The 1885 Criminal Law Amendment Act in Britain, after all, had criminalized homosexuality in Britain and was the statute used to sentence Oscar Wilde to hard labor in 1895. Government censors fearful of art's power exercised similar power across the arts. Some American cities banned jazz, for example, fearing that it promoted sinful, licentious behavior, while Nazi Germany declared most kinds of modernist painting "degenerate" and banned its sale, exhibition, and sometimes even creation.[8]

The struggle over the increasingly fraught boundary between art and obscenity remains a topic of central concern in the New Modernist Studies. Much of the recent work in this field, however, has shifted away from the idea that art has been locked in a gradually liberating struggle against the law and into some idealized state of absolute freedom. Instead, critics now look much more carefully at the way various kinds of laws have helped shape, circulate, and define a range of aesthetic practices. Celia Marshik's *British Modernism and Censorship* (2006), for example, explores the strategies writers like Woolf and Rhys used to test the limits of obscenity law while still trying to ensure that their works could be printed. She argues, in fact, that such strategies account in significant ways for the difficulty of such works, contending that modernism "owes many of its trademark aesthetic qualities—such as self-reflexivity, fragmentation, and indirection—to censorship" (6). Focusing specifically on Joyce, whose *Ulysses* remains the most famously banned book of the early twentieth century, Katherine Mullin argues that the graphic depictions of sex and sexuality in the book's final chapters were added only because its author realized the book would be banned. Paul Vanderham and Rachel Potter, meanwhile, argue that the dense, often baffling, wordplay in *Finnegans Wake* is part of a deliberate strategy Joyce used to embed even more aggressively obscene writing in an aesthetic form no censor could decipher. In Soviet Russia, the history of Mikhail Bulgakov's masterpiece novel *The Master and Margarita*'s battles with censorship, suppression, and forced revision spans nearly four decades, from the late twenties to 1967. In this sense, the laws governing censorship become not just repressive obstacles, but spurs to invention and creativity that helped enable aesthetic innovation. Codes governing both the behavior and the representation of homosexuality led many modernists to formulate codes of their own in queer poetics. Such laws, furthermore, extend well beyond those governing the graphic representation of the human body and its career. Sean Latham's *The Art of Scandal: Modernism, Libel Law, and the Roman à Clef* (2009), for example, explores the ways in which dozens of modernist works became entangled with libel laws governing the boundary between fiction and reality.

The public and private political lives of cultural figures also became subject to prosecution: W. E. B. Du Bois was threatened with prosecution under the Foreign Agents Registration Act, J. Edgar Hoover attempted to undermine Orson Welles's career at several junctures, and Langston Hughes was forced to testify in a McCarthy hearing about his communist affiliations even while his own books were being circulated abroad by the United States in its Cold War cultural diplomacy. The censorial regimes in dictatorial and totalitarian states forced countless figures to transmute their politics through a variety of expressive strategies, while the FBI's surveillance of black authors such as James Baldwin and Claude McKay, William J. Maxwell argues, led them to both experimentation and self-censorship. Indeed, new work based on the release of FBI files has begun to reveal just how pervasive the American surveillance apparatus became across the twentieth century as it built files on nearly every artist, writer, and actor of note. This burgeoning interest in modernism's intersection with law is now also leading well beyond censorship and obscenity (themes which became paramount as signs of Western freedom during the Cold War) to other legal regimes that can't be easily sorted into a narrative of aesthetic emancipation. These include the use of trademarks, battles over patents, and the publication of celebrity images in advertising, film, and other visual media across uneven legal contexts globally.

The expansion of modernism's imbrication in the law has also opened up a new and wide-ranging set of questions about copyright and intellectual property. Such concerns were initially stirred in the 1990s, when modernism's value as an economic as well as cultural good became apparent. As a result, authors, their publishers, and their estates began to assert their copyrights more aggressively, sometimes demanding exorbitant fees for quotations, controlling the creation of new editions, limiting access to private archives, and even intervening to stop books, anthologies, biographies, and adaptations deemed offensive or inappropriate. Debates about the rights of authors and how these rights affect the production and circulation of work from the early twentieth century became even more intense when the United States extended the duration of copyright protections with the passage of the Sonny Bono Copyright Extension Act in 1998, and when the European Union similarly moved to extend and harmonize their own laws governing intellectual property. All of this was further complicated by the fact that many modernist figures left their estates in disarray and their papers dispersed in a thousand sites, many of them still unknown. These legal changes, when coupled with the activism of some authors' estates, led to a crisis in modernist scholarship: new editions became increasingly expensive or could not be produced at all, while the assertion of copyright has limited access to many archives and thus constrained many kinds of scholarly work (biographies, editions of letters or manuscript drafts, studies of pirated editions of famous works) that has become common in fields covering works dating before the late nineteenth century.

Initially, Robert Spoo identified many of the key issues surrounding the growing assertion of intellectual property rights and the effect this had on our understanding of modernism. In "Copyright Protectionism and Its Discontents" (1998), he called attention to the ways in which rights holders deform our understanding of modernism and its contexts. The irony of these contemporary debates over intellectual property is that many early twentieth-century writers and artists were themselves often citing and recycling material from the past. In *The Cantos*, after all, Pound draws on an extraordinary range of borrowed material; Dada collages celebrated their capacity to use nothing new in the process of artistic creation; Walt Disney built his film empire by animating common fairy tales; and Cyril Connolly's elegiac *The Unquiet Grave* (1944) is nothing but a collection of quotations fashioned into a kind of poetic narrative. In *The Copywrights: Intellectual Property and the Literary Imagination* (2003), Paul Saint-Amour contends that part of modernism's innovation came from its voracious borrowing and thus its implicit rejection of strict definitions of intellectual property. As was the case with obscenity, here too the laws regulating copyright become both a spur and a limit to creative expression, opening up a dense set of connections that we are just now beginning to understand. And many of the writers and artists were themselves aware of these contradictions and found themselves waging sometimes odd legal battles in courtrooms, the press, and public letters. Spoo's *Without Copyrights: Piracy, Publishing, and the Public Domain* (2013), for example, tackles the history of book piracy and the efforts of writers, publishers, and lawyers to regulate, escape, or monopolize the public domain. And Caren Irr's *Pink Pirates* (2010) looks more broadly across the twentieth century to discern the ways in which copyright regimes—themselves rooted in property laws—have often proven especially harmful to women writers and artists.

The increasing focus on the nexus of the law and literature in the early twentieth century is now beginning to extend well beyond the regimes of obscenity, libel, and copyright that explicitly regulate the circulation and control of printed and visual works. Indeed, matters of law, rights, and jurisprudence touch on almost all of the topics this book series will explore. The suffragist cause, access to the ballot box in the Jim Crow South, and the endless struggle between individual rights and the powers of the state all mark sites where the law becomes deeply entwined with different modes of aesthetic expression and experimentation. There are, of course, spectacular sites of intersection: Oscar Wilde's trial for indecency, the ban placed on Hall's lesbian novel *The Well of Loneliness* in 1928, and the horrific book burnings in fascist Germany and Italy. As Allan Hepburn's collection *Troubled Legacies: Narrative and Inheritance* (2007) reminds us, however, the law works in more subtle ways as well by crafting the definition of families and the rights of inheritance. The concept, practice, and canons of law, in fact, underwent extraordinary innovations of their own in the early twentieth century, a point Ravit Reichman makes in *The Affective*

*Life of Law: Legal Modernism and the Literary Imagination* (2009). Far from a governor or limit of cultural production, in other words, the law itself endured a seismic transformation of its own that can best be described as modernist in its range and consequence.

# Modernism, war, and violence

War and violence raged across the modernist era, from the Boer Wars of South Africa to the two world wars, from civil wars in Ireland, China, and Spain to wars of independence in Cuba and Turkey. War provided the content and themes of a host of modernist works, whether Wilfred Owen's poetry, Rebecca West's *Return of the Soldier* (1918), or Hemingway's *Farewell to Arms* (1929), and it sparked aesthetic innovation too—the collage at the end of the postwar epic *The Waste Land* seems in some ways a commentary on Henry James's lament that "the war has used up words" (4). Most famously, the Futurists glorified war, and Henri Gaudier-Brzeska declared in Wyndham Lewis's *BLAST* (1915), "THIS WAR IS A GREAT REMEDY" (33). The technologies of mechanized war and the devastation they wrought fostered the angular, metallic, and antinatural look seen in works like Lewis's *A Battery Shelled* (1919) and Picasso's *Guernica* (1937). War underlies the shellshock that ripples across Woolf's *Mrs Dalloway* (1925) and Erich Maria Remarque's *All Quiet on the Western Front* (1929); and looking to less canonical or to forgotten figures, we can find a number of such conjunctions in works ranging from David Jones's *In Parenthesis* (1937) to José Martí's writings on the Cuban War of Independence (1895–98). Wars also ended prematurely the careers of influential figures, including Gaudier-Brzeska, T. E. Hulme, Rupert Brooke, Guillaume Apollinaire, and Umberto Boccioni, while state violence claimed Lorca, Osip Mandelstam, and Bruno Schulz.

Scholars have long placed the First World War—the War to End All Wars—at the center of high modernism. The disillusioned, cynical, ironic attitude toward the war has been read as a signature modernist break with the purported celebratory jingoism of late Victorian war writers. But it was not until 1975 that Paul Fussell's *The Great War and Modern Memory* (1975) reshaped the canon of modernist studies by highlighting writers who were involved in the war, and by providing a fresh context for reading the works of noncombatant writers. Fussell described the war, as many modernists did, in antiromantic, gritty terms, and he noted that the previous romanticization of war sparked modernist aesthetics. For Fussell, the great figures of modernism were the noncombatants, while veteran writers such as Siegfried Sassoon, Robert Graves, Wilfred Owen, and Edmund Blunden were lesser talents. These lesser talents, however, were responding to the war through the same modes of irony and allusion that their more celebrated peers were, in an attempt to capture their shock and bewilderment.

In the years since Fussell's work appeared, the importance of war to the formation of modernism has been studied from a number of angles. Some have claimed that "the modern" was born in the First World War, and that modernism actually gave its sensibilities *to* the First World War, as Modris Eksteins asserted. Vincent Sherry's *The Great War and the Language of Modernism* (2003) argues that high modernism's technical achievements in language were a result of the rewriting and revising of the discourse about the war in newspapers and other media. Jay Winter, on the other hand, has sought to sever the connection between modernism-as-rupture and war, arguing that the continuities in representations of public mourning, in fact, outweigh the radical ruptures and breaks so often associated with modernism. For Robert Buch, scenes of agony and destruction forced figures including Kafka, Georges Bataille, and Claude Simon to create works that offer no compassion, no mourning, and not even catharsis—only an unresolvable tension between unrest and paralysis in the reader. Focusing more closely on this critique of war and its effects on culture allows some critics to stretch the limits of modernism to include the caustically antiwar writings of Mark Twain on America's overseas imperial wars of 1898–1902 and Thomas Hardy's disgust at the Boer Wars in South Africa. Others have placed the literary effects of the First World War in new contexts; for James Dawes, the language of Anglo-American modernism must be read alongside the rhetoric of the Geneva Conventions, the documents that created human rights law, and the founding statements of a variety of social and professional organizations. Moving the focus of the First World War research beyond the Euro-American experience, Santanu Das's collection *Race, Empire, and First World War Writing* (2011) features essays on war writings by Chinese, Maori, Jamaican, Vietnamese, and many other figures who were affected by the war as soldiers, medics, indentured laborers, civilians, or prisoners.

New attention to the Second World War and the Cold War has expanded modernism's temporal boundaries once again, challenging the idea that 1945 marked a decisive break in intellectual and aesthetic history. Instead, 1939 has been seen as marking a new phase of modernism that lasted arguably into the 1950s. Marina MacKay and Jed Esty have reconceived a "late modernism" that turned inward, examined national culture in light of decolonization, and translated itself into new fields of inquiry such as cultural studies. Furthermore, after the war, a wide array of official and semi-official institutions promulgated an understanding of modernism as apolitical formal experimentation, in an effort to counteract the leftist reading of modernism as socially and politically radical. The magazine *Encounter*, founded in 1953 by Stephen Spender and Irving Kristol and later edited by Frank Kermode, was a key site for reinterpreting modernism and its legacies; the revelations in 1967 that its sponsor, the Congress for Cultural Freedom, had enjoyed CIA funding undermined the magazine's credibility and prompted the resignations of Spender and Kermode. The US Department of State and United States Information Agency contributed to the political instrumentalization of high modernism as well, circulating Abstract Expressionist paintings abroad and sending William Faulkner on cultural diplomatic missions to Europe, Latin America, and Japan. These projects opposed the fertile artistic experiments of modernism to the putatively stale, deterministic, even kitschy Socialist Realism mandated for Eastern Bloc artists and writers, and proposed one strand of high modernism as a kind of international language of freedom. Thus, it's not simply the case that modernist writers were still working after the Second World War, though that is important. Rather, modernist literature—famously seen as apolitical—was now recruited and interpreted for state politics. The opposition had become not only the tradition, as scholars like Harry Levin and Harold Rosenberg noted, but also the mouthpiece for dominant government regimes.

Further questions about war, aesthetics, and modernism are now branching out in many directions: What about war as it was experienced domestically, or wars that were watched from afar? What aesthetics were inspired by aerial photography (used in reconnaissance and in bombardments), and how were masculinity, femininity, and race recast by war propaganda? What commonalities exist among the treatments of the modern state's use of violence, from Max Weber's *Politics as a Vocation* (1919) to Lorca's "Ballad of the Spanish Civil Guard" (1936)? And how did violence and terrorism in undeclared or nonstatist wars intersect with art, from the fears of anarchist spies depicted in Conrad's *The Secret Agent* (1907) to the commentary on vigilante lynching in Billie Holliday's "Strange Fruit" (1939)? If we look beyond modernism's relationship with specific wars, what happens if we think comparatively at the types of wars that modernism grew from and responded to, as Sarah Cole does in *At the Violet Hour: Modernism and Violence in England and Ireland* (2012)? In short, can modernism itself be constituted in and around the disastrous suffering of a century that raised war to global levels, produced industrialized genocide, and made violence itself an integral part of modernity?

An illustrative example of the new and enlarged approaches to war and violence in modernist studies is the way in which scholars have looked to the manifesto as a vital conjunction of aesthetic and political revolutions in the modernist era. Nearly every avant-garde movement in the twentieth century declared its complete break from the past in such documents and, in perhaps the most famous of these manifestos, the Futurists used the genre to declare art itself a kind of war. Such writings found almost no place within the canonical high modernism that was built after the New Criticism; if anything, the manifesto was seen as a short, bombastic, and often overstated prelude to the development of more "serious" works. But the manifesto is also a document with a poetics that, Martin Puchner has argued, originates in the *Communist Manifesto* (1848). Marx and Engels's short book, he explains, ushered in a new type of declaration that "seeks to produce the arrival of the 'modern revolution' through an act of self-foundation and self-creation"; in doing so, they created a new genre in which figures with ideologies far removed from communism would participate (*Poetry* 2). Puchner traces the translation and dissemination of this document as it became—to use the term *Communist Manifesto* itself employs—a work of "world literature." Thus, a text that would seem to be on the border of modernism has now become central, which allows us not only to read Mina Loy's "Feminist Manifesto" (1914), Benedetto Croce's "Manifesto of the Anti-Fascist Intellectuals" (1925), and Oswald de Andrade's "Cannibal Manifesto" (1928), but also to better map the processes by which texts from *Ulysses* to *Things Fall Apart* (1958) became works of "world literature." Scholars like Mary Ann Caws have recovered and republished hundreds of manifestos, and they are now featured regularly in anthologies of modernist texts as both declarations and texts that belong in a history of sociopolitical *poiesis*. For Janet Lyon, this history extends from the pamphlet wars of seventeenth-century England to the statements of contemporary minority performance groups, while for Laura Winkiel, the crucial articulations of race in transnational and postcolonial contexts in the twentieth century came in manifestos that pitched themselves formally and aesthetically against proclamations issued from the metropole. These documents, in effect, offer one particularly striking example of the ways in which war and violence permeate a radically expanded modernism—one that no longer rotates only around the First War World or reaches an abrupt end with the Second.

# Modernism, science, and technology

As we have seen throughout this book, the term "modernism" has most commonly been used to describe the profound changes that touched nearly every aspect of art and culture in the first half of the twentieth century. These changes, however, were both enabled and accompanied by equally transformative work in science and engineering that altered the human perception of the physical world. Rather than marking off modernism as a period that runs from the turn of the twentieth century to the start of the Second World War, we could instead trace a roughly contemporaneous arc that begins with Albert Einstein's publication of the equation $E = mc^2$ in 1905 and ends with the detonation of the world's first nuclear weapon at the White Sands Proving Ground in 1945. Other such technological arcs might run from the first projected film shown by the Lumière brothers in 1895 to the standardization of broadcast television in 1941, or from Lord Kelvin's invention of the first analog computer in 1872 to Alan Turing's conception of the first modern computer in 1936. In this same period, the germ theory of medicine came into wide acceptance; Marie Curie revealed a hidden world of radioactive waves; Werner Heisenberg postulated his theory of uncertainty, which claimed that the outcome of some experiments depended on our observation of them; Ernest Rutherford postulated a groundbreaking new theory of atomic structure; the Wright brothers launched one of the first airplanes while Henry Ford popularized the automobile; new fields like psychology, psychoanalysis, and sociology set out to fashion a new field of human science; and Edwin Hubble explained the awe-inspiring scope of an extragalactic universe that was still expanding. The artists and writers of the period were well aware of these groungbreaking changes. In *The Waste Land*, for example, Eliot captures the sound of a skipping record in the phrase "that Shakespeherian Rag," and he wrote of Stravinsky's music that "it did seem to transform the rhythm of the steppes into the scream of the motor horn, the rattle of machinery, the grind of wheels, the beating of iron and steel, the roar of the underground railway, and the other barbaric cries of modern life; and to transform these despairing noises into music" ("London" 453). Margaret Heap, one of the coeditors of the *Little Review*, organized the Machine-Age Exhibition in 1927, which displayed objects like propellers, ball bearings, and industrial springs as works of modern art. And magazines like the *New Age* and the *Egoist* often devoted more space to new theories of science and society than they did to art and poetry.

Despite this interchange between science and aesthetics in the first half of the twentieth century, however, critics of modernism rarely considered the two in relation to each other—despite the fact that many artists and writers proposed theories of aesthetics in overtly scientific terms. A handful of thinkers like Marshall McLuhan, his student Hugh Kenner, Rosalind Krauss, and Jonathan Crary attempted to draw out some potential connections, but the dominant sense of high modernism as an isolated, autonomous, and purely aesthetic occupation imposed another kind of divide between art and science. Initially, work on modernism, science, and technology centered on film history, as we've already seen in the section on modernism and mass media. This contributed, in part, to new studies of the way discoveries about the physiology of perception underwrote particular avant-garde techniques. Crary's *Techniques of the Observer* (1990), for example, though not explicitly about modernism, contends that the revolution in vision associated with the camera actually resulted from new kinds of knowledge about the anatomy of perception. His still controversial argument shifts attention away from technological determinism and toward the objectification of the human body and its processes. This joined a number of similar studies about how the human became an object of both objective study and technological instrumentalization in the nineteenth and twentieth centuries. These include Anson Rabinbach's *The Human Motor* (1990), Wolfgang Schivelbusch's *The Railway Journey* (1986), and Stephen Kern's *The Culture of Time and Space, 1880-1918* (1983). More recently, the widely influential work of Friedrich Kittler pointed less to cultural studies and more toward nuanced histories of innovation that assign a kind of agency to technological objects themselves. His *Gramophone, Film, Typewriter* (1986; English 1999), for example, argues that these three devices "exploded Gutenberg's writing monopoly" and thereby relocated the human "essence . . . into apparatuses" (16). This simultaneous mechanization of perception and fragmentation of information into different substrates then becomes a way of understanding the radical aesthetic experiments associated with a much-expanded modernism.

Some of the most compelling work on modernism and science remains lodged at this interface between the instrumentalization of the human body and the attempts to represent the fundamentally new experiences made possible by technology. Enda Duffy's *The Speed Handbook: Velocity, Pleasure, Modernism* (2009), for instance, argues that key aspects of modernism were formed around what he calls "adrenaline aesthetics" (9). Linking the new experience of speed made possible by the automobile, the airplane, and the rollercoaster to biomedical discoveries about the endocrine system, Duffy argues that speed was "the only new pleasure of modernity" and that the experiences it produced became synonymous with modernism (11). This way of understanding aesthetic innovation as an attempt to both mediate and modulate new technologies is an important part of the New Modernist Studies. Tim Armstrong's foundational study, *Modernism, Technology, and the Body* (1998) explores the ways in which writers like Henry James, Nathaniel West, and Djuna Barnes all reconfigured the body, in an era when it was being increasingly policed by governmental regimes and opened to modification and even innovation. The horrors of the First World War, in particular, led to a new science of prosthetics that seemed to reduce the body to functional pieces that could be replaced, modified, and sometimes even improved by mechanical devices.

Prostheses then became part of the design movements of postwar European avant-gardes, and radical contortions of the human body and its forms—even turning bodies into "machines"—were at the heart of revolutions in modern performance arts. Other critics look not at the effects of technology of aesthetic production, but at the new theories about matter and time that seemed to erase the stable boundaries and structures of the physical world. Daniel Albright's *Quantum Poetics* (1997) thus demonstrates the ways in which these poets used new ideas about the atom and the nature of matter to theorize new kinds of symbolism and units of poetic force. Treating many of the same figures, Michael Golston in *Rhythm and Race in Modernist Poetry and Science* (2008) argues that physiological studies of rhythm contributed to key innovations in modernist twentieth-century prosody.

Alongside these studies of mainstream science and canonical modernism, however, there has also developed a new interest in spiritualism and magic. In the early twentieth century, the boundary between these two fields of endeavor was by no means clear. Thus, Conan Doyle, whose Sherlock Holmes is a master of objective observation, regularly attended séances and devoted a significant portion of his career to documenting the existence of fairies. In a cultural moment characterized by the discovery of otherwise invisible forces and rays, this uncertain boundary surrounding scientific knowledge should not be surprising. Indeed, many writers and artists saw themselves as explorers who were crafting in their work new ways of representing the world. The hazy vision images of Impressionist painting, the fragmented patterns of stream-of-consciousness writing, and the clashing montages of avant-garde poetry and film all seemed to align with a cacophonous new zeitgeist to which artists might attune themselves. Studies like Helen Sword's *Ghostwriting Modernism* (2002) and Alex Owen's *The Darkened Room: Women, Power, and Spiritualism in Late Victorian England* (1990) have mapped the ways in which spiritualism and modernism intersected with one another, noting the important role women were able to play as mediums who attained power through their ability to connect different worlds. And now, critics are beginning to turn their attention to the long-ignored connection between modernism and magic. Yeats famously joined the Hermetic Order of the Golden Dawn and drew on its beliefs about the mystical power of words to fashion his own theory of poetic symbolism. Other writers and artists in the period also helped develop new, and often still controversial, religions and spiritual practices, including Aleister Crowley and L. Ron Hubbard. Recent studies like Mark Morrisson's *Modern Alchemy* (2007) and Leigh Wilson's *Modernism and Magic* (2013) both are leading innovative new forays into this rich nexus between science, spiritualism, and art.

Alongside the attention to the borderline sciences has come a renewed interest in the pseudoscience of eugenics and its predecessors and offshoots, such as social Darwinism and phrenology. Versions of eugenics enjoyed support from figures as diverse as H. G. Wells, G. B. Shaw, J. M. Keynes, Margaret Sanger, Theodore Roosevelt, and W. E. B. Du Bois. Sterilization and population control programs reached far beyond the infamous campaigns in Germany and Anglo-America, to Japan, Brazil, the USSR, Switzerland, and elsewhere. Before eugenics was largely discredited, three international conferences on the idea were held between 1912 and 1932 (one in London, two in New York), each drawing respected figures from around the world. This movement's obsession with categories like race, inheritance, and purification often aligned in hazardous ways with racist, imperialist, classist, and misogynist ideologies. The tragic mulatto/a, for example, became an especially anxious figure in Nella Larsen's fiction because of the pervasive and frightening new discourses—supported by "science" and governments—about maternity and miscegenation in the early twentieth century. By contrast, Du Bois's plans for racial uplift held that African Americans, who had been "unbred" by slavery, must prepare for the "modern world" by "train[ing] and breed[ing] for brains, for efficiency, for beauty" ("Opinion" 152, 153). Looking to the rhetoric shared by eugenicists and modernists, scholars have also found clear points of exchange between the two, especially around high modernist metaphors used to describe rebirth, purification, and renewal in the arts. Likewise, the apocalyptic tones of some famous modernist works—Eliot's poems of the early 1920s, for instance, have been singled out—are indebted not only to the horrors of the First World War, but also to anxieties about the "breeding" of the future human race. At the intersection of pressing and volatile issues concerning race, bodies, technologies, social theory, politics, and representation, eugenics darkly gathers a host of contemporary approaches to the cultures of modernism.

# Modernism and environments

Many of the earliest critics and scholars of modernism declared it a quintessential aesthetic product of the industrial metropolis, where one could find the full range of the experience of modernity. As we saw, Raymond Williams attributed the movement's development of an "international language" to the conglomeration of immigrants, especially in the late nineteenth century, from far-flung sites that the metropolis tethered, while Fredric Jameson saw the fragmentation of mental life in the city as conditioned by the "unknowability" of the imperial periphery. The metropolis produced both high and low modernisms, ranging from Baudelaire's essays and poems about the flâneur to Benjamin's attempt to imagine an archaeology of nineteenth-century Paris in *The Arcades Project*. In Leopold Bloom's passage through Dublin or Clarissa Dalloway's shopping trip, the everyday fragments of modern urban life are given new symbolic, sometimes even mythic correspondences. The contrasting portraits of a single city in Döblin's *Berlin Alexanderplatz* (1929), Ruttmann's film *Berlin: Symphony of a Metropolis* (1927), Dos Passos's *Manhattan Transfer* (1925), and Dostoevsky's *Notes from Underground* (1864) suggest the ways by which the modern metropolis itself can become a protagonist—one often more vital and alive than the humans it presumably enfolds. The transformations of the categories of interior and exterior in the metropolis inspired sociological analysis from Georg Simmel, philosophical examination from Georges Sorel, and psychoanalytic research from Sigmund Freud. New cities came to prominence: New York was the first new metropolis in the twentieth century, while Los Angeles went from an outpost of the American West to a center of cultural production with the rise and dominance of Hollywood cinema. And new, often futuristic or utopian, cities also appeared across all media, ranging from Lang's Metropolis to H. G. Wells's Everytown in the proto-science fiction film *Things to Come* (1936).

In modernist depictions of cities we can see a compression of time-space that also became one of the movement's most studied formal legacies. Indeed, many twentieth-century artists came from peripheries to metropolises, especially to Paris: the French capital attracted Joyce from the colonial outpost of Dublin, Tzara from Bucharest via Moldavia, the Lost Generation from scattered parts of the United States, and black figures including Hughes, McKay, and the *Négritude* movement writers from the Americas and Africa. Conrad and Apollinaire emigrated from Poland to London and Paris, respectively; Ibsen from Norway to Italy and Germany; and C. L. R. James and other West Indian intellectuals also made London home. In modernism's famed urban sites, the divisions of high and low culture, private and public life, wealth and deprivation, machine age and organic life blurred. Crime, harems, brothels, cabarets, and opium dens could be found blocks away from museums and academies as the metropolis became an emblem of a headlong rush into the future. The city produced crowds and thus the anonymous "man of the crowd," life above and underground (Pound's "In a Station of the Metro" captures the latter), congregations of minority groups, and a mass consumer culture that created the debris and detritus recycled into art by Cubists and Dadaists. The metropolis, in short, gathers almost every topic vital to modernist studies, and as with the topic of war, this vitality has rarely been questioned— most every European and American metropolis has been treated as an engine of modernism.

Thanks, in part, to the rapidly developing field of eco-criticism and its increasingly complex theorization of "environments," scholars have developed new ways of thinking about the way *space* itself was more broadly produced in the early twentieth century. The inspiration for some of this work in modernism's literary geographies, such as Andrew Thacker's *Moving Through Modernity: Space and Geography in Modernism* (2003), comes from French thinker Henri Lefebvre, especially in his seminal publication *The Production of Space* (1974). Lefebvre argued that in the history of social articulations of spaces, "the fact is that around 1910 a certain space was shattered. It was the space of common sense, of knowledge (*savoir*), of social practice, of political power, a space thitherto enshrined in everyday discourse, just as in abstract thought, as the environment of and the channel for communications" (25). Lefebvre's timing aligns with Woolf's claim that "on or about December 1910 human character changed," and it points to a reorientation in space that was continually revised throughout the era. This reorientation affected everything from large-scale spaces such as skyscrapers to interior spaces designed with new furniture and decorations suited for "modern life." The implications of Lefebvre's work, along with that of Gaston Bachelard on the "poetics of space," Michel de Certeau on the "practices of everyday life," and David Harvey on the means by which capitalism structures the physical spaces of modern life, are apparent in much new work in the New Modernist Studies. William Sharpe's *New York Nocturne* (2008), for example, examines the ways in which the new urban architecture created a vital new kind of night life, while Victoria Rosner's *Modernism and the Architecture of Private Life* (2005) contends that home design itself was the source of innovative aesthetic and social practices.

Even as old spaces like the city and home underwent modernizing changes, entirely new and harrowing ones such as "no man's land" and the "concentration camp" came into existence. Meanwhile, stateless peoples and lands without a definitive government or state apparatus became increasingly common amid the seismic shifts of war and the constant redrawing of political boundaries. These include occupations and changes in government, from the leasing of Guantánamo in 1903 to the partitioning of British Palestine over several decades. Colonial expositions and national demonstration-projects attempted to recreate other spaces, as in the Poble Espanyol in Barcelona or the attempted Nazification of Łódź in Poland. Elsewhere, many modernists were involved in acts of spatial reinvention such as urban planning, public works projects, and cartography. Michael Rubenstein, in fact, argues in *Public Works: Infrastructure, Irish Modernism, and the Postcolonial* (2010) that the sewer is as essential to the invention of modern urban space and to the modernist aesthetic as is the skyscraper or the cinema. Even the notion of "nature" was transformed by writers who held that the Romantics did not have a singular claim to its power or its significance. Rather, modernists, as Bonnie Kime Scott argues, took "an abiding interest in nature, human interdependencies with it, and even in its preservation: think of the odor of lilies in Marcel Proust's *A la recherche* . . .; the walk on the beach in T. S. Eliot's 'Prufock'," and much more ("Green" 219). Here we can think, too, of Tahiti for Gauguin or Mexico for D. H. Lawrence, the Hebrides of Woolf's *To the Lighthouse* or Conrad's invented Costaguana in *Nostromo*, and the urban-rural blends in Brecht's theater or the settings of Manet's *Déjeuner sur l'herbe* and Monet's haystacks.

The emphasis on modernist spaces and the environments that writers inhabited furthermore included those of the burgeoning anthropological movement seen in Bronisław Malinowski and in Lucien Lévy-Bruhl, in Victor Segalen in Polynesia, or Zora Neale Hurston in the Everglades. This era was one in which the National

Park Service was created in 1916, in which public parks became increasingly common space, and in which the Works Progress Administration and New Towns Act made new cities in the United States and the United Kingdom from nothing. "Regional modernism" has emerged as a term for characterizing the movements that came from sites such as New Mexico, the British Midlands, or Kolkata; their ambivalent embraces and eschewals of the universalizing tendencies of much metropolitan modernism have opened new lines of inquiry into the nature of modernism itself. If we look beyond the London-Paris-Berlin-New York nexus, and beyond the Euro-American core, we see more uneven "development" that necessitates new modes of inquiry. For one, many other cities were destroyed or left in ruins, as Eliot imagines in *The Waste Land* ("Falling towers/Jerusalem Athens Alexandria/Vienna London"), in the wake of falling imperial dynasties and aristocratic orders and the redrawing of maps after the First World War. There were devastated spaces: the waste lands of the First World War and, later, Nanking, Japan, or Abyssinia; the falling estate of the Compsons in Faulkner's Yoknapatawpha County in Mississippi; the decline of Madrid, center of a former empire barely clinging to life around 1900; or Vienna, destroyed and rebuilt after the Second World War. On the other hand, Mexico City was at the center of a revolution in 1910 that captured the world's attention and became intellectually modernized alongside an influx of foreigners and exiles too; Prague was Kafka's muse, while New Orleans gave birth to jazz; old and new clashed in Moscow and in Beijing, in Delhi and in Cairo. These are topics that many scholars of global modernisms have taken up at length.

Finally, we could also think of the importance of the spaces in which modernist works were created: Proust in his cork-lined room; Eliot's writing *The Waste Land* while on a rest cure at Lausanne; Gramsci in his prison cell; Hurston's composition of *Their Eyes Were Watching God* while conducting anthropological fieldwork in the West Indies; Paul Celan's writing from a Nazi internment camp; Pound's beginning the *Pisan Cantos* on toilet paper while held in a detention cage in Italy, and his later *Cantos* from St. Elizabeth's asylum. Taking as a whole what these sections have outlined, we can see the stereotypical Harlem cabaret of the 1920s as a site where nearly every phenomenon examined by the New Modernist Studies intersected: race relations, high and low culture, patronage and commerce, music and nonliterary media, diasporic expression, "deviant" sexualities and gender identities, illegal activities (during Prohibition), and the technologies of modern life.

This tumultuous change in the experience and representation of the lived environment was shaped in profound ways by the work of architects and engineers who developed new materials and new designs for an era of machine-driven industrial modernity. The Crystal Palace in London and the Eiffel Tower in Paris rejected traditional decorative motifs and boasted of their prefabricated elements, their iron, steel, and glass composition. New kinds of steel and concrete, the invention of the elevator, the domestic use of electricity, and steam-driven ventilation led to the first skyscrapers like the Home Insurance Building in Chicago (1884) and the American Surety Building in New York (1895). The Russian Constructivist Vladimir Tatlin's planned Monument to the Third International (1919), a twinned helix made of these same materials, was to extend 400 meters high in order to stand as an unabashed symbol of modernity's triumph over traditional style. The signature Bauhaus-designed products combined form and function in buildings and chairs, homes and pottery alike. The European architects Le Corbusier (who called houses "machines for living") and Ludwig Mies van der Rohe attempted to adapt man-made structures, with clarity, simplicity, and harmony, to the bewildering environments and needs of contemporary life. Meanwhile, Frank Lloyd Wright sought to develop an identifiable "American" form of building and design that first embodied his idea of the nuclear family then moved to harmonize interior and exterior spaces, as in the Falling Water house, which sits over a waterfall, and the Johnson and Johnson building, which appears to open up to a cloud-filled sky. Such work coincided, of course, with the rapid expansion of structures as factories and warehouses, which reshaped urban and rural landscapes globally.

One of the most complicated issues in conceiving of "modernism," in fact, inheres in the history, and especially in the historiography, of architecture. In 1932, Alfred Barr held an exhibition at MoMA called "Modern Architecture—International Exhibition," in which the curators, Henry-Russell Hitchcock and Phillip Johnson defined the "International Style." Using examples from Le Corbusier, Bauhaus, Erich Mendelsohn, Mies van der Rohe, and many others, Hitchcock and Johnson validated modern experiments with clean, sharp lines and rectilinear forms, a rejection of ornament and symmetry, and open interior spaces that had characterized avant-garde architecture through the 1920s. Thus we see that a parallel conversation on "modernism" took place, even within the space of MoMA under Barr's direction in the mid-1930s when he also drew his famous diagram (Figure X). This style persisted, and yet was greatly revised, as it became more dominant in a still vaguely defined period called "Midcentury modernism," which runs roughly from 1945 to the mid-1970s. Here, modernism not only became popular—for the masses— but also, far from being oppositional, was employed in urban planning for postwar sprawl. Loosely congruent but nevertheless distinct from its place in painting, literature, and film, the concept of "modernism" in architecture, then, stretches at least from the 1920s until the 1970s. In the early seventies, those planned urban modernist projects were often torn down and new kinds of oppositional movements (now typically called postmodern) began to take their place. Robert Venturi's landmark treatise *Learning from Las Vegas: The Forgotten Symbolism of Architectural Form* (1972; revised 1977), for example, embraced the gaudy, ornamental, allegedly meretricious styles of popular culture against what it deemed a heroic, self-glorifying aesthetic promulgated by modernist architecture. Here again we are reminded that, as with the impact of postcolonial modernisms and Cold War modernisms, 1945 is an increasingly difficult cut-off point to maintain for modernism, and different fields bring about different temporalities. Only recently in the largely literary field of modernist studies have scholars such as David Spurr in *Architecture and Modern Literature* (2012), Jennifer Scappettone in *Killing the Moonlight: Modernism in Venice* (2014), and Jed Rasula and Tim Conley in the collection *Burning City: Poems of Metropolitan Modernity* (2012) taken more seriously the consequences of bringing together these disparate forms of modernism.

# Conclusion

This book began with the question "what is modernism?" And we arrive now at a desultory, if nevertheless provocative, answer: "We don't know." The term has a long, complex history that we have attempted to trace by looking at its multivalent origins, its initial consolidation, its gradual expansion, and its current fragmentation across numerous different fields of cultural and aesthetic inquiry. It has served as a call to arms and a way of organizing movements, discerning innovative practices, and driving innovative representations of the modern world. But it also carved up the complexity of modern culture in order to insulate an elite group of practitioners from the larger public while often silencing the voices of artists marginalized by gender, race, sexuality, and geography. Along the way it has also helped fashion and reform canons of taste and memory enshrined in literary anthologies, art museums, and college classrooms. It has become an institutionalized profession, self-regulating and fitted somewhat uncomfortably between the nineteenth-century and the always-moving present. Its manifest success as a concept plainly owes something to its unusual malleability. Cut free from precise historical or geographical markers, it has been able to morph constantly into new forms, contracting into a tightly defined historical period at times and expanding deep into the past and present at others. Modernism, it seems, is everywhere, but nevertheless always wriggling away from any attempt to pin it down and fix it in the amber of periodization or professionalization.

This book is meant merely to offer a kind of starting place for those curious about what modernism has meant and how the term has changed across the decades. As we've seen, it has served at times as a rigid cable that has managed to link a set of particularly powerful practices and ideas to a much larger set of ever-unfolding debates about the nature of human expression. Thus can the term "modernism" still name a set of uniquely innovative works in literature, film, art, drama, and architecture that have broken with the canons of classicism and realism to remake a fundamentally new world. At other times, modernism can instead act as a powerful magnet, capable of pulling together seemingly disparate works of cultural expression drawn from different genres, eras, media, and geographies. These fields of force allow us to see modernism nearly everywhere and to understand it as part of a massive attempt to make sense of a restless, voracious, and ever-expanding modernity.

There is, finally, no right way to define modernism, just as there is finally no right way to carve up the rich multiplicity of human expression. The nine other books that follow in this series all offer different ways of exploring this dynamic concept, weaving it into often sprawling networks that range across fields like architecture, science, technology, and feminism. Far from definitive statements, they offer an array of critical strategies for thinking about cultural responses to modernity in the twentieth century. They are, in short, invitations to our ongoing examination of what it means to be modern. There will inevitably be some points of convergence as well as moments of dissonance and disagreement among them. Individually, they offer accessible accounts of the ways in which modernism has mutated across different fields of intellectual inquiry while offering a powerful way of thinking about major cultural and social formations including gender, race, media, nation, science, and the law. Taken as a whole, they reveal the richness of modernism as a concept and its ongoing importance to nearly every aspect of a now global modernity.

# Notes

1   A precursor to this conference called "Modernism/Modernity" was organized by Robert Scholes at Brown University in 1997. It drew several hundred participants and featured talks by many of the editorial board members of the new journal.

2   Almost from the start, the MSA discouraged applications for papers and panels at its annual conference that focused on single authors—and particularly on canonical figures like Joyce, Pound, and Woolf. Until the formation of organizations like BAMS (the British Association of Modernist Studies) and EAM (the European Network for Avant-Garde and Modernism Studies), the MSA also imagined itself as a global organization that would encompass modernist studies across national and continental boundaries.

3   Although *Modernism/modernity* is now affiliated with the MSA, the two organizations have had a fraught relationship. The journal is run by three editors, one of whom is appointed to a limited term by the organization. For a time, each editor maintained an independent office, which contributed to a lack of coherent policy that, in turn, made the journal's offerings so diverse.

4   More recently, *Affirmations: of the Modern*, the official journal of the Australian Modernist Studies Network, was founded digitally in 2013.

5 The first Norton edition of *Cane*, edited by Darwin Turner, was 246 pages in length and included 80 pages of commentary; Byrd and Gates's edition is 472 pages and contains over 300 pages of letters, archival resources, biography, and commentary.

6 These changes are not only contextual but also structural: when Faulkner later republished the story, he shifted various sections to place a new emphasis on the epistemological uncertainty surrounding the un-narrated event that led to the lynching.

7 The stories are each numbered independently, making it impossible to tell which one actually begins the book. Thus, each page has two numbers depending on the direction in which the reader is moving.

8 In banning such work, the Nazis accidentally ended up producing one of the most famous modernist art displays of the era: the *Entartete Kunst* (degenerate art) exhibition of 1937, derived from the over 5,000 items a special commission had seized from galleries, museums, and private collections throughout Germany.

# GLOSSARY

**Abstract Expressionism:** a movement in the visual arts roughly from the 1940s through the early 1960s, most closely identified with the work of Jackson Pollock, Willem de Kooning, and Franz Kline. Its artists often used large canvases, abstract shapes, spontaneous or improvised techniques, and vivid, dynamic color combinations captured most famously in Pollock's dripping of paint ("Action Painting," as it was known). Abstract Expressionism figures significantly in the critical history of modernism for several reasons: it was championed by Clement Greenberg and Harold Rosenberg, who read it as an extension of modernism beyond the Second World War, when many literary critics had declared modernism "over." Furthermore, it was the first distinctly American artistic movement to influence Europe and beyond, and its influence coincided with the rise of US global power during the Cold War. This connection has prompted many scholars to investigate the ways by which it was promoted in the American state's anti-Soviet cultural diplomatic efforts as an emblem of creativity and freedom in the United States—despite the fact that Abstract Expressionists themselves mostly critiqued American culture, from which they felt a rebellious alienation.

**Aestheticism (art for art's sake, *l'art pour l'art*):** a movement, and a name used as an umbrella term for various other movements, that originated primarily in France and England in the late nineteenth century. Reacting against moralism, utilitarianism, and Realism in the arts, Aestheticists argued for the autonomy of art from legal as well as academic structures and for the development of a specific set of criteria—derived entirely from the media and language of art itself—for evaluating art-objects, whether novels or paintings. Its key figures, such as Walter Pater, Oscar Wilde, and Algernon Charles Swinburne, often praised ornate, decorative works that highlighted their own artifice, as opposed to organic or natural forms, and they advocated hedonistic, pleasure-filled lifestyles. The movement's origins are debated; the French readings of Edgar Allan Poe's arguments for aesthetic autonomy are vital, Arthur Rimbaud's and Charles Baudelaire's lives and works were inspirations, and Théophile Gautier is credited with the slogan *l'art pour l'art*. At the same time, Aestheticism's exchanges with the Decadent movement were critical too. The legacy of Aestheticism in modernist works is vast, perhaps most notable in the work of the Bloomsbury Group; even those who rejected it as a movement, such as T. E. Hulme, clearly drew on its precepts.

**Alienation:** generally, a sense or condition of non-belonging from society and culture at large, which became a prominent theme in modernist works at least since the Industrial Revolution. In Marxist criticism, the term refers more specifically to the estrangement of social relations because of class and because modern modes of capitalist production separate people from their works, and in the end, from their abilities to control their destinies. Alienated figures in modernist literature range from Charles Baudelaire's flâneur to Zora Neale Hurston's ostracized Janie Crawford.

**Autonomy:** in aesthetics, the idea that art functions according to its own rules, which are determined by the form, nature, and medium of the art-object alone. Art must therefore be judged and criticized according to properties inherent to art, rather than those drawn from the spheres of morality, politics, economics, or utility. A central concept in debates over the nature of modernism, modern autonomy theory is often said to originate in the work of Immanuel Kant, who emphasized a disinterested approach to aesthetic theory grounded in a belief that true art separated itself, by way of its form, from other cultural productions; for this reason, Clement Greenberg claimed that Kant was the first modernist. The autonomy of art was asserted by a number of modernists, and also attacked by avant-garde groups such as Dada.

**Avant-garde:** a concept originating in military terminology, meaning "advance-guard," that has been used to denote experimental, oppositional, and iconoclastic (often controversial) aesthetics. The relationship between modernism and the avant-garde has been fiercely debated by critics like Renato Poggioli, Peter Bürger, and Matei Călinescu. In modernist studies, the avant-garde is most often associated with Dada, Surrealism, and interwar experimentalism. Bürger, for instance, claimed that these groups sought to launch an assault on the notion of "art" itself, whereas modernists sought only to change art. Some consider postmodernism a neo-avant-garde that responded to the institutionalization and cultural absorption of modernism.

**Bauhaus:** a school of architecture and design founded by Walter Gropius in Germany in 1919, and a strong influence on modernist and postmodernist aesthetics even after its closure by the Nazi regime in 1933. Bauhaus artists sought to integrate "high" art and its formal elements with the design of objects for everyday life, bringing form and function together and training artists for a range of creative, practical applications. Rejecting both ornate, decorative aesthetics and uniform, mass-produced patterns, Bauhaus sought a middle ground, known as International Style, that would create harmony between design and use.

**Black Arts movement:** an influential movement, originating in the mid-1960s and closely linked to the civil rights and Black Power movements, that emphasized the distinctly African American character of its texts. Founded by LeRoi Jones (Amiri Baraka) and including Nikki Giovanni and Maya Angelou, the Black Arts movement ranged in its productions from radical, sometimes violent messages to less politically charged projects that recovered suppressed African American aesthetic traditions. Black Arts figures generally rejected black modernism (most notably, the New Negro Renaissance) for its alleged capitulation to the demands of white reading publics and wealthy white patrons. But as the arguments of Black Arts thinkers helped establish African American Studies departments in universities in the following decades, they indirectly led to the revaluation of black modernism in the 1980s. Scholars since then have found both continuities and divergences between a wide range of early twentieth-century modernisms and Black Arts productions, especially in theater.

**Bloomsbury Group:** a coterie based at Virginia and Leonard Woolf's home in London whose aesthetic experiments, social thought, and sexual politics were fundamental to the development of English modernism. The group included the Woolfs, E. M. Forster, Lytton Strachey, Vanessa and Clive Bell, Roger Fry, and J. M. Keynes. Their work was wide-ranging, from novels to visual art, economic tracts to translations of Freud. They were united by a belief in the autonomy of art, and they advocated for a variety of antifascist, pacifist, feminist, and humanitarian causes. In the history of modernist studies, Bloomsbury has been both celebrated for its innovations and, on several occasions, condemned or discounted, most notably by Hugh Kenner and Raymond Williams, both of whom saw them as a disaffected, provincial, bourgeois minority. In recent decades, scholars have turned their attention to marginal Bloomsbury figures; to the Woolfs' Hogarth Press, which published T. S. Eliot's *The Waste Land* alongside Virginia Woolf's own novels and a host of political education pamphlets; and to the Dreadnought Hoax, a stunt of political critique engineered by Bloomsbury members with Horace de Vere Cole in 1910 in which they dressed in blackface and successfully passed with the Royal Navy as a delegation of Abyssinian royalty.

**Bourgeoisie:** in Marxist criticism, a concept that refers to the class that owns the means of production and seeks to accumulate capital and property. Modernism's relationship to this class has been a topic of debate for decades: some have seen modernism as an elitist assault on bourgeois values, habits of consumption, and readerly/viewing expectations, while others have argued for a complicated relationship in which modernism moves across the class spectrum. Likewise, Marxist critics have long debated whether modernist works—sometimes seen as representing the alienated bourgeoisie—seek to liberate bourgeois individuals from their "false consciousness" or simply to condemn their worldview and replace it with another one.

**Commodification:** a concept in Marxist criticism that denotes the process of converting ideas, aesthetics, objects, and even parts of the natural world into goods that can be assigned value then bought and sold. The modernist era saw the commodification of everything from intellectual property to historical cultural artifacts, alongside works of art, sculptures, and books, often as part of the pervasive culture of mass consumption in the wake of the Industrial Revolution. Modernists responded to this in a variety of ways; the doctrine of aesthetic autonomy was asserted and revised by some to remove art and literature from the marketplace, while others engaged fully in efforts to give a price and exchange value to their works (and some figures did both). Certain postmodernists critiqued modernism for its hostility to commodification and instead engaged directly with the marketplace, as with Andy Warhol's Campbell's soup cans.

**Constructivism:** a movement largely in visual art and architecture that originated in Russia in the wake of the Russian Revolution (1917). The Constructivists included Vladimir Tatlin, Alexander Rodchenko, Kurt Schwitters, and many others, and they sought to replace the autonomy of the art-object with its social utility—specifically, in service of the revolution. Their works in the 1920s, which ranged from propaganda posters to modern buildings, strongly influenced the efforts to combine form and function seen in a wide range of twentieth-century movements, perhaps most visibly in the Bauhaus school. Constructivist art is characterized by simple, clean lines and shapes, often assembled with an analytic, utopian purpose.

**Critical theory:** see Frankfurt School

**Cubism:** an avant-garde movement in painting, led by Pablo Picasso and Georges Braque, that dramatically influenced the course of twentieth-century aesthetics. Noted for its use of jagged, fragmented, and reassembled collisions of multiple perspectives within a single plane, Cubism employed geometric forms and hard angles to move further away from Realism and

Naturalism in painting. Its most famous, and arguably first, example is Picasso's *Les Demoiselles d'Avignon* (1907), and the movement underwent many revisions and shifts over the following years. Its presence was felt in literature in the works of Gertrude Stein and Ernest Hemingway, in the architecture of Le Corbusier, and in poetry ranging from Guillaume Apollinaire to Wallace Stevens.

**Dada:** an international avant-garde arts movement, roughly from 1915–24, that emphasized irrationality, anti-aesthetics, and often radical leftist politics. Its key figures included Tristan Tzara, Hugo Ball, and Marcel Duchamp. United by their response to the horrors of the First World War, Dadaists presented a signal assault on the autonomy of art and coordinated demonstrations that sought to shock the public conscience. As the most influential of the avant-gardes of the early twentieth century, Dada has figured in a number of discussions of modernism, particularly the latter's relationship to revolutionary aesthetics, as studied by Peter Bürger and by scholars of postmodernism. Others have suggested that Dada's avant-garde practices and modernism's experimentalism exist in a continuum defined by the consumption, rather than the production, of art-objects.

**Decolonization:** a term used to describe the overthrow of colonial regimes, most often those of the post-1500 European empires. Decolonization movements arguably began with the United States's War of Independence (1776–83), spread across the Americas in the 1800s, and then became a global force following the breakup of several empires in the First World War and the dismantling of others after the Second. The relationship between modernism and decolonization is especially complex: anticolonialism fueled early modernist works such as Joseph Conrad's novels, Irish modernist works from those of W. B. Yeats to James Joyce, and modernism in late colonial India (as in Rabindranath Tagore's poetry), the Caribbean (José Martí, Kamau Brathwaite, Derek Walcott), and across Africa (Tayeb Salih, Ngũgĩ wa Thiongo, Léopold Sédar Senghor). In all of these cases, this relationship is made more complex because of the uneven incorporation and rejection of European modernist aesthetics in these and other writers' and artists' works. The temporal and conceptual boundaries of modernism have been questioned in many ways by scholars of anticolonial and postcolonial modernisms.

*Écriture féminine* ("feminine writing"): a concept developed in French feminist literary theory in the 1970s to denote a style of writing that incorporates, accounts for, or attends to the female body as a unique source of creativity. The term was coined by Hélène Cixous, who reinterpreted the theories of Sigmund Freud, Jacques Lacan, and Jacques Derrida to point to the ways in which the structure of language itself encoded—and reinforced—femininity as a lack, with respect to masculinity. *Écriture féminine* does not mean writing by women; indeed, Molly Bloom's monologue in James Joyce's *Ulysses* (1922) was read as a key example. It often refers to nonlinear work that subverts rationality and teleology. Alongside the broader work of Cixous, Julia Kristeva, Monique Wittig, and Luce Irigaray, *écriture féminine* was a central concept in the theorization and articulation of feminist modernism across the 1980s and early 1990s.

**Edisonian era:** a term used to describe the conditions of modern life in the wake of the technologies and inventions most closely identified with Thomas Edison. Edison's light bulbs, phonographs, and motion picture cameras, along with his improvements to the telephone, telegraph, and energy-production technologies, not only revolutionized daily life, but also gave rise to new industries that became major sources of modernist cultural productions, from movie studios to the music recording industry. The history of these technologies in modernist works is profound; early critics of modernism often pointed to this fact, while schools such as the New Critics considered cinema, for instance, a nonaesthetic field identified with mass culture, wholly separate from the autonomous literary works of the modernists. The recovery and treatment of modernist cinematic, sound, and technological cultural productions has been a significant project in modernist studies, at least since the 1980s.

**Enlightenment:** a broad international movement beginning in the late eighteenth century, in which intellectuals, political figures, artists, and many others argued for the superiority of human reason over tradition and divine authority. For this reason, and because it was linked both to political and to aesthetic revolutions, the Enlightenment has been identified by some critics as the origin of "modernity" and therefore a starting point for modernism. Others—most famously Theodor Adorno—critiqued the Enlightenment not as the liberation of humanity, but as the beginning of a new hyper-rationalized form of domination and deception, with its pervasively dehumanizing effects ultimately finding horrifying expression in the Holocaust.

***Entartete Kunst* ("Degenerate Art"):** a German term used extensively by the Nazi regime to characterize most aesthetic movements now recognized as "modernist." The Nazi government, which banned such art, produced an exhibition entitled *Entartete Kunst* in Munich in 1937. Modernist art, including works by Marc Chagall, was hung haphazardly on the walls, with denigrating descriptions of each piece below, in an effort to convince the public that it was created by psychopaths and criminals, and that it represented a Jewish, Bolshevist conspiracy against the German people. The show, and the Nazi repression of modernism and confiscation of modernist works, was taken by many critics at the time to show that modernist art was by nature hostile to totalitarianism, especially given that the Stalin regime had purged similar styles.

**Epic theater:** a movement in early twentieth-century theater, mostly closely identified with Bertolt Brecht and including Vladimir Mayakovsky and Vsevolod Meyerhold. Epic theater seeks to heighten the viewer's awareness of the fact that she is watching a play, and thus to elucidate the nature of the construction and performance of the spectacle before her. For Brecht, this was an enlightening political critique that would throw back the curtain on the mystification of theater; the audience must be alienated, he argued, rather than engrossed in the plot and characters, as proponents of naturalist, mimetic theater had aimed. The famous "fourth wall" of theater would be broken as actors step out of character in various ways and would incorporate the audience in the action.

**Ethnic studies:** an umbrella term for a variety of fields that examine cultural productions through the lens of ethnicity, generally understood as a combination of racial, historical, linguistic, and geographical elements. Ethnic studies thus includes African American studies, Asian studies, Latino/a studies, and much more, and has significant overlaps with fields defined by national and linguistic histories, and with postcolonial studies. Having arisen in the wake of the multicultural movements of the 1960s and 1970s, ethnic studies came to bear on modernist studies by pointing to the limitations of definitions of modernism that were held together by a common language, by critiquing the "invisible" whiteness of the canon, and by expanding and revising the canon with studies of nonwhite figures.

**Expressionism:** an avant-garde movement in literature, visual and plastic arts, dance, and cinema, centered in pre–First World War Germany, that emphasized individual, subjective perspectives through which "reality" was distorted according to an emotional state. Rather than a coterie or group, Expressionists were loosely affiliated and often at odds with one another; the most famous figures were Franz Kafka, Gottfried Benn, Fritz Lang, and Wassily Kandinsky, with Edvard Munch being an important forerunner. Expressionism was largely metropolitan, a response to the rapid rise of German industrialization and its alienating, socially fragmenting effects.

**Fauvism:** a movement in French painting just after the turn of the twentieth century, led by Henri Matisse and André Derain, which sought to push Impressionism further by exploring paint, color, and the canvas without regard for the natural world as inspiration. Closely related to both Post-Impressionism and Expressionism, Fauvism (from the French *les Fauves*, "the wild beasts") used bold, bright, often unnatural, colors combined with wild, seemingly uncontrolled brush strokes.

**Formalism:** a school of literary criticism that seeks to treat form and understand its mechanics in relative isolation, bracketing cultural contexts, authorial intent, and ideological critique. Formalism arose in the early twentieth century as a rejection of previous modes of criticism and scholarship such as belletrism and philology. It aimed to account for the literariness of the textual object and to emplace it in the history of genres and forms. The Russian Formalists and the New Critics are the two most prominent advocates of this approach, which fell out of favor beginning in the 1950s, but still significantly informs a number of schools of contemporary thought on literature, most notably through its emphasis on close reading.

**Frankfurt School:** the name given to an evolving group of Marxist cultural critics who, in the 1920s, broke with thinkers they considered overly partisan, orthodox communists and instead gathered around the German Institute for Social Research. Its principal figures include Theodor Adorno, Max Horkheimer, Herbert Marcuse, and later, Jürgen Habermas. Walter Benjamin and György Lukács were vital interlocutors with the school as well. Especially during the interwar period, Frankfurt School thinkers, disillusioned both by Western capitalism and by Soviet dogma, produced rich cultural analyses of avant-garde and modernist works by focusing on the sociopolitical contexts of their experiments with form. Unwilling to see aesthetic autonomy as ideologically neutral, they engaged in protracted debates with literary critics and with one another about the politics of modernism. They paid special attention to the rise of mass media and the fragmentation of social relations under modern capitalism as contexts for reading modernism. Their mode of analysis, known as critical theory and still practiced in contemporary scholarship, eschews the notion of dispassionate examination of a text in favor of political critique as an end. The school's founding members were dispersed into exile when Hitler came to power; several critics landed in the United States.

**Futurism:** the name of several movements, most famously the one launched by F. T. Marinetti, an Italian writer who published "The Futurist Manifesto" in the Parisian newspaper *Le Figaro* in 1909. Futurists celebrated technology, speed, force, violence, hypermasculinity, and modern commodities such as cars. In turn, they loathed women, museums, libraries, and any notion of "tradition." Their aesthetics, which emphasized hard angles, geometric forms, and dynamism, strongly influenced English Vorticism. Many Italian Futurists were nationalists who became fascists in the 1920s and 1930s, though Marjorie Perloff's work influentially argues that the movement, especially before the onset of the First World War, was politically complex.

**Gender studies:** a wide-ranging school of criticism that includes women's and feminist studies, queer studies, and analyses of concepts such as masculinity and family structures. Much of the impetus for gender studies came from feminism in the 1960s and 1970s, when scholars interrogated the ways in which femininity had been portrayed, constructed, and disparaged in cultural history. Within modernist studies, this prompted attacks on the misogyny of writers such as Wyndham Lewis, D. H. Lawrence, T. E. Hulme, and Ezra Pound, and the canonization of women modernists such as Virginia Woolf, Gertrude Stein, and Amy Lowell. In subsequent decades, gender studies has both recovered hundreds of neglected women writers and moved away from exploring gendered identities to examining the imbrication of femininity, masculinity, queerness, and other similar concepts in modernity.

**Genre fiction:** a term applied, often dismissively or pejoratively, to certain works of literature that rely heavily on predetermined conventions of plot and form. Most genre fiction is written and marketed for cheap, mass, popular consumption. Early theories of modernism often held that modernists cast their works in stark opposition to genre fiction, which they associated with sentimentality, romance, feminine writing, and a hostility to aesthetic innovation of any type. More recently, new attention has been paid to these modes of writing since many of the most familiar genres— including detective fiction, science fiction, and the Western—evolved alongside modernist fiction.

**Greenwich Village:** a neighborhood in New York City, home to diverse immigrant and international groups in the early twentieth century. Before the First World War and in the interwar period, Greenwich Village was the gathering point of many bohemian leftist, radical, and dissident artists and writers, including John Dos Passos, Waldo Frank, and Randolph Bourne. These and other figures were connected to the avant-garde revolution in the visual arts in New York in the 1910s, expressed most famously in Alfred Stieglitz's 291 and the 1913 Armory Show.

**Harlem Renaissance:** a movement centered in the largely African American neighborhood of Harlem in New York City, primarily in the 1920s and 1930s. As part of the New Negro movement, the international pan-African and black diaspora movements, the queer aesthetic movement, and white patronage of the black arts at the time, the Harlem Renaissance was a gathering point for the best-known black writers and artists of the era, including Langston Hughes, Zora Neale Hurston, Claude McKay, Countee Cullen, Jessie Redmon Fauset, and Jean Toomer. Its relationship to modernism was divided by critics along racial lines for decades, as it was rarely considered before the 1980s to have been part of the international modernist movement. Since then, it has been seen as vital to modernist aesthetic developments and, at the same time, apart from them, sometimes even in opposition to the most famous formal experiments of white, European figures.

**Imagism:** a poetic movement in English in the early twentieth century, first elaborated by T. E. Hulme and then consolidated by Ezra Pound, F. S. Flint, H. D. (Hilda Doolittle), and Richard Aldington. Their aims were a concision and precision in language, an exploration of free verse, and a rejection of "ornament" or rhetoric in poetry. Many critics have considered Imagism an heir to Symbolism, the first avant-garde in twentieth-century Anglophone letters, and (as T. S. Eliot claimed) the starting point of modernist poetry. Published first in *Poetry* magazine in featured sections in 1912, then emerging in various anthologies (*Des Imagistes* in 1914, *Some Imagist Poets* in 1915), the movement grew to include figures ranging from Amy Lowell to James Joyce. As it splintered into factions—Pound disparaged Lowell's version as "Amygism"—it went on to influence a wide variety of modernist aesthetics.

**Imperialism:** see New Imperialism

**Impersonal Theory of Poetry:** an influential ideal outlined by T. S. Eliot in his essay "Tradition and the Individual Talent" (1919). Eliot argues, against William Wordsworth, that poetry is not a "turning loose of emotion, but an escape from emotion," and indeed from "personality." Eliot argued that the poet must instead find his or her expression by ordering the past monuments of literary history with a strong "historical sense." *The Waste Land* is often seen as his greatest application of this theory. Eliot's Impersonal Theory helped inspire the New Critical approach to literary texts.

**International Style:** a term coined in 1932 by Henry-Russell Hitchcock and Alfred Johnson to describe a group of movements in early twentieth-century architecture. Exemplified by the works of Le Corbusier, Walter Gropius, and Ludwig Mies van der Rohe, International Style featured clean lines, no ornament, rectilinear designs, and modern materials such as steel, concrete, and glass. In critical history, "International Style" became synonymous with "modernism" in architecture.

**Irish Literary Revival:** a flourishing of poetry, fiction, and theater in the late nineteenth and early twentieth centuries in Ireland, most often associated with the revival of the Gaelic language and the rise of Irish nationalism and anticolonial fervor. Its most famous figures include W. B. Yeats, George Russell ("AE"), and John Millington Synge, all of whom synthesized English literary forms with native Irish ballads, songs, and content. The preeminent Irish figure of English-language modernism, James Joyce, often placed himself in opposition to these figures and their celebrations of Irish cultural history.

**Jazz:** musical form that originated in the polyglot, multicultural atmosphere of New Orleans in the early 1900s, blending Southern American, African, and European styles into a distinct musical idiom that relied on syncopation, improvisation, and dissonance. Its most famous early figures were Duke Ellington and Louis Armstrong, and it rapidly spread globally to create a host of other musical forms and genres. Because of its association with low or popular culture, and its origins in black America, jazz was not seen for decades as part of modernist musical or cultural history; it was famously denigrated by critics such as Theodor Adorno and Clive Bell. However, since the 1980s, scholars have seen jazz as a distinctive modernist form, one whose rhythms surface in the poetry of T. S. Eliot and Langston Hughes alike.

**Kitsch:** a term of German-language origin used to characterize cheap, mass-produced art that is meant for popular consumption. Kitsch, in the modernist era, was often synonymous with treacly, sentimental, often gaudy pseudo-art; that is, objects that *imitate* art, by way of their appearance and cultural references, rather than actually *being* art. For this reason, kitsch was held in opposition to high modernist literature but was integrated into the work of avant-garde groups such as the Dadaists, who used tabloid newspapers in their collages. Postmodernists often critiqued modernism's hostility to kitsch and, like the early twentieth-century avant-garde, incorporated, and even celebrated, it in their works, drawing on styles such as camp in order to dislodge the notion of "high" art.

**Left Bank (*La Rive Gauche*):** an area on the western banks of the Seine in Paris, used as a term to denote the congregation of a fantastic array of modernist artists, writers, and thinkers roughly between 1910 and 1945. The international scene included countless expatriates such as James Joyce, Ezra Pound, Gertrude Stein, Ernest Hemingway, Nancy Cunard, Sylvia Beach, Langston Hughes, and others, all of whom lived in this bohemian atmosphere alongside French figures ranging from Henri Matisse to Jean-Paul Sartre. For this reason, accounts of modernism have often emphasized the metropolitan, cosmopolitan nature of the movement and the social and aesthetic liberalism that many figures adopted from interwar Parisian culture.

**Little magazines:** a term used to describe periodicals such as *Poetry*, the *Little Review*, *BLAST*, and the *Egoist*, which promoted experimental writing and published many of the key texts of the modernist movement. Little (or "small") magazines were so called because they often had tiny circulations relative to popular publications. They were often supported primarily by private backers rather than by subscriptions or advertisements, and they tended to position themselves and their writers in opposition to popular culture. Many had short but very influential runs that featured heterogeneous combinations of poetry, fiction, art, editorials and manifestos, and even commerce. The rise of materialist histories in modernist studies has led scholars to see the magazines as objects of analysis themselves, rather than as disposable sites in which serialized works first appeared.

**Lost Generation:** a group of American modernist writers who settled or spent significant time in Paris after the First World War. Ernest Hemingway, F. Scott Fitzgerald, John Dos Passos, and others congregated around Gertrude Stein's apartment at 27 rue de Fleurus on the Left Bank, and their works are characterized by a disillusion and alienation developed, in many cases, from their experiences with the war. These writers experimented with a variety of techniques, including Cubism (influenced by Stein's close relationship with Picasso), unreliable narration, stream of consciousness, and cinema-style montage. The writers of the Lost Generation were among the first Americans, along with T. S. Eliot and Ezra Pound, to be recognized as modernist by critics who located modernism chiefly in European arts.

**Manifesto:** a text that outlines the aims, demands, and views of a particular political or aesthetic group. The manifesto form became immensely popular in the modernist era, with almost every group, from the Symbolists to the Futurists to the Surrealists, having their own, often linking politics and aesthetics. Scholars have traced the rise of manifestos in the late nineteenth and early twentieth centuries to the success of the *Communist Manifesto* (1848), by Karl Marx and Friedrich Engels.

**Marxist criticism:** a mode of cultural analysis derived from the works of Karl Marx, emphasizing historical (especially social, political, and economic) contexts, ideology, material conditions, the production and consumption of aesthetic objects as goods, and the interplay of form and content, among many other elements. Marxist critics since the modernist era paid special attention to these elements in modernist works that allegedly attempted to disavow or obscure them, replacing reality with myth, or production with the impersonality of the author. From the start, Marxist critics argued that modernist experiments with form had a political content that could not be isolated in an autonomous aesthetic realm. Marxist criticism informed or inspired a number of other fields, from media studies to postcolonialism.

**Men of 1914:** a term coined by Wyndham Lewis in reference to himself, T. S. Eliot, James Joyce, and Ezra Pound. Lewis's term helped solidify the reputations of these four figures as central to the modernist revolution, creating a mystique around them that he grounded in the claim that they were the legitimate heirs to T. E. Hulme's aesthetic program. It also placed pre–First World War aesthetics—especially formal innovation—at the point of origin of modernism and made the onset of the war a vital juncture in its history. The exclusivity (especially along gender lines) of this grouping has been challenged by a number of critics since the 1980s.

*Modernisme:* a term used most often to refer to the Catalan aesthetic movement around the turn of the twentieth century, most famous for its architecture, as in the work of Antoni Gaudí. *Modernisme* also refers in French loosely to the works of Paris's bohemian figures of the latter half of the nineteenth century, and sometimes to the developments in painting since Édouard Manet. The term *modernisme* is far less common in Francophone criticism than "modernism" is in English, highlighting one of the crucial challenges in conceiving of a unified, transnational conception of "modernism."

*Modernismo:* an international movement in Latin American letters of the late nineteenth and early twentieth centuries, whose principal figures were Rubén Darío, José Martí, Leopoldo Lugones, and others. The *modernistas* drew on French Symbolism, Parnassianism, Decadentism, and Aestheticism in order to launch an attack on what they saw as the stale, tradition-bound writing that prevailed in Hispanophone letters. They were, notably, the first aesthetic group to self-consciously name themselves as "modernists," when Darío assigned them the term in 1890. The relationship between *modernismo* and modernism has been debated fiercely for decades: the former was previously dismissed as derivative and inferior, thus separate from modernism. More recently, *modernismo* has been seen as one of many global modernisms, and is seen by some as providing a blueprint for international modernism by having been the first postcolonial literature to overtake the literary world of its former colonizer.

**Modernity:** a broad concept that resists definition and remains one of the most fiercely debated topics of contemporary scholarship. Used loosely to refer to dynamic shifts in societies, politics, technologies, and aesthetics, modernity can refer to anything from the idea of being modern (which dates at least to the sixth century AD), to the Renaissance, to the Age of Enlightenment, to the Industrial Revolution, to the post–Second World War global condition, to world history since colonialism, or even, as some critics argue, to any period in any location in which rapid, exhilarating change takes place. The connection between modernity and modernism is unresolved, as is the question of whether modernity is singular or plural, or even a meaningful concept at all.

**Museum of Modern Art (MoMA):** founded in New York City, first opened to the public in 1929. Alfred Barr was the museum's most influential figure during the interwar period. Under his directorship, MoMA became famous not only for collecting and promoting modern art—its holdings in modernist painting are unparalleled—but also for serving as an institutional home for modernist works that, in many cases, were considered too experimental or controversial to find a broad audience. The museum often serves as a touchstone in debates about the dialectic between the revolutionary oppositionality of modernist works and their absorption into both bourgeois and popular cultures.

**Naturalism:** a movement in literature, visual arts, and theater in the late nineteenth and early twentieth centuries that extended the work of Realism by focusing on specific social and familial environments and the ways in which they determine human fate. Naturalism was made famous by the novelist Émile Zola and the playwrights August Strindberg and Henrik Ibsen, who emphasized the details of quotidian life and often portrayed characters who lived in abject conditions of various types. Modernism's relationship to Naturalism has been debated for decades by critics; the former was first seen as a rejection of the latter, but canonical modernists such as James Joyce also wrote in largely Naturalistic styles (as in his *Dubliners*).

**New Criticism:** a school of formalist literary criticism focused on the techniques of close reading. Its principal figures were I. A. Richards (who developed the similar "Practical Criticism"), William Empson, R. P. Blackmur, and a subgroup known as the Southern New Critics: John Crowe Ransom, Allen Tate, Cleanth Brooks, and the interrelated Fugitive and Agrarian collectives. New Critics understood texts as autonomous, self-sufficient objects; thus, they dismissed criticism that took into account politics, ideology, or biography. Poems especially were explicable as organic forms that used the innate properties of literary language to create irony, paradox, and other effects that separated them from everyday writing and speech. Modernist poetry was exceptionally valuable to the New Critics, who often championed T. S. Eliot and drew on his essays in formulating their program. New Criticism was—and remains—enormously influential in university studies of literature. For that reason, especially in the 1940s and 1950s, it helped consolidate the first canon of modernist texts and authors using the criteria of form, difficulty, and autonomy. The responses to and rejections of New Critical approaches have been many since the 1960s, from cultural studies to gender studies, though their precepts remain important to much scholarship and pedagogy.

**New Imperialism:** a term used to describe the era of European imperialism lasting roughly from the mid-1800s, through the Scramble for Africa and the Berlin Conference (1884), and ending with the Second World War. During this period, the United Kingdom rose to the preeminent position of global territorial domination. Many Marxist critics, such as Fredric Jameson, hold that the fragmentation and unknowability present in the form of modernist novels is a symptom of the metropolitan inability to comprehend peripheral subjects with whom citizenship was now shared.

**New Journalism:** a term used most famously by Matthew Arnold to describe the seismic shifts in late Victorian English print culture. The New Journalism came about in the final decades of the nineteenth century with the convergence of several factors: the Elementary Education Act of 1870 and other school reforms that increased literacy rates, the availability of cheap materials for newspaper printing, the invention of halftone image reproduction, and the popularity of sensationalist and tabloid journalism. A new type of newspaper and magazine, meant for mass, popular consumption, often at a cheap price subsidized by ubiquitous advertisements, emerged and, in the minds of many elite writers and thinkers, threatened to dumb down culture and the power of literature. T. E. Hulme was foremost among the modernists who were hostile to the effects of the New Journalism on the English language. (Distinct from the New Journalism movement associated with Tom Wolfe, Hunter S. Thompson, and American writers of the 1960s and 1970s.)

**New Modernist Studies:** a term used to describe the changes in the field of modernist studies roughly since the mid-1990s. Critics often point to the founding of *Modernism/modernity* in 1994 and the MSA in 1998 as two key events in its history. It now refers very broadly to scholarship produced after the postmodernist attacks on modernism; much of this work challenges the previous, longstanding critical axioms about modernism's commitment to apolitical, ahistorical formal experimentation and its reliance on myth, allusion, and difficulty.

New Negro: a movement formed in response to Jim Crow laws and enduring racism in the United States in the early twentieth century. Its key figures—W. E. B. Du Bois, Alain Locke, Booker T. Washington, and Hubert Harrison—along with most every writer and artist of the Harlem Renaissance, advocated for a new African American identity grounded both in political rights and in social respectability and dignity. The New Negro peaked in the interwar period as it came into contact with the international, pan-African, and diaspora understandings of modern black subjectivity and social existence.

New Woman: an international movement of the late nineteenth and early twentieth centuries that consolidated and advanced many feminist ideals, including the rights to vote, hold public offices, own property, pursue postsecondary education, and enter professional society. The works of Henrik Ibsen and Henry James famously depicted (and gave a name to) New Women, and a number of women modernists and proto-modernists, including Kate Chopin, Olive Schreiner, and Sarah Grand, were involved in various components of the movement. The New Woman faced a great deal of resistance and was, in some cases, blamed by the male establishment for "modernism" itself, as it sought to overthrow a host of sociopolitical traditions.

New York Intellectuals: a loosely affiliated group of thinkers and cultural critics whose work was launched in New York in the 1930s, primarily in the *Partisan Review* (1934–2003). Spanning several generations, its best-known figures included Clement Greenberg, Hannah Arendt, Leslie Fiedler, Susan Sontag, Lionel Trilling, Harold Rosenberg, Irving Howe, and Alfred Kazin, though many others were associated either by publications or by sympathetic politics. The New York Intellectuals were, in the beginning, mostly Jewish Marxists who were anti-Stalinists and often at odds with the Communist Party USA. Their view of modernism is famously ambivalent: while they celebrated its oppositionality and experimentalism, they were wary of the conservatism and anti-Semitism of some of its key figures.

Ontology: a branch of philosophy that investigates the nature of reality or being, often paired with epistemology, which investigates the nature of knowledge and how humans access it. Ontology is a core concept in modernist studies because many modernist writers asserted the ontological value—the self-sufficiency, without relying on other objects or concepts for its existence—of the work of art. This assertion, fundamental to theories of aesthetic autonomy, was then translated into a doctrine by the New Critics, most famously John Crowe Ransom, who held that the poem could access a deeper reality than normal human perceptions could, and thus must be analyzed scientifically—as a distinct, real object.

*Poésie pure* ("**Pure poetry**"): a concept in French Symbolist poetry, most often associated with Paul Valéry and derived from his readings of Stéphane Mallarmé's work, that argues for poetry developed according to internal, "purely" poetic laws. Poets must create works that resist paraphrase in prose by containing structural and formal elements that are untranslatable outside of the poems themselves. This implicit argument for the autonomy of the aesthetic object in poetry influenced a number of modernist writers, most notably T. S. Eliot.

**Postcolonial studies:** a branch of study that investigates the complex relationships between colonialism and imperialism across history, ranging from epistemology to aesthetic forms to political solidarities. Its influence in modernist studies has been immense, both in studies of colonialism in the works of canonical figures like Joyce and in the dramatic expansion of the field of modernism around non-Western sites of cultural production. Postcolonialist thought was key to most all Marxist scholars of modernism from the 1980s onward, and within the New Modernist Studies, it has informed studies of poetics, fashion, race, gender, media networks, and much more.

**Postmodernism:** a term that has been used to define a style of aesthetics, a cultural condition associated with contemporary capitalism, a mode of criticism, and much more. In literature and art, postmodernism typically refers to the use of pastiche, parody, kitsch, semiotic play, and metanarratives, all in ways that modernism was said to abjure. In architecture, its history is different, involving a rejection of mid-century modernism and its centrality to urban planning. These and other senses are often held together by an abandonment of grand narratives (of civilization, art, symbolism, and more) and by their critique of the institutionalization of modernism, whether in universities or in government. The postmodernist critiques of modernism helped energize the formation of the New Modernist Studies, and at the same time, postmodernist projects such as ethnic studies and postcolonial studies have been widely incorporated into it.

**Poststructuralism:** a term used to describe the works of many, mostly French philosophers of the 1960s and 1970s, but with important roots in the works of earlier figures such as Friedrich Nietzsche. Poststructuralists argued for the instability of deep or fundamental "structure" in the human sciences (as the Structuralists of the 1950s and early 1960s had used it), an antihumanist perspective, and an opposition to binaries (male/female, reason/madness).

Its best-known figures include Jacques Derrida, Michel Foucault, Julia Kristeva, and Jacques Lacan, and its influence spread widely, especially in Anglo-American literary studies in the 1970s and 1980s. Poststructuralism informed many of the cultural critiques, mostly from the left, that came during and after the worldwide revolutions of the late 1960s. Certain modernists and avant-gardists held a privileged place in poststructuralist thought because of their "decentered" and radically subversive (especially revolutionary) approaches to language or to theatrical performance.

**Post-Impressionism:** a movement primarily in the visual arts of late 1800s and early 1900s, emphasizing geometric forms and bright, unnatural colors; its key figures were Paul Cézanne, Vincent van Gogh, Georges Seurat, and, Édouard Manet. The term "Post-Impressionism" was coined in 1910 by the Bloomsbury art critic Roger Fry, who organized the groundbreaking exhibition "Manet and the Post-Impressionists" in London that year. Many have speculated that Virginia Woolf's claim that "on or about December 1910, human character changed" is a reference to this show, which introduced new French aesthetics to a British public she and Fry considered too traditional in taste.

**Practical criticism:** see New Criticism

**Primitivism:** a fascination with exotic, often indigenous cultures, which became a prominent theme in a variety of modernist works. Primitivist aesthetics were the result of a convergence of factors, including the New Imperialism, colonial exhibitions across Europe, anthropological investigations of "primitive" cultures, and a desire among artists and writers to explore non-Western aesthetics. Pablo Picasso's use of African masks and Antonin Dvorak's use of Native American musical idioms represent two of the more famous examples. The politics of primitivism and its implicit desire to connect with a certain past have been primary topics in postcolonial modernist studies of the past two decades.

**Psychoanalytic criticism:** a term used to describe a varied set of approaches to literature and culture that draw inspiration from Sigmund Freud and his many interpreters and interlocutors across the twentieth century. Psychoanalytic criticism often emphasizes concepts such as the unconscious and repression; perhaps most important for the history of modernist studies was its influence on the development of gender studies, race studies, and French Theory in the 1970s and 1980s.

**Quarrel of the Ancients and the Moderns (*Querelle des Anciens et des Modernes*):** a debate that began in late sixteenth-century France over whether modern life—thanks to the developments, inventions, and discoveries of the Renaissance era—was now superior to the wisdom and traditions of the classical world. The debate spread to several other countries and was famously depicted in "The Battle of the Books," Jonathan Swift's prolegomenon to his satire *A Tale of the Tub* (1704). The debate is notable for historians of modernism because it involved the extensive use of the term "modernist," often to describe disparagingly a figure with a naive faith in progress and little sense of the grandeur of history.

**Queer studies:** a field of criticism that arose in the 1990s, through the work of Eve Kosofsky Sedgwick, Judith Butler, and others, that examines the constructions and performance of gender identities, sexual orientations, same-sex desire, and social norms with an eye to "queerness" or "deviance." Its impact on modernist studies has been profound, including studies of homosexual writers (Marcel Proust, Virginia Woolf, Langston Hughes, Gertrude Stein, E. M. Forster, and many others), homosexual anxieties in the works of a number of figures, and the historical figuration of "the homosexual" around the turn of the twentieth century.

**Race studies:** see Ethnic studies

**Realism:** a movement that dominated the arts and much of literature in the second half of the nineteenth century. Realism emphasized a careful and faithful attention to "reality," understood as material conditions of human existence without the kind of fantasy or distortion Romanticism had advocated. It was made famous by figures such as George Eliot, William Dean Howells, and Gustave Courbet, among many others. Modernism has often been understood as a reaction against Realism, and in particular, to the commercialization of Realism as it became the dominant style of popular and genre fiction in the late Victorian era. Modernists also drew heavily on elements of Realism, revised it through subgenres such as psychological realism, and themselves gave inspiration to movements such as Magical Realism, which combined modernist and realist techniques.

**Revolutions of 1848:** a wave of large-scale revolts across Europe and Latin America that, in the space of just one year, led to dramatic changes in the political shape of the West. The revolutions shared many principles but were not tightly coordinated; most agitated for political rights and improved conditions for working people, the lower and middle classes, peasants, and serfs. A host of factors led to the revolts, including industrialism, urbanization, technological advances, rising literacy rates and education, dramatic income inequality, nationalist fervor, and political suppression. The groups involved often sought to overthrow or significantly reform absolutist, monarchic, or imperial states and governments, and to dismantle the power of the aristocracy and nobility. Because of the widespread *cultural* shifts that the Revolutions of 1848 introduced—*political* victories were less common—scholars have pointed to them as an origin of the modernist ethos. Charles Baudelaire, for example, had been a revolutionary in France in 1848, an experience that shaped his influential writings on "modernity" and the arts.

**Romanticism:** a movement in the arts and literature that occupied most of the first half of the nineteenth century. Made most famous in English by figures such as William Wordsworth, Percy Shelley, and John Keats, Romanticism reacted against the rationalism of the Enlightenment and the onset of industrial modernity. The Romantics turned, instead, to emotion, experience, nature, and the imagination as the sources of meaning. Because it was seen as a genuine aesthetic revolution—as opposed to a continuation or modification of preexisting styles—and was linked to the French Revolutions, Romanticism has often been seen as the forerunner of modernism. Some critics have argued that modernism was an extension (and perhaps the final one) of Romanticism's treatment of symbols and objects, while others see modernism, following T. S. Eliot's denigration of Romantic poetry, as a repudiation of its emphasis on the author's emotional state.

**Southern New Critics:** see New Criticism

**Surrealism:** an aesthetic movement launched in the late 1910s and early 1920s, emphasizing irrationality, dream content, explorations of the unconscious, automatic writing, and shock or surprise. Led by André Breton, author of two versions of *The Surrealist Manifesto* (1924 and 1929), Surrealism's most familiar figures include Salvador Dalí, Joan Miró, and Marcel Duchamp. Surrealism came just after Dada and carried with it a similar assault on bourgeois culture, materialism, conformity, and traditional aesthetics—especially those of Realism. A robustly international movement, Surrealism has been read both as integral to modernist aesthetics and as an avant-garde assault on modernism's elevation of autonomy.

**Symbolism:** often said to begin with Charles Baudelaire's poetry collection *Les fleurs du mal* (1857), a movement that reacted against the prevailing Realism of mid-nineteenth-century European arts. Symbolists rejected the idea that art should correspond to the external or material world and argued instead for the autonomy of art and literature by glorifying symbols and words themselves. They celebrated ideas and experience as ends in themselves, against what they saw as the increasing utilitarianism, materialism, and rationalism of modernity. Many critics have seen Symbolism, as it was subsequently developed by Stéphane Mallarmé, Paul Valéry, and Jean Moréas, as the point of origin for modernism across a number of languages. One of the first major scholars of modernism, Edmund Wilson, characterized Proust, Valéry, Joyce, Eliot, Yeats, and Stein as part of a French-English Symbolist movement.

**Taylorization:** a term used to describe the modern approach of scientific management in the labor and production of goods. Named for Frederick Taylor, this approach was especially popular in the early twentieth century, and it emphasized rationalism, efficiency, and mass production over craft. Modernism has been seen largely as a rejection of Taylorization and its effects on society.

**Tradition:** an important concept in modernist aesthetics and modernist studies primarily because it has often been taken to represent the inverse of "modernism." Whether in the Quarrel of the Ancients and the Moderns, the Enlightenment, the debates over Modernism in the Catholic church, or the aesthetic revolutions advocated by a host of figures and groups, tradition was often the enemy. However, the relationship is more complicated: T. S. Eliot's famous essay "Tradition and the Individual Talent" (1919) actually argued for an embrace of a certain type of tradition—just not the reigning traditions of English poetry at the time. Later, modernism itself became a "tradition of the new," as Harold Rosenberg called it. Modernism's transformation from marginal and oppositional to dominant and traditional after the Second World War prompted a series of revaluations of the movement and its particular investments in or rejections of the notion of tradition.

**Vernacular, popular, and "low" modernisms:** a set of terms used to refer to modernisms that emerged away from, or even in opposition to, high or elite culture. Modernism, for decades, was held by critics to have been a highbrow movement that cast itself against art of the commercial world and of rural, allegedly uncultured peoples. In the past two decades, however, scholars have shown that modernism was deeply entwined with these worlds, and that certain modernists actually crafted their aesthetic idioms *through* vernacular or popular forms, such as local dialects, folk ballads, indigenous traditions, advertising trends, pulp and sensationalist fictions, and mass-produced music.

**Victorian era:** strictly speaking, the period of the reign of Queen Victoria of the United Kingdom, which lasted from 1837 to 1901. In cultural history, the term is used to denote a highly conservative age that elevated the refinement of taste and manners, the repression of sexual expression, the further domestication of women, and the jingoistic celebration of the expansion of British Empire. While this characterization is reductive and in many ways inaccurate, it served as a crucial tool for argument among modernist figures who saw their own aesthetic revolutions as emblems of a new "era" of modern life that would overthrow the persistence of Victorianism. The near-coincidence of Victoria's death and Joseph Conrad's publication of *Heart of Darkness* (1899) and *Lord Jim* (1900), both of which critiqued the political and cultural atmospheres of the Victorian era, led many critics to date the beginning of English-language modernism from this "break."

**Vorticism:** an English avant-garde movement headed by Wyndham Lewis and named by Ezra Pound, launched around 1913 and centered on the journal *BLAST* (1914–15). Drawing on Futurist and Cubist aesthetics, Vorticists favored geometric forms and abstract shapes over human forms and natural settings. Its literature also celebrated machines, modern technologies, and dynamism, often with a political conservativism and cultural misogyny akin to that of Futurism. Vorticism spread internationally, but dissipated quickly during the First World War. Some argue that it was the only true avant-garde movement in English visual arts of the early twentieth century.

# CRITICAL BIBLIOGRAPHIES FOR THE NEW MODERNIST STUDIES

Below we offer brief lists of key and representative studies in the fields within the New Modernist Studies that we outline in Chapter 4. The bibliographic information for works and authors that we mention in that chapter, but do not cite directly, can be found here too. These lists are by no means comprehensive; rather, we hope they will serve as starting points for scholars seeking to delve further into any number of topics. The books that will follow in the New Modernisms series will provide more capacious bibliographies for each of these and other related fields.

## Modernism as a concept (including surveys, anthologies, and introductions)

Armstrong, Tim. *Modernism: A Cultural History*. Cambridge: Polity, 2005.
Ayers, David. *Modernism: A Short Introduction*. Malden, MA: Blackwell, 2004.
Bradshaw, David and Kevin J. H. Dettmar, eds. *A Companion to Modernist Literature and Culture*. London: Wiley-Blackwell, 2008.
Brooker, Peter, Andrzej Gasiorek, and Andrew Thacker, eds. *The Oxford Handbook of Modernisms*. Oxford: Oxford University Press, 2010.
Butler, Christopher. *Modernism: A Very Short Introduction*. New York: Oxford University Press, 2010.
Clark, T. J. *Farewell to an Idea: Episodes from a History of Modernism*. New Haven: Yale University Press, 1999.
Cuddy-Keane, Melba, Adam Hammond, and Alexandra Peat. *Modernism: Keywords*. Malden, MA: Wiley-Blackwell, 2014.

Dettmar, Kevin J. H., ed. *Rereading the New: A Backward Glance at Modernism*. Ann Arbor: University of Michigan Press, 1992.

Eysteinsson, Astradur and Vivian Liska, eds. *Modernism*. 2 vols. Amsterdam: Benjamins, 2007.

Friedman, Susan Stanford. "Planetarity: Musing Modernist Studies." *Modernism/modernity* 17.3 (September 2010): 471–99.

Kolocotroni, Vassiliki, Jane Goldman, and Olga Taxidou, eds. *Modernism: An Anthology of Sources and Documents*. Edinburgh: Edinburgh University Press, 1998.

Levenson, Michael, ed. *The Cambridge Companion to Modernism*. 2nd ed. Cambridge: Cambridge University Press, 2011.

Lewis, Pericles. *The Cambridge Introduction to Modernism*. Cambridge: Cambridge University Press, 2007.

Mao, Douglas and Rebecca L. Walkowitz. "The New Modernist Studies." *PMLA* 123.3 (May 2008): 737–48.

Middleton, Tim, ed. *Modernism: Critical Concepts in Literary and Cultural Studies*. 5 vols. New York: Routledge, 2003.

Murray, Alex and Philip Tew, eds. *The Modernism Handbook*. London: Continuum, 2009.

Nicholls, Peter. *Modernisms: A Literary Guide*. Berkeley: University of California Press, 1995.

Rabaté, Jean-Michel, ed. *A Handbook of Modernism Studies*. Hoboken, NJ: John Wiley & Sons, 2013.

Rainey, Lawrence, ed. *Modernism: An Anthology*. Malden, MA: Blackwell, 2005.

Wicke, Jennifer. "Appreciation, Depreciation: Modernism's Speculative Bubble." *Modernism/modernity* 8.3 (September 2001): 389–403.

# Modernism, gender, and sexuality

Ardis, Ann L. and Leslie W. Lewis, eds. *Women's Experience of Modernity, 1875 – 1945*. Baltimore: Johns Hopkins University Press, 2003.

Boone, Joseph. *Libidinal Currents: Sexuality and the Shaping of Modernism*. Chicago: University of Chicago Press, 1998.

Cheng, Anne Anlin. *Second Skin: Josephine Baker and the Modern Surface*. New York: Oxford University Press, 2011.

Conor, Liz. *The Spectacular Modern Woman: Feminine Visibility in the 1920s*. Bloomington: University of Indiana Press, 2004.

Delap, Lucy. *The Feminist Avant-garde: Transatlantic Encounters of the Early Twentieth Century*. Cambridge: Cambridge University Press, 2007.

Doan, Laura. *Fashioning Sapphism: The Origins of a Modern English Lesbian Culture*. New York: Columbia University Press, 2001.

Doyle, Laura. *Bordering on the Body: The Racial Matrix of Modern Fiction and Culture*. New York: Oxford University Press, 1994.
Felski, Rita. *The Gender of Modernity*. Cambridge, MA: Harvard University Press, 1995.
Friedman, Susan Stanford. *Mappings: Feminism and the Cultural Geographies of Encounter*. Princeton, NJ: Princeton University Press, 1998.
Frost, Laura. *Sex Drives: Fantasies of Fascism in Literary Modernism*. Ithaca: Cornell University Press, 2002.
Froula, Christine. *Modernism's Body: Sex, Culture, and Joyce*. New York: Columbia University Press, 1996.
Froula, Christine. *Virginia Woolf and the Bloomsbury Avant-garde: War, Civilization, Modernity*. New York: Columbia University Press, 2005.
Garrity, Jane. *Step-daughters of England: British Women Modernists and the National Imaginary*. New York: Palgrave, 2003.
Green, Barbara. "Feminist Periodical Culture." *Literature Compass* 6.1 (2009): 191–205.
Jay, Karla. "Lesbian Modernism: (Trans)forming the (C)Anon." *Professions of Desire: Lesbian and Gay Studies in Literature*. Ed. George Haggerty and Bonnie Zimmerman. New York: MLA, 1995. 73–7.
Marcus, Jane. *Hearts of Darkness: White Women Write Race*. New Brunswick, NJ: Rutgers University Press, 2004.
Pease, Allison. *Modernism, Feminism, and the Culture of Boredom*. Cambridge: Cambridge University Press, 2012.
Rado, Lisa, ed. and intro. *Rereading Modernism: New Directions in Feminist Criticism*. New York: Garland, 1994.
Scott, Bonnie Kime, ed. *Gender in Modernism: New Geographies, Complex Intersections*. Urbana: University of Illinois Press, 2007.
Snaith, Anna. *Modernist Voyages: Colonial Women Writers in London, 1890-1945*. Cambridge: Cambridge University Press, 2014.
Stevens, Hugh and Caroline Howlett. *Modernist Sexualities*. Manchester: Manchester University Press, 2000.
Trask, Michael. *Cruising Modernism: Class and Sexuality in American Literature and Social Thought*. Ithaca, NY: Cornell University Press, 2003.
Wachman, Gay. *Lesbian Empire: Radical Crosswriting in the Twenties*. New Brunswick, NJ: Rutgers University Press, 2001.
Ziarek, Ewa Płonowska. *Feminist Aesthetics and the Politics of Modernism*. New York: Columbia University Press, 2012.

# Modernist races

Baker, Houston A. *Turning South Again: Re-thinking Modernism/Re-reading Booker T.* Durham, NC: Duke University Press, 2001.

Blair, Sara. *Harlem Crossroads: Black Writers and the Photograph in the Twentieth Century.* Princeton, NJ: Princeton University Press, 2007.

Chinitz, David E. *Which Sin to Bear? Authenticity and Compromise in Langston Hughes.* New York: Oxford University Press, 2013.

Chu, Patricia. *Race, Nationalism and the State in British and American Modernism.* Cambridge: Cambridge University Press, 2006.

Douglas, Ann. *Terrible Honesty: Mongrel Manhattan in the 1920s.* New York: Farrar, Straus, and Giroux, 1995.

Edwards, Brent Hayes. *The Practice of Diaspora: Literature, Translation, and the Rise of Black Internationalism.* Cambridge, MA: Harvard University Press, 2003.

Foley, Barbara. *Jean Toomer: Race, Repression, and Revolution.* Urbana: University of Illinois Press, 2014.

Francis, Jacqueline. *Making Race: Modernism and "Racial Art" in America.* Seattle: University of Washington Press, 2012.

Gilroy, Paul. *The Black Atlantic: Modernity and Double Consciousness.* Cambridge, MA: Harvard University Press, 1993.

Goldsby, Jacqueline. *A Spectacular Secret: Lynching in American Life and Literature.* Chicago: University of Chicago Press, 2006.

Lemke, Sieglinde. *Primitivist Modernism: Black Culture and the Origins of Transatlantic Modernism.* New York: Oxford University Press, 1998.

Michaels, Walter Benn. *Our America: Nativism, Modernism, and Pluralism.* Durham, NC: Duke University Press, 1995.

Miller, Joshua L. *Accented America: The Cultural Politics of Multilingual Modernism.* New York: Oxford University Press, 2011.

Miller, Monica L. *Slaves to Fashion: Black Dandyism and the Styling of Black Diasporic Identity.* Durham, NC: Duke University Press, 2009.

Nielsen, Aldon Lynn, ed. *Reading Race in American Poetry: "An Area of Act."* Urbana: University of Illinois Press, 2000.

Patterson, Anita. *Race, American Literature and Transnational Modernisms.* Cambridge: Cambridge University Press, 2008.

Platt, Len, ed. *Modernism and Race.* Cambridge: Cambridge University Press, 2011.

Seshagiri, Urmila. *Race and the Modernist Imagination.* Ithaca, NY: Cornell University Press, 2010.

Smethurst, James. *The African American Roots of Modernism: From Reconstruction to the Harlem Renaissance.* Chapel Hill: University of North Carolina Press, 2011.

Sollors, Werner. *Ethnic Modernism.* Cambridge, MA: Harvard University Press, 2008.

Thaggert, Miriam. *Images of Black Modernism: Verbal and Visual Strategies of the Harlem Renaissance.* Amherst: University of Massachusetts Press, 2010.

Vogel, Shane. *The Scene of the Harlem Cabaret: Race, Sexuality, Performance*. Chicago: University of Chicago Press, 2009.
Wilson, Sarah. *Melting-Pot Modernism*. Ithaca: Cornell University Press, 2010.

# Modernism in a global context

Begam, Richard, and Michael Moses. *Modernism and Colonialism: British and Irish Literature, 1899–1939*. Durham: Duke University Press, 2007.
Berman, Jessica. *Modernist Commitments: Ethics, Politics, and Transnational Modernism*. New York: Columbia University Press, 2012.
Boehmer, Elleke. *Empire, the National, and the Postcolonial, 1890–1920: Resistance in Interaction*. Oxford: Oxford University Press, 2002.
Booth, Howard J. and Nigel Rigby, eds. *Modernism and Empire*. Manchester: Manchester University Press, 2000.
Bush, Christopher. *Ideographic Modernism: China, Writing, Media*. New York: Oxford University Press, 2010.
Casanova, Pascale. *The World Republic of Letters*. Trans. M. B. DeBevoise. Cambridge, MA: Harvard University Press, 2004.
Doyle, Laura. *Freedom's Empire: Race and the Rise of the Novel in Atlantic Modernity, 1640-1940*. Durham, NC: Duke University Press, 2008.
Doyle, Laura and Laura Winkiel, eds. *Geomodernisms: Race, Modernism, Modernity*. Bloomington: Indiana University Press, 2005.
Eagleton, Terry, Fredric Jameson, and Edward W. Said. *Nationalism, Colonialism, and Literature*. Ed. Seamus Deane. Minneapolis: University of Minnesota Press, 1990.
Emery, Mary Lou. *Modernism, the Visual, and Caribbean Literature*. Cambridge: Cambridge University Press, 2009.
Esty, Jed. *Unseasonable Youth: Modernism, Colonialism, and the Fiction of Development*. New York: Oxford University Press, 2012.
Gikandi, Simon. *Writing in Limbo: Modernism and Caribbean Literature*. Ithaca: Cornell University Press, 1992.
GoGwilt, Christopher. *The Passage of Literature: Genealogies of Modernism in Conrad, Rhys, and Pramoedya*. New York: Oxford University Press, 2011.
Hart, Matthew. *Nations of Nothing But Poetry: Modernism, Transnationalism, and Synthetic Vernacular Writing*. New York: Oxford University Press, 2010.
Hayot, Eric. *The Hypothetical Mandarin: Sympathy, Modernity, and Chinese Pain*. New York: Oxford, 2009.

Jameson, Fredric. *The Modernist Papers*. London: Verso, 2007.
Kalliney, Peter. *Commonwealth of Letters: British Literary Culture
and the Emergence of Postcolonial Aesthetics*. New York: Oxford
University Press, 2013.
Lewis, Pericles. *Modernism, Nationalism, and the Novel*. Cambridge:
Cambridge University Press, 2000.
Lloyd, David. *Anomalous States: Irish Writing and the Post-Colonial
Moment*. Durham, NC: Duke University Press, 1993.
Mejías-López, Alejandro. *The Inverted Conquest: The Myth of Modernity
and the Transatlantic Onset of Modernism*. Nashville, TN: Vanderbilt
University Press, 2009.
Mitter, Partha. *The Triumph of Modernism: India's Artists and the Avant-
Garde, 1922-47*. London: Reaktion, 2007.
Pollard, Charles W. *New World Modernisms: T. S. Eliot, Derek Walcott,
and Kamau Brathwaite*. Charlottesville: University of Virginia Press,
2004.
Qian, Zhaoming. *Orientalism and Modernism: The Legacy of China in
Pound and Williams*. Durham, NC: Duke University Press, 1995.
Ramazani, Jahan. *A Transnational Poetics*. Chicago: University of
Chicago Press, 2009.
Rogers, Gayle. *Modernism and the New Spain: Britain, Cosmopolitan
Europe, and Literary History*. New York: Oxford University Press,
2012.
Rosenberg, Fernando. *The Avant-Garde and Geopolitics in Latin
America*. Pittsburgh: University of Pittsburgh Press, 2006.
Said, Edward. *Culture and Imperialism*. New York: Knopf, 1993.
Walkowitz, Rebecca L. *Cosmopolitan Style: Modernism beyond the
Nation*. New York: Columbia University Press, 2006.
Wollaeger, Mark, ed. *The Oxford Handbook of Global Modernisms*.
New York: Oxford University Press, 2012.
Yao, Steven G. *Translation and the Languages of Modernism: Gender,
Politics, Language*. New York: Palgrave Macmillan, 2002.

# Modernism's print cultures

Ardis, Ann. *Modernism and Cultural Conflict, 1880–1922*. Cambridge:
Cambridge University Press, 2002.
Bornstein, George. *Material Modernism: The Politics of the Page*.
Cambridge: Cambridge University Press, 2001.
Braddock, Jeremy. *Collecting as Modernist Practice*. Baltimore: Johns
Hopkins University Press, 2012.

Brooker, Peter and Andrew Thacker. *The Oxford Critical and Cultural History of Modernist Magazines.* 3 vols. Oxford: Oxford University Press, 2009–13.

Carey, John. *The Intellectuals and the Masses: Pride and Prejudice among the Literary Intelligentsia, 1880-1939.* London: Faber and Faber, 1992.

Churchill, Suzanne W. *The Little Magazine* Others *and the Renovation of Modern American Poetry.* Aldershot: Ashgate, 2006.

Collier, Patrick. *Modernism on Fleet Street.* Aldershot: Ashgate, 2006.

Cooper, John Xiros. *Modernism and the Culture of Market Society.* Cambridge: Cambridge University Press, 2004.

Culter, Edward S. *Recovering the New: Transatlantic Roots of Modernism.* Hanover, NH: University Press of New England, 2003.

Dettmar, Kevin and Stephen Watt, eds. *Marketing Modernisms: Self-Promotion, Canonization, Rereading.* Ann Arbor: University of Michigan Press, 1996.

Earle, David M. *Re-covering Modernism: Pulps, Paperbacks, and the Prejudice of Form.* Burlington, VT: Ashgate, 2009.

English, James F. *The Economy of Prestige: Prizes, Awards, and the Circulation of Cultural Value.* Cambridge, MA: Harvard University Press, 2005.

Ferrall, Charles. *Modernist Writing and Reactionary Politics.* Cambridge: Cambridge University Press, 2001.

Hammill, Faye. *Sophistication: A Literary and Cultural History.* Liverpool: Liverpool University Press, 2010.

Jaffe, Aaron. *Modernism and the Culture of Celebrity.* Cambridge: Cambridge University Press, 2005.

Jaffe, Aaron and Jonathan Goldman. *Modernist Star Maps: Celebrity, Modernity, Culture.* Burlington, VT: Ashgate, 2010.

Latham, Sean. *"Am I a Snob?": Modernism and the Novel.* Ithaca: Cornell University Press, 2003.

Lutes, Jean Marie. *Front-Page Girls: Women Journalists in American Culture and Fiction, 1880–1930.* Ithaca: Cornell University Press, 2006.

Marek, Jayne E. *Women Editing Modernism: "Little" Magazines and Literary History.* Lexington: University of Kentucky Press, 1995.

McGann, Jerome J. *Black Riders: The Visible Language of Modernism.* Princeton, NJ: Princeton University Press, 1993.

Morrisson, Mark S. *The Public Face of Modernism: Little Magazines, Audiences, and Reception, 1905–1920.* Madison: University of Wisconsin Press, 2001.

North, Michael. *Reading 1922: A Return to the Scene of the Modern.* New York: Oxford University Press, 1999.

Ohmann, Richard. *Selling Culture: Magazines, Markets, and Class at the Turn of the Century.* London: Verso, 1996.

Peppis, Paul. *Literature, Politics, and the English Avant- Garde: Nation and Empire, 1901–1918.* Cambridge: Cambridge University Press, 2000.

Rainey, Lawrence. *Institutions of Modernism: Literary Elites and Public Culture.* New Haven: Yale University Press, 1998.

Rosenquist, Rod. *Modernism, the Market and the Institution of the New.* Cambridge: Cambridge University Press, 2009.

Scholes, Robert and Clifford Wulfman. *Modernism in the Magazines: An Introduction.* New Haven: Yale University Press, 2010.

Tratner, Michael. *Modernism and Mass Politics: Joyce, Woolf, Eliot, Yeats.* Stanford: Stanford University Press, 1995.

Villis, Tom. *Reaction and the Avant-garde: The Revolt Against Liberal Democracy in Early Twentieth-century Britain.* New York: St. Martins, 2006.

Wicke, Jennifer. *Advertising Fictions: Literature, Advertisement, and Social Reading.* New York: Columbia University Press, 1988.

# Modernism and mass media

Avery, Todd. *Radio Modernism: Literature, Ethics, and the BBC, 1922–1938.* Aldershot: Ashgate, 2006.

Bolter, Jay David and Richard Grusin. *Remediation: Understanding New Media.* Cambridge, MA: MIT Press, 1999.

Campbell, Timothy. *Wireless Writing in the Age of Marconi.* Minneapolis: University of Minnesota Press, 2006.

Charney, Leo and Vanessa R. Schwartz, eds. *Cinema and the Invention of Modern Life.* Berkeley: University of California Press, 1995.

Cohen, Debra Rae, Michael Coyle, and Jane Lewty, eds. *Broadcasting Modernism.* Gainesville: University of Florida Press, 2009.

Doane, Mary Ann. *The Emergence of Cinematic Time: Modernity, Contingency, the Archive.* Cambridge, MA: Harvard University Press, 2002.

Elsaesser, Thomas. "Tales of Sound and Fury." *Film Theory and Criticism.* Ed. Gerald Mast, Marshall Cohen, and Leo Braudy. New York: Oxford University Press, 1992. 244–58.

Goble, Mark. *Beautiful Circuits: Modernism and the Mediated Life.* New York: Columbia University Press, 2010.

Gunning, Tom. "The Cinema of Attractions: Early Film, Its Spectator and the Avant-Garde." *Wide Angle* 8.3–4 (Fall 1986): 63–70.

Hansen, Miriam. "The Mass Production of the Senses: Classical Cinema as Vernacular Modernism." *Modernism/modernity* 6.2 (April 1999): 59–77.

Marcus, Laura. *The Tenth Muse: Writing about Cinema in the Modernist Period*. Oxford: Oxford University Press, 2007.

McCabe, Susan. *Cinematic Modernism: Modernist Poetry and Film*. New York: Cambridge University Press, 2005.

Murphet, Julian. *Multimedia Modernism: Literature and the Anglo-American Avant-garde*. Cambridge: Cambridge University Press, 2009.

Naremore, James and Patrick Brantlinger, eds. *Modernity and Mass Culture*. Bloomington: Indiana University Press, 1991.

North, Michael. *Camera Works: Photography and the Twentieth-Century Word*. New York: Oxford University Press, 2005.

North, Michael. *Machine-Age Comedy*. New York: Oxford University Press, 2009.

Pressman, Jessica. *Digital Modernism: Making It New in New Media*. New York: Oxford University Press, 2014.

Sconce, Jeffrey. *Haunted Media: Electronic Presence from Telegraphy to Television*. Durham, NC: Duke University Press, 2000.

Sterne, Jonathan. *The Audible Past: Cultural Origins of Sound Reproduction*. Durham, NC: Duke University Press, 2003.

Taussig, Michael. *Mimesis and Alterity: A Particular History of the Senses*. New York: Routledge, 1993.

Trotter, David. *Cinema and Modernism*. Malden, MA: Blackwell, 2007.

Weheliye, Alexander G. *Phonographies: Grooves in Sonic Afro-Modernity*. Durham, NC: Duke University Press, 2005.

Wollaeger, Mark. *Modernism, Media, and Propaganda*. Princeton: Princeton University Press, 2006.

Young, Paul. *The Cinema Dreams Its Rivals: Media Fantasy Films from Radio to the Internet*. Minneapolis: University of Minnesota Press, 2006.

# Modernism and the law

Bru, Sascha. *Democracy, Law and the Modernist Avant-gardes: Writing in the State of Exception*. Edinburgh: Edinburgh University Press, 2009.

Hepburn, Allan, ed. *Troubled Legacies: Narrative and Inheritance*. Toronto: University of Toronto Press, 2007.

Irr, Caren. *Pink Pirates: Contemporary American Women Writers and Copyright*. Iowa City: University of Iowa Press, 2010.

Latham, Sean. *The Art of Scandal: Modernism, Libel Law, and the Roman à Clef*. New York: Oxford University Press, 2009.

Marshik, Celia. *British Modernism and Censorship*. Cambridge: Cambridge University Press, 2006.

Maxwell, William J. *F. B. Eyes: How J. Edgar Hoover's Ghostreaders Framed African American Literature*. Princeton, NJ: Princeton University Press, 2015.

Medd, Jodie. *Lesbian Scandal and the Culture of Modernism*. Cambridge: Cambridge University Press, 2012.

Miller, Andrew John. *Modernism and the Crisis of Sovereignty*. New York: Routledge, 2012.

Mullin Katherine. *James Joyce, Sexuality and Social Purity*. Cambridge: Cambridge University Press, 2003.

Parkes, Adam. *Modernism and the Theater of Censorship*. New York: Oxford University Press, 1996.

Potter, Rachel. *Obscene Modernism: Literary Censorship and Experiment, 1900-1940*. Oxford: Oxford University Press, 2013.

Reichman, Ravit. *The Affective Life of Law: Legal Modernism and the Literary Imagination*. Stanford, CA: Stanford University Press, 2009.

Saint-Amour, Paul. *The Copywrights: Intellectual Property and the Literary Imagination*. Ithaca, NY: Cornell University Press, 2003.

Saint-Amour, Paul, ed. *Modernism and Copyright*. New York: Oxford University Press, 2010.

Spoo, Robert. "Copyright Protectionism and Its Discontents: The Case of James Joyce's *Ulysses* in America." *Yale Law Journal* 108 (1998): 633–67.

Spoo, Robert. *Without Copyrights: Piracy, Publishing, and the Public Domain*. New York: Oxford University Press, 2013.

Strychacz, Thomas. *Modernism, Mass Culture, and Professionalism*. Cambridge: Cambridge University Press, 1993.

Trotter, David. *Paranoid Modernism: Literary Experiment, Psychosis, and the Professionalization of English Society*. Oxford: Oxford University Press, 2001.

Vanderham, Paul. *James Joyce and Censorship: The Trials of* Ulysses. New York: New York University Press, 1998.

# Modernism, war, and violence

Barnhisel, Greg. *Cold War Modernists: Art, Literature, and American Cultural Diplomacy*. New York: Columbia University Press, 2015.

Bonikowski, Wyatt. *Shell Shock and the Modernist Imagination: The Death Drive in Post-World War I British Fiction*. Burlington, VT: Ashgate, 2013.

Booth, Allyson. *Postcards from the Trenches: Negotiating the Space between Modernism and the First World War*. New York: Oxford, 1996.

Buch, Robert. *The Pathos of the Real: On the Aesthetics of Violence in the Twentieth Century*. Baltimore: Johns Hopkins University Press, 2010.

Caws, Mary Ann, ed. *Manifesto: A Century of Isms*. Lincoln: University of Nebraska Press, 2001.

Cobley, Evelyn. *Representing War: Form and Ideology in First World War Narratives*. Toronto: University of Toronto Press, 1993.
Cole, Sarah. *At the Violet Hour: Modernism and Violence in England and Ireland*. New York: Oxford University Press, 2012.
Cole, Sarah. *Modernism, Male Friendship, and the First World War*. New York: Cambridge University Press, 2003.
Das, Santanu, ed. *Race, Empire and First World War Writing*. Cambridge: Cambridge University Press, 2011.
Das, Santanu. *Touch and Intimacy in First World War Literature*. Cambridge: Cambridge University Press, 2005.
Davis, Thomas. *The Extinct Scene: Late Modernism and Everyday Life*. New York: Columbia University Press, 2015.
Dawes, James. *The Language of War: Literature and Culture in the U.S. from the Civil War through World War II*. Cambridge, MA: Harvard University Press, 2002.
Deer, Patrick. *Culture in Camouflage: War, Empire, and Modern British Literature*. Oxford: Oxford University Press, 2009.
Esty, Jed. *A Shrinking Island: Modernism and National Culture in England*. Princeton, NJ: Princeton University Press, 2004.
Eksteins, Modris. *Rites of Spring: The Great War and the Birth of the Modern Age*. Boston: Houghton Mifflin, 1989.
Fussell, Paul. *The Great War and Modern Memory*. New York: Oxford University Press, 1975.
Houen, Alex. *Terrorism and Modern Literature from Joseph Conrad to Ciaran Carson*. New York: Oxford University Press, 2002.
Krockel, Carl. *War Trauma and English Modernism: T. S. Eliot and D. H. Lawrence*. New York: Palgrave Macmillan, 2011.
Lyon, Janet. *Manifestoes: Provocations of the Modern*. Ithaca: Cornell University Press, 1999.
MacKay, Marina. *Modernism and World War II*. Cambridge: Cambridge University Press, 2007.
Mellor, Leo. *Reading the Ruins: Modernism, Bombsites and British Culture*. Cambridge: Cambridge University Press, 2011.
Miller, Tyrus. *Late Modernism: Politics, Fiction, and the Arts between the Wars*. Berkeley: University of California Press, 1999.
Puchner, Martin. *Poetry of the Revolution: Marx, Manifestos, and the Avant-Gardes*. Princeton: Princeton University Press, 2006.
Saint-Amour, Paul K. *Tense Future: Modernism, Total War, Encyclopedic Form*. New York: Oxford University Press, 2015.
Saunders, Frances Stonor. *The Cultural Cold War: The CIA and the World of Arts and Letters*. New York: New Press, 2000.
Sherry, Vincent. *The Great War and the Language of Modernism*. New York: Oxford University Press, 2003.

Tate, Trudi. *Modernism, History, and the First World War*. Manchester: Manchester University Press, 1998.

Végsö, Roland. *The Naked Communist: Cold War Modernism and the Politics of Popular Culture*. New York: Fordham University Press, 2013.

Winkiel, Laura. *Modernism, Race and Manifestos*. New York: Cambridge University Press, 2008.

Winter, Jay. *Sites of Memory, Sites of Mourning: The Great War in European Cultural History*. Cambridge: Cambridge University Press 1998.

# Modernism, science, and technology

Albright, Daniel. *Quantum Poetics: Yeats, Pound, Eliot, and the Science of Modernism*. New York: Cambridge University Press, 1997.

Armstrong, Tim. *Modernism, Technology, and the Body: A Cultural Study*. New York: Cambridge University Press, 1998.

Blanco, María del Pilar. *Ghost-watching American Modernity: Haunting, Landscape, and the Hemispheric Imagination*. New York: Fordham University Press, 2012.

Childs, Donald J. *Modernism and Eugenics: Woolf, Eliot, Yeats and the Culture of Degeneration*. Cambridge: Cambridge University Press, 2001.

Crary, Jonathan. *Techniques of the Observer: On Vision and Modernity in the Nineteenth Century*. Cambridge, MA: MIT Press, 1990.

Danius, Sara. *The Senses of Modernism: Technology, Perception, and Aesthetics*. Ithaca, NY: Cornell University Press, 2002.

Duffy, Enda. *The Speed Handbook: Velocity, Pleasure, Modernism*. Durham, NC: Duke University Press, 2009.

English, Daylanne K. *Unnatural Selections: Eugenics in American Modernism and the Harlem Renaissance*. Chapel Hill: University of North Carolina Press, 2004.

Foster, Hal. *Prosthetic Gods*. Cambridge, MA: MIT Press, 2004.

Golston, Michael. *Rhythm and Race in Modernist Poetry and Science*. New York: Columbia University Press, 2008.

Kern, Stephen. *The Culture of Time and Space, 1880-1918*. Cambridge, MA: Harvard University Press, 1983.

Kittler, Friedrich. *Gramophone, Film, Typewriter*. Trans. and Intro. Geoffrey Winthrop-Young and Michael Wutz. Stanford: Stanford University Press, 1999.

Lewis, Pericles. *Religious Experience and the Modernist Novel*. New York: Cambridge University Press, 2010.

Materer, Timothy. *Modernist Alchemy: Poetry and the Occult*. Ithaca, NY: Cornell University Press, 1995.

Morrisson, Mark. *Modern Alchemy: Occultism and the Emergence of Atomic Theory*. New York: Oxford University Press, 2007.

Owen, Alex. *The Darkened Room: Women, Power, and Spiritualism in Late Victorian England*. Philadelphia: University of Pennsylvania Press, 1990.

Rabinbach, Anson. *The Human Motor: Energy, Fatigue, and the Origins of Modernity*. New York: Basic Books, 1990.

Salisbury, Laura and Andrew Shail, eds. *Neurology and Modernity: A Cultural History of Nervous Systems, 1800-1950*. New York: Palgrave Macmillan, 2010.

Schivelbusch, Wolfgang. *The Railway Journey: The Industrialization of Time and Space in the Nineteenth Century*. Berkeley: University of California Press, 1986.

Surette, Leon and Demetres Tryphonopoulos, eds. *Literary Modernism and the Occult Tradition*. Orono, ME: University of Maine Press, 1996.

Thurschwell, Pamela. *Literature, Technology and Magical Thinking, 1880-1920*. Cambridge: Cambridge University Press, 2001.

Tiffany, Daniel. *Radio Corpse: Imagism and the Cryptaesthetic of Ezra Pound*. Cambridge, MA: Harvard University Press, 1995.

Wilson, Leigh. *Modernism and Magic: Experiments with Spiritualism, Theosophy and the Occult*. Edinburgh: Edinburgh University Press, 2013.

# Modernism and environments

Bachelard, Gaston. *The Poetics of Space*. Trans. Maria Jolas. Foreword Étienne Gilson. Boston: Beacon, 1969.

Blanchot, Maurice. *The Space of Literature*. Trans. and Intro. Ann Smock. Lincoln: University of Nebraska Press, 1982.

Buckler, Julie A. *Mapping St. Petersburg: Imperial Text and Cityshape*. Princeton, NJ: Princeton University Press, 2005.

Certeau, Michel de. *The Practice of Everyday Life*. Trans. Steven Rendall. Berkeley: University of California Press, 1984.

Clark, T. J. *The Painting of Modern Life: Paris in the Art of Manet and His Followers*. New York: Knopf, 1984.

Gleason, William. *Sites Unseen: Architecture, Race, and American Literature*. New York: New York University Press, 2011.

Grosz, Elizabeth. *Architecture from the Outside: Essays on Virtual and Real Space*. Foreword by Peter Eisenman. Cambridge, MA: MIT Press, 2001.

Harvey, David. *Paris, Capital of Modernity*. New York: Routledge, 2003.

Jencks, Charles. *The Language of Post-modern Architecture*. New York: Rizzoli, 1977.

Lefebvre, Henri. *The Production of Space*. Trans. Donald Nicholson-Smith. Malden, MA: Wiley-Blackwell, 1992.

Mao, Douglas. *Solid Objects: Modernism and the Test of Production*. Princeton, NJ: Princeton University Press, 1998.

Mendelson, Jordana. *Documenting Spain: Artists, Exhibition Culture, and the Modern Nation, 1929-1939*. University Park: Pennsylvania State University Press, 2005.

Parsons, Deborah L. *Streetwalking the Metropolis: Women, the City, and Modernity*. Oxford: Oxford University Press, 2000.

Raine, Anne. "Ecocriticism and Modernism." *The Oxford Handbook of Ecocriticism*. Ed. Greg Garrard. New York: Oxford University Press, 2014. 98–117.

Rasula, Jed and Tim Conley, eds. *Burning City: Poems of Metropolitan Modernity*. Notre Dame, IN: Action Books, 2012.

Rosner, Victoria. *Modernism and the Architecture of Private Life*. New York: Columbia University Press, 2005.

Rubenstein, Michael. *Public Works: Infrastructure, Irish Modernism, and the Postcolonial*. Notre Dame, IN: University of Notre Dame Press, 2010.

Scappettone, Jennifer. *Killing the Moonlight: Modernism in Venice*. New York: Columbia University Press, 2014.

Schulze, Robin. *The Degenerate Muse: American Nature, Modernist Poetry, and the Problem of Cultural Hygiene*. New York: Oxford University Press, 2013.

Scott, Bonnie Kime. "Green." *Modernism and Theory: A Critical Debate*. Ed. Ross. New York: Routledge, 2009. 219–24.

Sharpe, William Chapman. *New York Nocturne: The City after Dark in Literature, Painting, and Photography, 1850-1950*. Princeton, NJ: Princeton University Press, 2008.

Spurr, David. *Architecture and Modern Literature*. Ann Arbor: University of Michigan Press, 2012.

Thacker, Andrew. *Modernism, Space and the City*. Edinburgh: Edinburgh University Press, 2014.

Thacker, Andrew. *Moving through Modernity: Space and Geography in Modernism*. Manchester: Manchester University Press, 2009.

Venturi, Robert, Denise Scott Brown, and Steven Izenour. *Learning from Las Vegas: The Forgotten Symbolism of Architectural Form* (1972; revised 1977). Cambridge, MA: MIT Press, 1977.

Walkowitz, Judith. *Nights Out: Life in Cosmopolitan London*. New Haven: Yale University Press, 2012.

Wolff, Janet. "The Invisible Flâneuse: Women and the Literature of Modernity." *Theory, Culture & Society* 2.3 (November 1985): 37–46.

# WORKS CITED

Adorno, Theodor. *Aesthetic Theory*. Trans. C. Lenhardt. Ed. Gretel Adorno and Rolf Tiedemann. London; Boston: Routledge and K. Paul, 1984.

Adorno, Theodor. *Minima Moralia: Reflections from Damaged Life*. Trans. E. F. N. Jephcott. London: New Left Books, 1974.

Adorno, Theodor. *Negative Dialectics*. Trans. E. B. Ashton. New York: Continuum, 1995.

Altieri, Charles. *The Art of Twentieth-century Poetry: Modernism and After*. Malden, MA: Blackwell, 2006.

Altieri, Charles. *Enlarging the Temple: New Directions in American Poetry*. Lewisburg, PA: Bucknell University Press, 1979.

Altieri, Charles. "How the 'New Modernist Studies' Fails the Old Modernism." *Textual Practice* 26.4 (2012): 763–82.

Altieri, Charles. "Objective Image and Act of Mind in Modern Poetry." *PMLA* 91.1 (January 1976): 101–14.

Altieri, Charles. *Painterly Abstraction in Modernist American Poetry: The Contemporaneity of Modernism*. New York: Cambridge University Press, 1989.

Anderson, Perry. *A Zone of Engagement*. London: Verso, 1992.

Antin, David. "Modernism and Postmodernism: Approaching the Present in American Poetry." *Radical Coherency: Selected Essays on Art and Literature, 1966-2005*. Chicago: Chicago University Press, 2012. 161–96.

Ardis, Ann L. *Modernism and Cultural Conflict, 1880-1922*. New York: Cambridge University Press, 2002.

Auerbach, Erich. *Mimesis: The Representation of Reality in Western Literature*. Intro. Edward W. Said. Princeton, NJ: Princeton University Press, 2003.

Baker, Houston. *Blues, Ideology, and Afro-American Literature: A Vernacular Theory*. Chicago: University of Chicago Press, 1984.

Baker, Houston. *Modernism and the Harlem Renaissance*. Chicago: University of Chicago Press, 1987.

Barth, John. "The Literature of Exhaustion." *The Friday Book: Essays and Other Nonfiction*. Baltimore: Johns Hopkins University Press, 1984.

Barthes, Roland. *Mythologies*. Trans. Annette Lavers and Richard Howard. New York: Hill and Wang, 2013.

Barthes, Roland. *S/Z: An Essay*. Trans. Richard Miller. New York: Hill and Wang, 1975.

Baudelaire, Charles. "The Painter of Modern Life." *Modernism: An Anthology of Sources and Documents*. Ed. Vassiliki Kolocotroni, Jane Goldman, and Olga Taxidou. Edinburgh: Edinburgh University Press, 1998. 102–8.

Beach, Joseph Warren. *The Twentieth Century Novel: Studies in Technique*. New York: The Century Co., 1932.

Beckett, Samuel. "Dante... Bruno. Vico... Joyce." *Our Exagmination Round His Factification For Incamination of Work in Progress*. Ed. Samuel Beckett, Frank Budgen, Eugene Jolas, et al. New York: New Directions, 1972. 1–22.

Beebe, Maurice. "What Modernism Was." *Journal of Modern Literature* 3.5 (July 1974): 1065–84.

Bell, Clive. *Art*. London: Chatto & Windus, 1931.

Bell, Michael. "F. R. Leavis." *The Cambridge History of Literary Criticism. Modernism and the New Criticism*. Ed. A. Walton Litz, Louis Menand, and Lawrence Rainey. 7 vols. Cambridge: Cambridge University Press, 2000. 7: 389–422.

Benjamin, Walter. "The Crisis of the Novel." Trans. Rodney Livingstone. *Selected Writings*. Ed. Michael W. Jennings, Howard Eiland, and Gary Smith. 4 vols. 2: Part 1. Cambridge, MA: Harvard University Press, 2005. 299–304.

Benjamin, Walter. "The Work of Art in the Age of Mechanical Reproduction." *Illuminations: Essays and Reflections*. Ed. and Intro. Hannah Arendt. Trans. Harry. New York: Schocken Books, 1969. 217–51.

Benstock, Shari. *Women of the Left Bank: Paris, 1900–1940*. Austin: University of Texas Press, 1986.

Berman, Marshall. *All That Is Solid Melts into Air: The Experience of Modernity*. London: Verso, 1983.

Blackmur, R. P. *New Criticism in the United States*. Folcroft, PA: Folcroft, 1971.

Blomfield, Reginald. *Modernismus*. London: Macmillan, 1934.

Bloom, Harold. *A Map of Misreading*. New York: Oxford University Press, 2003.

Bogan, Louise. "Modernism in American Literature." *American Quarterly* 2.2 (Summer 1950): 99–111.

Bornstein, George. *Material Modernism: The Politics of the Page*. Cambridge: Cambridge University Press, 2001.

Bornstein, George. "The Once and Future Texts of Modernist Poetry." *The Future of Modernism*. Ed. Hugh Witemeyer. Ann Arbor: University of Michigan Press, 1997. 161–79.

Bourdieu, Pierre. "The Field of Cultural Production, or: The Economic World Reversed." *The Field of Cultural Production*. Ed. and Intro. Randal Johnson. New York: Columbia University Press, 1993. 29–73.

Bradbury, Malcolm. "Modernity in Modern English Literature." *Modernism: Critical Concepts in Literary and Cultural Studies*. Ed. Tim Middleton. 5 vols. New York: Routledge, 2003. 68–94.

Bradbury, Malcolm and James McFarlane. "The Name and Nature of Modernism." *Modernism: A Guide to European Literature, 1890-1930*. London: Penguin, 1991. 19–55.

Breslin, James E. B. *From Modern to Contemporary: American Poetry, 1945-65*. Chicago: University of Chicago Press, 1984.

Brooks, Cleanth. "The Heresy of Paraphrase." *Twentieth-Century Literary Theory: An Introductory Anthology*. Ed. Vassilis Lambropoulos and David Neal Miller. Albany: State University of New York Press, 1987. 239–53.

Brooks, Cleanth. *Modern Poetry and the Tradition*. Chapel Hill: University of North Carolina Press, 1939.

Brzezinski, Max. "The New Modernist Studies: What's Left of Political Formalism?" *minnesota review* 76 (Spring 2011): 109–25.

Bürger, Peter. *The Decline of Modernism*. Trans. Nicholas Walker. Cambridge: Polity Press, 1992.

Bürger, Peter. *The Theory of the Avant-Garde*. Trans. Michael Shaw. Minneapolis: University of Minnesota Press, 1984.

Călinescu, Matei. *Five Faces of Modernity: Modernism, Avant-Garde, Decadence, Kitsch, Postmodernism*. Durham, NC: Duke University Press, 1987.

Casanova, Pascale. *The World Republic of Letters*. Trans. M. B. DeBevoise. Cambridge, MA: Harvard University Press, 2004.

Chase, William Merritt. "Velasquez." *The Quartier Latin* 1 (July 1896): 4–5.

Cheng, Anne Anlin. *Second Skin: Josephine Baker and the Modern Surface*. New York: Oxford University Press, 2011.

Clark, T. J. *Farewell to an Idea: Episodes from a History of Modernism*. New Haven: Yale University Press, 1999.

Conor, Liz. *The Spectacular Modern Woman: Feminine Visibility in the 1920s*. Bloomington: Indiana University Press, 2004.

Conrad, Joseph. "Travel: Preface to Richard Curle's *Into the East*." *Last Essays*. Ed. Harold Ray Stevens and J. H. Stape. Cambridge: Cambridge University Press, 2010. 64–70.

Cuddy-Keane, Melba, Adam Hammond, and Alexandra Peat. *Modernism: Keywords*. Malden, MA: Wiley-Blackwell, 2014.

Davidson, Harriet. "Improper Desire: Reading *The Waste Land*." *The Cambridge Companion to T. S. Eliot*. Ed. A. David Moody. Cambridge: Cambridge University Press, 1995. 121–31.

DeKoven, Marianne. *Rich and Strange: Gender, History, Modernism*. Princeton, NJ: Princeton University Press, 1991.

DeVree, Howard. "Modernism Under Fire." *New York Times* (September 11, 1949): X6.

Doan, Laura and Jane Garrity, eds. *Sapphic Modernities: Sexuality, Women, and National Culture*. New York: Palgrave Macmillan, 2006.

Doyle, Laura. *Freedom's Empire: Race and the Rise of the Novel in Atlantic Modernity, 1640-1940*. Durham, NC: Duke University Press, 2008.

Du Bois, W. E. B. "Criteria of Negro Art." *The Wiley Blackwell Anthology of African American Literature*. Ed. Gene Andrew Jarrett. 2 vols. Malden, MA: Wiley Blackwell, 2014. 2: 157–63.

Du Bois, W. E. B. "Opinion." *Crisis* 24.4 (August 1922): 151–5.

Du Bois, W. E. B. *The Souls of Black Folk*. Rockville, MD: Arc Manor, 2008.

Duffy, Enda. *The Speed Handbook: Velocity, Pleasure, Modernism*. Durham, NC: Duke University Press, 2009.

Eagleton, Terry. *Exiles and Émigrés: Studies in Modern Literature*. London: Chatto & Windus, 1970.

Edwards, Brent Hayes. *The Practice of Diaspora: Literature, Translation, and the Rise of Black Internationalism*. Cambridge, MA: Harvard University Press, 2003.

Eliot, T. S. "Commentary." *Criterion* 2.7 (April 1924): 231–5.

Eliot, T. S. "The Function of Criticism." *Selected Prose of T. S. Eliot*. Ed. and Intro. Frank Kermode. New York: Harcourt Brace Jovanovich, 1975. 68–76.

Eliot, T. S. "London Letter." *Dial* 71.4 (October 1921): 452–5.

Eliot, T. S. "The Metaphysical Poets." *Selected Prose of T. S. Eliot*. Ed. and Intro. Frank Kermode. New York: Harcourt Brace Jovanovich, 1975. 59–67.

Eliot, T. S. *The Sacred Wood*. 2nd ed. London: Metheun, 1928.

Eliot, T. S. *To Criticize the Critic and Other Writings*. New York: Farrar, Straus and Giroux, 1965.

Eliot, T. S. "Tradition and the Individual Talent." *Selected Prose of T. S. Eliot*. Ed. and Intro. Frank Kermode. New York: Harcourt Brace Jovanovich, 1975. 37–44.

Eliot, T. S. "*Ulysses*, Order, and Myth." *Selected Prose of T. S. Eliot*. Ed. and Intro. Frank Kermode. New York: Harcourt Brace Jovanovich, 1975. 175–8.

Eliot, T. S. "The Waste Land." *The Complete Poems and Plays, 1909-1950*. New York: Harcourt, Brace and Company, 1980. 37–55.

Ellmann, Richard. *James Joyce*. Rev. ed. Oxford: Oxford University Press, 1982.

Ellmann, Richard and Charles Feidelson. "Preface." *The Modern Tradition: Backgrounds of Modern Literature*. Ed. Ellmann and Feidelson. New York: Oxford University Press, 1965. v–ix.

English, James F. *The Economy of Prestige: Prizes, Awards, and the Circulation of Cultural Value.* Cambridge, MA: Harvard University Press, 2005.

Eysteinsson, Astradur. *The Concept of Modernism.* Ithaca: Cornell University Press, 1990.

Faulkner, Peter. *Modernism.* New York: Harper and Row, 1977.

Feidelson, Charles. *Symbolism and American Literature.* Chicago: University of Chicago Press, 1953.

Felski, Rita. *The Gender of Modernity.* Cambridge, MA: Harvard University Press, 1995.

Fiedler, Leslie A. "The Death of Avant-Garde Literature." *The Collected Essays of Leslie Fiedler,* 2 vols. New York: Stein and Day, 1971. 2: 454–60.

Fiedler, Leslie A. "The New Mutants." *The Collected Essays of Leslie Fiedler,* 2 vols. New York: Stein and Day, 1971. 2: 379–400.

Filreis, Alan. *Counter-revolution of the Word: The Conservative Attack on Modern Poetry, 1945-1960.* Chapel Hill: University of North Carolina Press, 2008.

Flaubert, Gustave. *The Letters of Gustave Flaubert, 1830-1857.* Ed. and Trans. Francis Steegmuller. Cambridge, MA: Harvard University Press, 1980.

Ford, Ford Madox [Ford Madox Hueffer]. *Thus to Revisit: Some Reminiscences.* New York: E. P. Dutton & Co, 1921.

Foster, Hal. "Introduction." *The Anti-Aesthetic: Essays on Postmodern Culture.* Ed. Foster. New York: The New Press, 1998. ix–xvii.

Frank, Joseph. "Spatial Form in Modern Literature." *Sewanee Review* 53.2 (Spring 1945): 221–40.

Frank, Joseph. "Spatial Form in Modern Literature: An Essay in Three Parts." *Sewanee Review* 53.4 (Autumn 1945): 643–53.

Fried, Michael. "Art and Objecthood." *Art and Objecthood: Essays and Reviews.* Chicago: University of Chicago Press, 1998. 148–72.

Friedman, Susan Stanford. "Definitional Excursions: The Meanings of Modern/Modernism/Modernity." *Modernism/modernity* 8.3 (September 2001): 493–513.

Friedman, Susan Stanford. "Periodizing Modernism: Postcolonial Modernities and the Space/Time Borders of Modernist Studies." *Modernism/modernity* 13.3 (Spring 2006): 425–43.

Friedman, Susan Stanford. "Planetarity: Musing Modernist Studies." *Modernism/modernity* 17.3 (September 2010): 471–99.

Friedman, Susan Stanford. "Theory." *Modernism and Theory: A Critical Debate.* Ed. Stephen Ross. New York: Routledge, 2009. 237–45.

Fry, Paul H. "I. A. Richards." *The Cambridge History of Literary Criticism. Modernism and the New Criticism.* Ed. A. Walton Litz, Louis Menand, and Lawrence Rainey. 7 vols. Cambridge: Cambridge University Press, 2000. 7: 181–99.

Fry, Roger. *A Roger Fry Reader.* Ed. and Intro. Christopher Reed. Chicago: University of Chicago Press, 1996.

Gates, Henry Louis, Jr. "The Black Man's Burden." *Fear of a Queer Planet: Queer Politics and Social Theory.* Ed. Michael Warner. Minneapolis: University of Minnesota Press, 1993. 230–8.

Gates, Henry Louis, Jr. *The Signifying Monkey: A Theory of Afro-American Literary Criticism.* New York: Oxford University Press, 1988.

Gaudier-Brzeska, Henri. "Vortex Gaudier-Brzeska." *BLAST* 2 (1915): 33–4.

George, W. L. "A Painter's Literature." *Modernism: Critical Concepts in Literary and Cultural Studies.* Ed. Tim Middleton. 5 vols. New York: Routledge, 2003. 1: 145–53.

Gikandi, Simon. *Maps of Englishness: Writing Identity in the Culture of Colonialism.* New York: Columbia University Press, 1996.

Gikandi, Simon. *Writing in Limbo: Modernism and Caribbean Literature.* Ithaca: Cornell University Press, 1992.

Gilbert, Geoff. *Before Modernism Was: Modern History and the Constituency of Writing.* Houndmills: Palgrave Macmillan, 2004.

Gilbert, Sandra and Susan Gubar. *No Man's Land: The Place of the Woman Writer in the Twentieth Century. Volume 3: Letters from the Front.* New Haven: Yale University Press, 1994.

Gilroy, Paul. *The Black Atlantic: Modernity and Double Consciousness.* Cambridge, MA: Harvard University Press, 1993.

Goble, Mark. *Beautiful Circuits: Modernism and the Mediated Life.* New York: Columbia University Press, 2010.

GoGwilt, Christopher. *The Passage of Literature: Genealogies of Modernism in Conrad, Rhys, and Pramoedya.* New York: Oxford University Press, 2011.

Golding, Alan. *From Outlaw to Classic: Canons in American Poetry.* Madison: University of Wisconsin Press, 1995.

Graff, Gerald. *Literature Against Itself: Literary Ideas in Modern Society.* Chicago: University of Chicago Press, 1979.

Greenberg, Clement. "Avant-Garde and Kitsch." *Clement Greenberg: The Collected Essays and Criticism.* Ed. John O'Brian. 4 vols. Chicago: University of Chicago Press, 1986. 1: 5–22.

Greenberg, Clement. "Modernist Painting." *Clement Greenberg: The Collected Essays and Criticism.* Ed. John O'Brian. 4 vols. Chicago: University of Chicago Press, 1986. 4: 85–93.

Greenberg, Clement. "Towards a Newer Laocoon." *Clement Greenberg: The Collected Essays and Criticism.* Ed. John O'Brian. 4 vols. Chicago: University of Chicago Press, 1986. 1: 23–41.

Greenberg, Clement. "An upside-down world?" In *Multiple Modernities, 1905-1970.* Press kit. Centre national d'art et de culture Georges Pompidou. 2013. 16–24.

Habermas, Jürgen. "Modernity—An Incomplete Project." Trans. Seyla Ben-Habib. *The Anti-Aesthetic: Essays on Postmodern Culture.* Ed. Hal Foster. New York: The New Press, 1998. 1–15.

Hardy, Thomas. *Tess of the D'Urbervilles: A Pure Woman Faithfully Presented*. New York: Harper & Brothers, 1895.

Harrison, John R. *The Reactionaries: Yeats, Lewis, Pound, Eliot, Lawrence: A Study of the Anti-Democratic Intelligentsia*. New York: Schocken, 1967.

Harvey, David. *The Condition of Postmodernity: An Enquiry into the Origins of Cultural Change*. Malden, MA: Wiley-Blackwell, 1990.

Hassan, Ihab. *The Dismemberment of Orpheus: Toward a Postmodern Literature*. 2nd ed. Madison: University of Wisconsin Press, 1982.

Hassan, Ihab. "POSTmodernISM: A Paracritical Bibliography." *New Literary History* 3.1 (Fall 1971): 5–30.

Hayot, Eric. *On Literary Worlds*. New York: Oxford University Press, 2012.

Hoffman, Frederick J., Charles Allen, and Carolyn F. Ulrich. *The Little Magazine: A History and a Bibliography*. Princeton, NJ: Princeton University Press, 1946.

Hough, Graham. *Reflections on a Literary Revolution*. Washington, DC: Catholic University of America Press, 1960.

Howe, Irving. "The Idea of the Modern." *Literary Modernism*. Ed. Howe. Greenwich, CT: Fawcett, 1967. 11–40.

Hughes, Langston. "The Negro Artist and the Racial Mountain." *The Wiley Blackwell Anthology of African American Literature*. Ed. Gene Andrew Jarrett. 2 vols. Malden, MA: Wiley Blackwell, 2014. 2: 210–13.

Hulme, T. E. "Cinders." *The Collected Writings of T. E. Hulme*. Ed. Karen Csengeri. Oxford: Clarendon, 1994. 7–22.

Hulme, T. E. "A Lecture on Modern Poetry." *The Collected Writings of T. E. Hulme*. Ed. Karen Csengeri. Oxford: Clarendon, 1994. 49–56.

Hulme, T. E. "Modern Art II: A Preface Note and Neo-Realism." *The Collected Writings of T. E. Hulme*. Ed. Karen Csengeri. Oxford: Clarendon, 1994. 286–93.

Hulme, T. E. "Romanticism and Classicism." *The Collected Writings of T. E. Hulme*. Ed. Karen Csengeri. Oxford: Clarendon, 1994. 59–83.

Hutchinson, George. *The Harlem Renaissance in Black and White*. Cambridge, MA: Harvard University Press, 1995.

Huyssen, Andreas. *After the Great Divide: Modernism, Mass Culture, Postmodernism*. Bloomington: University of Indiana Press, 1986.

Huyssen, Andreas. "High/Low in an Expanded Field." *Modernism/ modernity* 9.3 (September 2002): 363–74.

Inge, W. R. *Modernism in Literature*. London: H. Millford, Oxford University Press, 1937.

Isherwood, Christopher. *The Berlin Stories*. Intro. Armistead Maupin. New York: New Directions, 2008.

Jackson, Holbrook. "A Plea for Revolt in Attitude." *Rhythm* 1.3 (Winter 1911): 6–10.

Jaffe, Aaron. *Modernism and the Culture of Celebrity*. New York: Cambridge University Press, 2005.

James, David and Urmila Seshagiri. "Metamodernism: Narratives of Continuity and Revolution." *PMLA* 129.1 (January 2014): 87–100.

James, Henry. "Henry James's First Interview." By Preston Lockwood. *New York Times* (March 21, 1915): 4.

Jameson, Fredric. "Baudelaire as Modernist and Postmodernist: The Dissolution of the Referent and the Artificial 'Sublime.'" *The Lyric Theory Reader: A Critical Anthology*. Eds. Virginia Jackson and Yopie Prins. Baltimore, MD: Johns Hopkins University Press, 2014. 350–61.

Jameson, Fredric. *Fables of Aggression: Wyndham Lewis, the Modernist as Fascist*. Berkeley: University of California Press, 1979.

Jameson, Fredric. "Modernism and Imperialism." *Nationalism, Colonialism, and Literature*. Ed. Seamus Deane. Minneapolis: University of Minnesota Press, 1990. 43–68.

Jameson, Fredric. *The Political Unconscious: Narrative as a Socially Symbolic Act*. Ithaca: Cornell University Press, 1981.

Jameson, Fredric. *A Singular Modernity: Essay on the Ontology of the Present*. London: Verso, 2002.

Jameson, Fredric. "*Ulysses* in History." *The Modernist Papers*. London: Verso, 2007. 137–51.

Jancovich, Mark. "The Southern New Critics." *The Cambridge History of Literary Criticism. Modernism and the New Criticism*. Ed. A. Walton Litz, Louis Menand, and Lawrence Rainey. 7 vols. Cambridge: Cambridge University Press, 2000. 7: 200–18.

Jarrell, Randall. "The End of the Line." *Kipling, Auden & Co.: Essays and Reviews, 1935-1964*. New York: Farrar, Straus and Giroux, 1980. 76–83.

Jencks, Charles. *The New Paradigm in Architecture: The Language of Post-modernism*. New Haven, CT: Yale University Press, 2002.

Jolas, Eugene. *Man from Babel*. Ed. and Intro. Andreas Kramer and Rainer Rumold. New Haven: Yale University Press, 1998.

Jolas, Eugene et al. "Proclamation ('Revolution of the Word,' 1929)." *Eugene Jolas: Critical Writings, 1924-1951*. Ed. and Intro. Klaus H. Kiefer and Rainer Rumold. Evanston, IL: Northwestern University Press, 2009. 111–12.

Jones, LeRoi [Amiri Baraka]. "Introduction." *The Moderns: An Anthology of New Writing in America*. New York: Corinth Books, 1963. ix–xvi.

Joyce, James. *The Letters of James Joyce*. Ed. Stuart Gilbert. 3 vols. New York: Viking Press, 1957–66.

Joyce, James. *Ulysses*. Ed. Hans Walter Gabler. New York: Vintage Books, 1984.

Karl, Frederick. *Modern and Modernism: The Sovereignty of the Artist, 1885-1925*. New York: Atheneum, 1985.

Kaufmann, Michael Edward. "T. S. Eliot's New Critical Footnotes to Modernism." *Rereading the New: A Backward Glance at Modernism*.

Ed. Kevin J. H. Dettmar. Ann Arbor: University of Michigan Press, 1992. 73–85.

Kazin, Alfred. *On Native Grounds: An Interpretation of Modern American Prose Literature*. New York: Reynal and Hitchcock, 1942.

Kenner, Hugh. *The Pound Era*. Berkeley: University of California Press, 1971.

Kermode, Frank. *Continuities*. London: Routledge & Kegan Paul, 1968.

Kermode, Frank. *History and Value: The Clarendon Lectures and the Northcliffe Lectures*. Oxford: Clarendon Press, 1987.

Kermode, Frank. *Romantic Image*. London: Routledge, 2002.

Kermode, Frank. *The Sense of an Ending: Studies in the Theory of Fiction*. Oxford: Oxford University Press, 2000.

Kittler, Friedrich. *Gramophone, Film, Typewriter*. Trans. and Intro. Geoffrey Winthrop-Young and Michael Wutz. Stanford: Stanford University Press, 1999.

Kracauer, Siegfried. "The Mass Ornament." *The Mass Ornament: Weimar Essays*. Trans., Ed., and Intro. Thomas Y. Levin. Cambridge, MA: Harvard University Press, 1995.

Krauss, Rosalind. *The Originality of the Avant-Garde and Other Modernist Myths*. Cambridge, MA: MIT Press, 1986.

Kristeva, Julia. *Séméiôtikè: Recherches pour une sémanalyse*. Paris: Éditions du Seuil, 1969.

Lacan, Jacques. *Le séminaire de Jacques Lacan: Livre XXIII, Le sinthome (1975-76)*. Ed. Jacques-Alain Miller. Paris: Éditions du Seuil, 2005.

Lavrin, Janko. *Aspects of Modernism: From Wilde to Pirandello*. Freeport, NY: Books for Library Press, 1968.

Leavis, F. R. "English Letter." *Poetry* 44.2 (May 1934): 98–102.

Leavis, F. R. *New Bearings in English Poetry: A Study of the Contemporary Situation*. London: Chatto & Windus, 1942.

Leavis, F. R. "Retrospect 1950." *New Bearings in English Poetry*. New York: George W. Stewart, 1950. 215–38.

Lefebvre, Henri. *The Production of Space*. Trans. Donald Nicholson-Smith. Malden, MA: Wiley-Blackwell, 1992.

Levenson, Michael. *A Genealogy of Modernism: A Study of English Literary Doctrine, 1908-1922*. New York: Cambridge University Press, 1984.

Levin, Harry. "What Was Modernism?" *Massachusetts Review* 1.4 (Summer 1960): 609–30.

Lewis, Wyndham. *Blasting & Bombardiering*. Berkeley: University of California Press, 1967.

Locke, Alain. "Negro Youth Speaks." *The New Negro: An Interpretation*. Ed. Locke. Intro. Arnold Rampersad. New York: Atheneum, 1992. 47–53.

Longenbach, James. *Modern Poetry after Modernism*. New York: Oxford University Press, 1997.

Longenbach, James. *Stone Cottage: Pound, Yeats, and Modernism*. New York: Oxford University Press, 1988.

Longworth, Deborah. "Gendering the Modernist Text." *The Oxford Handbook of Modernisms*. Eds. Peter Brooker, Andrzej Gasiorek, and Andrew Thacker. Oxford: Oxford University Press, 2010. 156–77.

Lowell, Amy. "Preface." *Some Imagist Poets: An Anthology*. Boston: Houghton Mifflin, 1915. v–viii.

Lowell, Amy. *Tendencies in Modern American Poetry*. New York: Macmillan, 1917.

Lukács, György. "The Ideology of Modernism." *The Meaning of Contemporary Realism*. Trans. John and Necke Mander. London: Merlin Press, 1963. 17–46.

Lunn, Eugene. *Marxism and Modernism: An Historical Study of Lukács, Brecht, Benjamin and Adorno*. Berkeley: University of California Press, 1982.

Lyotard, Jean-François. *The Postmodern Condition: A Report on Knowledge*. Trans. Geoff Bennington and Brian Massumi. Foreword by Fredric Jameson. Minneapolis: University of Minnesota Press, 1984.

MacCabe, Colin. *James Joyce and the Revolution of the Word*. New York: Harper, 1979.

Man, Paul de. "Literary History and Literary Modernity." *Blindness and Insight: Essays in the Rhetoric of Contemporary Criticism*. Intro. Wlad Godzich. New York: Routledge, 1983. 142–65.

Mao, Douglas and Rebecca L. Walkowitz. "The New Modernist Studies." *PMLA* 123.3 (May 2008): 737–48.

Marinetti, F. T. "The Foundation and Manifesto of Futurism." *Critical Writings: New Edition*. Ed. Günter Berghaus. Trans. Doug Thompson. New York: Farrar, Straus & Giroux, 2008. 11–17.

Marshik, Celia. *British Modernism and Censorship*. Cambridge: Cambridge University Press, 2006.

Matthiessen, F. O. *The Achievement of T. S. Eliot*. Boston: Houghton Mifflin, 1935.

Michaels, Walter Benn. *Our America: Nativism, Modernism, and Pluralism*. Durham, NC: Duke University Press, 1995.

Miller, Tyrus. *Late Modernism: Politics, Fiction, and the Arts between the Wars*. Berkeley: University of California Press, 1999.

"Mimeograph." Advertisement for the Edison-Dick Mimeograph. *Life* (February 22, 1929): 2.

"moderne." *Dictionnaire Historique de la Langue Française*. Ed. Alain Rey. 2 vols. Paris: Dictionnaires Le Robert, 1992. 2: 1258–9.

"modernism." *The International English and French Dictionary*. Ed. Leon Smith and Henry Hamilton. Paris: Ch. Fouraut, 1866. 391.

"modernism." *Oxford English Dictionary*. www.oed.com. Accessed May 18, 2013.

"modernist." *Oxford English Dictionary*. www.oed.com. Accessed May 21, 2013.

Modernist Studies Association. "Member Services." http://msa.press.jhu.
    edu/members/. Accessed July 25, 2013.
Monroe, Harriet. "Imagism Today and Yesterday." Review of *Imagist
    Anthology 1930–New Poetry* by Richard Aldington et al. *Poetry*
    35.4 (July 1930): 213–18.
Nelson, Cary. *Repression and Recovery: Modern American Poetry and
    the Politics of Cultural Memory, 1910-1945*. Madison: University of
    Wisconsin Press, 1989.
North, Michael. *The Dialect of Modernism: Race, Language, and
    Twentieth-Century Literature*. New York: Oxford University Press,
    1994.
North, Michael. *Novelty: A History of the New*. Chicago: University of
    Chicago Press, 2013.
Paz, Octavio. *Children of the Mire: Modern Poetry from Romanticism
    to the Avant-Garde*. Trans. Rachel Phillips. Cambridge, MA: Harvard
    University Press, 1974.
Perkins, David. *History of Modern Poetry, Volume 1: From the 1890s to the
    High Modernist Mode*. Cambridge, MA: Harvard University Press, 1976.
Perloff, Marjorie. *The Futurist Moment: Avant-Garde, Avant Guerre, and
    the Language of Rupture*. Chicago: University of Chicago Press, 2003.
Perloff, Marjorie. "Modernist Studies." *Redrawing the Boundaries: The
    Transformation of English and American Literary Studies*. Ed. Stephen
    Greenblatt and Giles Gunn. New York: Modern Language Association,
    1992. 154–78.
Perloff, Marjorie. *The Poetics of Indeterminacy: Rimbaud to Cage*.
    Princeton: Princeton University Press, 1981.
Perloff, Marjorie. "Pound/Stevens: Whose Era?" *New Literary History*
    13.3 (Spring 1982): 485–514.
Perloff, Marjorie. *21st-Century Modernism: The "New" Poetics*. Malden,
    MA: Blackwell, 2002.
Poggioli, Renato. *The Theory of the Avant-Garde*. Trans. Gerald
    Fitzgerald. Cambridge, MA: Harvard University Press, 1968.
Pope Pius X. "Pascendi dominici gregis" [1907]. http://www.vatican.va/
    holy_father/pius_x/encyclicals/documents/hf_p-x_enc_19070908_
    pascendi-dominici-gregis_en.html. Accessed August 2, 2013.
Pound, Ezra. *ABC of Reading*. Intro. Michael Dirda. New York:
    New Directions, 2010.
Pound, Ezra. "Affirmations: Vorticism." *New Age* 16.11 (January 14,
    1915): 277–8.
Pound, Ezra. *Cantos*. New York: New Directions, 1996.
Pound, Ezra. *Gaudier-Brzeska: A Memoir*. New York: New Directions, 1974.
Pound, Ezra. "Harold Monro." *Criterion* 11.45 (July 1932): 581–92.
Pound, Ezra. *Literary Essays of Ezra Pound*. Ed. and Intro. T. S. Eliot.
    New York: New Directions, 1968.

Pound, Ezra. "Manifesto," *Poetry* 41.1 (October 1932): 40–3.

Pound, Ezra. "The Renaissance." *Literary Essays of Ezra Pound.* New York: New Directions, 1968. 214–26.

Pound, Ezra. "A Retrospect." *Literary Essays of Ezra Pound.* New York: New Directions, 1968. 3–14.

Pound, Ezra. *The Selected Letters of Ezra Pound, 1907-1941.* Ed. D. D. Paige. London: Faber and Faber, 1982.

Pound, Ezra. *The Spirit of Romance.* New York: New Directions, 1974.

Pound, Ezra. "Through Alien Eyes," *New Age* 12.11 (January 16, 1913): 252.

Puchner, Martin. "The New Modernist Studies: A Response." *minnesota review* 79.1 (2012): 91–6.

Puchner, Martin. *Poetry of the Revolution: Marx, Manifestos, and the Avant-gardes.* Princeton, NJ: Princeton University Press, 2006.

Rado, Lisa, "Introduction." *Rereading Modernism: New Directions in Feminist Criticism.* Ed. Rado. New York: Garland, 1994. 3–19.

Rainey, Lawrence. "Introduction." *Modernism: An Anthology.* Ed. Rainey. Malden, MA: Blackwell, 2005. xix–xxix.

Rainey, Lawrence and Robert von Hallberg. "Editorial/Introduction." *Modernism/modernity* 1.1 (January 1994): 1–3.

Ransom, John Crowe. "Apologia for Modernism." *Kenyon Review* 2.2 (Spring 1940): 247–51.

Ransom, John Crowe. "Criticism Inc." *Selected Essays of John Crowe Ransom.* Ed. and Intro. Thomas Daniel Young and John Hindle. Baton Rouge: Louisiana State University Press, 1984. 93–106.

Ransom, John Crowe. "The Future of Poetry." *Fugitive* 3.1 (February 1924): 2–4.

Ransom, John Crowe. "The Making of a Modern: The Poetry of George Marion O'Donnell." *Southern Review* 1 (Autumn 1936): 864–74.

Ransom, John Crowe. "Modern with the Southern Accent." *Virginia Quarterly Review* 11.2 (Spring 1935): 184–200.

Ransom, John Crowe. "Poetry: A Note on Ontology." *Selected Essays of John Crowe Ransom.* Ed. and Intro. Thomas Daniel Young and John Hindle. Baton Rouge: Louisiana State University Press, 1984. 74–92.

Ransom, John Crowe. "Wanted: An Ontological Critic." *Selected Essays of John Crowe Ransom.* Ed. and Intro. Thomas Daniel Young and John Hindle. Baton Rouge: Louisiana State University Press, 1984. 147–79.

Rasula, Jed. "Make It New." *Modernism/modernity* 17.4 (November 2010): 713–33.

Read, Herbert. *Art Now: An Introduction to the Theory of Modern Painting and Sculpture.* London: Faber & Faber, 1948.

Richards, I. A. *The Philosophy of Rhetoric.* Oxford: Oxford University Press, 1965.

Richards, I. A. *Poetries and Sciences: A Reissue of* Science and Poetry (1926, 1935) *with Commentary.* London: Routledge and Kegan Paul, 1970.

Richards, I. A. *Principles of Literary Criticism.* New York: Routledge, 2001.

Riding, Laura and Robert Graves. *A Survey of Modernist Poetry.* Garden City, NY: Doubleday Doran & Co., 1928.

Rimbaud, Arthur. "Letter to Paul Demeny." *Modernism: An Anthology of Sources and Documents.* Ed. Vassiliki Kolocotroni, Jane Goldman, and Olga Taxidou. Edinburgh: Edinburgh University Press, 1998. 109–11.

Robinson, Lillian and Lise Vogel. "Modernism and History." *New Literary History* 3.1 (Autumn 1971): 177–99.

Rodker, John. *The Future of Futurism.* New York: E. P. Dutton & Co., 1927.

Rodker, John. "The 'New' Movement in Art." *The Dial Monthly* (May 1914): 184–8.

Rosenberg, Harold. *The Tradition of the New.* New York: McGraw-Hill, 1965.

Ross, Stephen. "Introduction: The Missing Link." *Modernism and Theory: A Critical Debate.* Ed. Ross. New York: Routledge, 2009. 1–17.

Sabatier, Paul and Catholic Church Congregatio Sancti Oficii. *Modernism.* Trans. C. A. Miles. New York: Scribner's, 1908.

Schorer, Mark. "Technique as Discovery." *Hudson Review* 1.1 (Spring 1948): 67–87.

Schwartz, Sanford. "The Postmodernity of Modernism." *The Future of Modernism.* Ed. Hugh Witemeyer. Ann Arbor: University of Michigan Press, 1997. 9–31.

Scott, Bonnie Kime. *Gender in Modernism: New Geographies, Complex Intersections.* Ed. Scott. Urbana: University of Illinois Press, 2007.

Scott, Bonnie Kime. "Green." *Modernism and Theory: A Critical Debate.* Ed. Ross. New York: Routledge, 2009. 219–24.

Scott, Bonnie Kime. "Introduction." *The Gender of Modernism: A Critical Anthology.* Ed. Scott. Bloomington: Indiana University Press, 1990. 1–18.

Scott, Bonnie Kime. *Refiguring Modernism. Volume 1: The Women of 1928.* Bloomington: Indiana University Press, 1995.

Scott-James, R. A. *Modernism and Romance.* London: John Lane, 1908.

Sedgwick, Eve. *Epistemology of the Closet.* Berkeley: University of California Press, 2008.

Seldes, Gilbert. "Nineties—Twenties—Thirties." *Dial* 73.5 (November 1922): 574–8.

Shapiro, Karl. *In Defense of Ignorance.* New York: Random House, 1960.

Shklovskii, Victor. "Art as Technique." *Modernism: An Anthology of Sources and Documents.* Ed. Vassiliki Kolocotroni, Jane Goldman, and Olga Taxidou. Edinburgh: Edinburgh University Press, 1998. 217–21.

Sitwell, Edith. *Aspects of Modern Poetry.* London: Duckworth, 1934.

Smith, Stan. *The Origins of Modernism: Eliot, Pound, Yeats and the Rhetorics of Renewal.* New York: Harvester Wheatsheaf, 1994.

Spender, Stephen. *The Struggle of the Modern*. Berkeley: University of California Press, 1963.

Stein, Gertrude. *Everybody's Autobiography*. New York: Copper Square Publishers, 1971.

Strindberg, August. *Miss Julie and Other Plays*. Trans. Michael Robinson. Oxford: Oxford University Press, 1998.

Symons, Arthur. *The Symbolist Movement in Literature*. London: Archibald, Constable & Co., 1908.

Trilling, Lionel. "On the Teaching of Modern Literature." *Beyond Culture: Essays on Literature and Learning*. New York: Harcourt Brace Jovanovich, 1965. 3–27.

West, Rebecca. "The Sex War: Disjointed Thoughts on Men." *Clarion* (April 18, 1913): 3.

Wicke, Jennifer. *Advertising Fictions: Literature, Advertisement, and Social Reading*. New York: Columbia University Press, 1988.

Wicke, Jennifer. "Appreciation, Depreciation: Modernism's Speculative Bubble." *Modernism/modernity* 8.3 (September 2001): 389–403.

Williams, Raymond. "The Bloomsbury Fraction." *Culture and Materialism: Selected Essays*. London: Verso, 2005. 148–69.

Williams, Raymond. *Culture and Society, 1780-1950*. New York: Columbia University Press, 1983.

Williams, Raymond. "Metropolitan Perceptions and the Emergence of Modernism." *The Politics of Modernism: Against the New Conformists*. Ed. and Intro. Tony Pinkney. London: Verso, 1989. 37–48.

Williams, Raymond. "When was Modernism?" *The Politics of Modernism: Against the New Conformists*. Ed. and Intro. Tony Pinkney. London: Verso, 1989. 31–5.

Wilson, Edmund. *Axel's Castle: A Study in the Imaginative Literature of 1870-1930*. New York: Charles Scribner's Sons, 1969.

Wimsatt, W. K. *The Verbal Icon: Studies in the Meaning of Poetry*. Lexington: University of Kentucky Press, 1954.

Winters, Yvor. *Primitivism and Decadence*. London: Haskell House, 1937.

Winters, Yvor "T. S. Eliot: The Illusion of Reaction (II)." *Kenyon Review* 3.2 (Spring 1941): 221–39.

Wollaeger, Mark. "Introduction." *The Oxford Handbook of Global Modernisms*. Ed. Wollaeger. New York: Oxford University Press, 2012. 3–22.

Woolf, Virginia. "Modern Fiction." *Collected Essays*. 4 vols. London: Hogarth Press, 1966. 2: 103–10.

Woolf, Virginia. "Mr. Bennett and Mrs. Brown." *Collected Essays*. 4 vols. London: Hogarth Press, 1966. 1: 319–37.

Woolf, Virginia. *Three Guineas*. New York: Harcourt, Brace, Jovanovich, 1966.

Yeats, W. B. "Man and the Echo." *The Collected Poems of W. B. Yeats*. Ed. Richard J. Finneran. New York: Scribner, 1996. 345–6.

# INDEX